This Wicked Rebellion

John Zimm

THIS

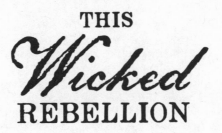

REBELLION

Wisconsin Civil War Soldiers Write Home

EDITED BY

John Zimm

FOREWORD BY

Michael Edmonds

WISCONSIN HISTORICAL SOCIETY PRESS

Published by the Wisconsin Historical Society Press
Publishers since 1855
© 2012 by State Historical Society of Wisconsin

wisconsinhistory.org

Printed in Canada
Cover design by Mark Skowron Design, LLC
Interior design and typesetting by Sara DeHaan

17 16 15 14 13 12   1 2 3 4 5

Library of Congress Cataloging-in-Publication Data

This wicked rebellion : Wisconsin Civil War soldiers write home / edited by John Zimm ;
foreword by Michael Edmonds.
   pages cm
Includes index.
   ISBN 978-0-87020-504-0 (hardcover : alk. paper) 1. United States—History—Civil War,
1861-1865—Personal narratives. 2. Wisconsin—History—Civil War, 1861-1865—Personal narratives. 3. Soldiers—Wisconsin—Correspondence. I. Zimm, John, editor.
   E464.T48 2012
   973.74'75—dc23

                                        2012009086

Front cover: Rebel works in front of Atlanta, WHi Image ID 78970.

Contents

Foreword

"I LOVE history," Roger Daltrey of the Who once remarked, "yet at school it was the most boring thing I've ever sat through in my life. It was about as exciting as a clam race. All they wanted to talk about was numbers and dates. It ceased to be about people."[1]

Well, this is a book about people. And not just *about* them, but by them. Here are the voices of everyday Wisconsin people who lived and died during the Civil War, brought to life in their personal letters.

"There never was an army like this for correspondence," remarked a Boston reporter visiting the troops in 1861:

> Go through the camp at any time, any hour of the day, and you will see hundreds of soldiers when off-duty—writing letters. It is a picturesque sight. Some lie at full length on the ground, beneath the shade of the trees, with a board or a book for a table, with pen and ink—though often only a pencil— writing the news to their friends. Some stand upright against the trunks of the trees; some lean forward with their papers upon their knees, and some with much painstaking stand up and write.[2]

Census records suggest about 85 percent of Union soldiers could read and write, and most of them put their skills to good use. Soldiers were sending forty-five thousand letters a day from the front during the fall of 1861.[3]

Mailing letters home was simple enough, in theory. In each regiment a chaplain, quartermaster, or soldiers assigned to mail duty would gather letters up and take them to brigade headquarters. Brigade staff would send them along to division headquarters, where a wagon would be loaded and sent to the nearest railroad. The train would carry them to Washington for dispersal around the country.

In reality, though, the process was usually more complicated.

First, writing material could be so hard to find that soldiers sometimes filled a sheet of paper, turned it ninety degrees, and then wrote across it a second time. Privacy was also in short supply. Chauncey Cooke of Buffalo County described a scene inside the barracks at Camp Randall in 1863:

> I can count more than 40 of the boys writing letters to their mothers or their girls. Mostly to their girls. Its [*sic*] easy to tell, if a fellow is writing to his mother he don't squirm and cover his paper when some guy looks over his shoulder.[4]

Once Private Cooke reached the front, though, the teasing ended. "I wrote you only day before yesterday," he told his sister,

> but all the boys have the fever, as it looks, of writing letters tonight. Cannons are booming both on the right and on the left, and as our Lieutenant says, things look mighty squally for tomorrow. I can't say that I am a bit nervous, but as the boys say, some of us may be where we can't send letters tomorrow and better send 'em now.[5]

Once a letter left camp, there was no telling how long it might take to reach its destination. If a soldier was stationed near a direct railroad to Washington, the letter could reach home in a few days. If his unit was on the march, though, it might take more than a month. Sometimes mail wagons were seized by the enemy, in which case letters never arrived at all. On average, most soldiers' letters probably reached their destinations within two weeks. Postage cost three cents (about seventy-seven cents today), more than many soldiers could afford. As the war progressed they were allowed to send unstamped letters home; the postage was paid by the recipient.

Since groups of men often enlisted together, once a letter reached home it was passed eagerly around a large circle of family and friends. Many were also printed in the local newspaper. Some were even intended for publication, sent as letters to the editor in towns like Oshkosh or Richland Center. The letters in this volume were all published in Wisconsin newspapers, from which they were clipped by the Quiner family of Madison.

Edwin B. Quiner (1816–1868) started his career as a thirteen-year-old printer's apprentice in New Haven, Connecticut. He moved steadily west as a journeyman printer, eventually reaching Milwaukee in the fall of 1839 and finding work at the *Milwaukee Sentinel*. By 1847 he had moved out to Waukesha, where he was chosen county register of deeds.

In 1850 Quiner bought a press of his own and launched the *Democratic*

State Register in Watertown. After he joined the fledgling Republican movement, Quiner's politics gradually diverged from those of his readers until
he was forced to close his paper and leave town. His personality may have
had something to do with it too. The historian of printing in Wisconsin
noted that Quiner "was described as irritable in temper, bitter and personal
editorially, and thus alienated those who would be his friends." In 1857 he
relocated his family to Madison, where he served as an assistant clerk to the
Wisconsin Assembly for two sessions.[6]

When war broke out in the spring of 1861, Quiner was appointed a private secretary to the governor. "During the time," the press noted afterward, "Mr. Quiner subscribed for every paper published in the state and
from these papers his daughters clipped the letters written by the soldiers
to their families." They pasted these into scrapbooks arranged by regiment
and, within that, by date. When the war ended, Quiner's daughters had
filled nearly four thousand scrapbook pages with approximately ten thousand letters sent home from the front. They were written not only by soldiers
but also by chaplains, civilian aid agents, and reporters embedded with the
troops (as we would say today).[7]

Quiner intended to use the letters as one of his sources for a history of
Wisconsin's participation in the war. His thousand-page *Military History of
Wisconsin: A Record of the Civil and Military Patriotism of the State, in the War
for the Union* . . . appeared in the spring of 1866. By then he was gravely ill
from overwork. He soon moved to Baraboo, where he died on February 28,
1868.

In 1867, perhaps while leaving Madison, Quiner donated his ten scrapbooks of letters to the Wisconsin Historical Society. In his annual report,
Society director Lyman Draper wrote, "We must next notice a very valuable contribution, which we cannot estimate too highly, from Edwin B.
Quiner—eleven [*sic*] quarto volumes of mounted newspaper scraps relative
to the important part Wisconsin enacted in the late war." Noting that they
"were used to only a limited extent, in the preparation of Mr. Quiner's elab-
orate work on the Rebellion," Draper predicts they will "prove one of the
very richest collections for historical reference on all matters pertaining to
Wisconsin's part in the war for the Union."[8]

He was right. Over the last century and a half, Quiner's scrapbooks have
been cited in nearly two hundred books and articles. The Wisconsin His-

torical Society microfilmed them in 1982 and digitized them in 2010. All ten thousand letters are now online for free at www.wisconsinhistory.org /civilwar, carefully indexed, along with the full text of his book.

The letters selected here are among the very best the Quiners saved. Each group of letters is preceded by a short explanation by editor John Zimm that sets the stage. After that, the modern world melts away, and you're sitting by the hearth on the family farm or around a barrel down at the general store, listening to a neighbor read the latest news from the South.

These letters will make you smile, sigh, recoil, and reflect. Here is the Civil War through the eyes and voices of real people. Sometimes we dismiss our predecessors as primitives who lacked the intelligence, good taste, or good luck to be born in our own time. But that's a mistake. They were just as smart, funny, thoughtful, and richly complicated as you and I are. Dip into this book anywhere, and see how they faced up to challenges as big as our own.

Michael Edmonds
Madison, Wisconsin

Notes

1. *New York Post*, October 4, 2003.
2. *Boston Daily Journal*, November 1861, in James W. Milgram, *Federal Civil War Postal History* (Lake Forest, IL: Northbrook, 2007), 136.
3. United States Census Office, 9th census, 1870, in *Compendium of the Ninth Census* (Washington, DC: Government Printing Office, 1872), 8, 456.
4. "Letters of a Badger Boy in Blue: Life at Old Camp Randall," *Wisconsin Magazine of History* 4, no. 2 (December 1920): 211.
5. "Letters of a Badger Boy in Blue: The Atlanta Campaign," *Wisconsin Magazine of History* 5, no. 1 (September 1921): 68.
6. *Wisconsin State Journal*, March 4, 1868; *Watertown Democrat*, July 5, 1860; *La Crosse Tribune*, August 16, 1913; Douglas McMurtrie, *Early Printing in Wisconsin* (Seattle: Frank McCaffrey, 1931), 129.
7. *La Crosse Tribune*, August 16, 1913.
8. *Wisconsin Historical Collections* (Madison, WI: Atwood & Rublee, 1868), 5:164.

Preface

DURING THE Civil War, from campgrounds and battlefields in the South to the riotous streets of Milwaukee and the wild frontier of Minnesota, men and women not very different from you or me had to learn to adapt in the face of trials for which their previous life experiences had not prepared them. In the clippings so carefully preserved by Edwin B. Quiner and his daughters, we are allowed the unique opportunity to step into the lives and thoughts of a diverse group of people and relive what they went through as the country fought to settle the questions of slavery and states' rights. In this book, what I've tried to assemble is not a chronological retelling of Wisconsin's role in the Civil War; rather, this collection should be viewed as a window through which we can experience the varied trials and happenings of Wisconsin's participants as they struggled to make it through arguably the nation's most demanding crucible.

I made selections using a variety of criteria. Many well-written accounts had to be excluded from the book simply because there were far too many of them. In fact, a book of equal size as this could have been assembled from accounts written by soldiers on picket duty alone. Clippings that tell a unique story about Wisconsin's role in the war were likely to be considered. How could I not include, for example, the account of Lieutenant Colonel Whipple disguising himself in a buffalo robe and recapturing two Confederate prisoners on the run from Camp Randall while wielding only a club? Too many accounts exist of famous battles to include every one, but you'll find stories from some of the most famous engagements. Accounts that express an array of divergent views on issues of the day—for example, on slavery or the draft—were included, while affected narratives full of flowery prose were set aside. I have tried to make selections I thought would give the clearest snapshot of the part played by Wisconsin's men and women in the variety of situations and challenges they faced.

During the course of the war, a vernacular developed that can be confounding today. Soldiers often wrote admiringly of their "Belgians," by which they meant their rifles, manufactured in Belgium and imported by the thousands as the army expanded from a few thousand to several hundred thousand in the early days of the war. Correspondents also used the now-obsolete terms "inst.," or "instant," and "ult.," or "ultimo," meaning "this month" and "last month" respectively. "Secesh," short for secessionist, was a common epithet applied to disloyal Southerners both in and out of the army. Occasionally, an explanatory footnote has been used to clarify ad hoc uses of archaic language or obscure references. Racialist terms that offend modern sensibilities were used at will in all manner of accounts, and have been retained. Readers can judge for themselves how much grace is due our forebears for the language they used.

One of the issues in working with these letters is that only the newspaper clippings remain. There is no way to return to the original handwritten letters in order to check seeming errors and variations in style. For this reason, unique spellings and misspellings and odd, dated styles were retained. The letters have passed through the filter of the original newspaper editors and typesetters, who made style and design choices that we can't see behind. Where a newspaper used small capital letters to indicate a stress, the letter writer may have simply underlined; where a name is given in all capital letters, the letter writer may have used lowercase. Because it is impossible to know what lies behind these design choices, I have kept much of them as they appear, even though they are likely different than the original writing, are unorthodox in the context of today's publishing practices, and vary widely from letter to letter. At the very least, this serves to give a sense of what Wisconsinites saw as they opened their papers in the 1860s. Silent edits were made when obviously unintentional errors in printing occurred—for example, when a type block was printed upside down—and some emendations or additions have been made, always in brackets, to clarify confusing passages or fill in spots where the clippings are difficult to read. So that readers can go back to the letters themselves, I note their location within the Quiner scrapbooks at the end of each selection.

Reading through Quiner's ten volumes of clippings has been eminently rewarding work. While it may be a fool's errand to attempt to boil down ten thousand letters into a book of about two hundred or so pages, I hope that reading the words of Wisconsin's participants will foster an appreciation for the men and women who had to navigate those complicated times. Far from being nameless, faceless, or powerless, these were very real human beings who gave up the comforts of home, lost friends and family, loved and hated, celebrated and censured, and did not know what the outcome of the conflict would be. The men and women you'll meet in these pages had dreams and plans for their lives until war interfered. Through the vivifying magic of the words that Edwin B. Quiner preserved, their lives can become real to us once again.

John Zimm
Madison, Wisconsin

CHAPTER 1

The War in the North

THE WINTER of 1860 to 1861 was an uncertain time. Southern states left the union every few days until by February 1, 1861, a total of seven had seceded. With the bombardment and surrender of Fort Sumter in mid-April, a tense war of words and bravado gave way to the raising and training of armies as President Abraham Lincoln called for 75,000 troops to subdue "combinations too powerful to be suppressed by the ordinary course of judicial proceedings, or by the powers vested in the marshals by law."

Initially asked to provide only one regiment of 780 men, Wisconsin would eventually send over 80,000 young men to war, 11,000 of whom did not return. Before they could go to war, however, these men had to be mustered into the army, given a uniform and a gun, and provided with a minimal amount of training. To this end, camps were constructed in Milwaukee and Madison where men were sent to become soldiers, the most famous being Madison's Camp Randall. Young men who had probably never ventured far from home found life in these camps at once tedious and entertaining, despising drill yet finding plenty of opportunities to entertain themselves with songs, dances, or tomfoolery about town.

Challenging times lay ahead for those at home left to work the fields, mind the stores, and keep Northern society functioning even as so many young men were away fighting the rebellion. Women were particularly affected as they raised families alone, endured separation from their husbands and fathers, and began to take on the work that men had traditionally done. Women had to rely on the kindness of their neighbors and sometimes found that promises of help did not materialize.

Nor were military affairs restricted to the South. In the fall of 1862, draft rioters raised havoc in several Wisconsin communities. Troops that had planned to go south in the fall of 1862 found themselves instead marching through Wisconsin, hunting down rioters and those evading the draft, or heading to the Wisconsin-Minnesota border to suppress Indian troubles. Other regiments were retained at Camp Randall to guard Confederate prisoners housed there or to suppress a mutiny among Wisconsin troops who refused to go to the front. Meanwhile, Wisconsin soldiers in the field were fighting and dying and being forever changed by the experience, as many mothers and fathers, wives and children found out when their loved ones returned home from the front.

Leaving Home

Having been accepted into service, companies were sent to Milwaukee or Madison to learn the basics of nineteenth-century soldiering. At railroad depots around the state, scenes like the following occurred as communities sent their young men off to become soldiers.

Departure of the Beloit City Guards.

Never did this city witness such a spectacle as was presented last Friday upon the departure of the Beloit City Guards, for their rendezvous at Milwaukee. The entire population of the city, and many persons from the adjacent country, assembled to witness the embarkation of the first company from Rock County. The streets were thronged with people, and every available position in the vicinity of the depot was occupied by spectators, long before the hour of departure had arrived. It was found necessary to stretch a rope from the depot to State street, in order to keep open a space between the crowd and the cars for the occupation of the troops. The rooms and platform of the depot were occupied by the relatives of the soldiers that were to leave. The Beloit Cadet Rifles, the Home Guard, the Firemen, and the Union Guards of Winnebago Co., Ill., under command of Capt Burroughs, were drawn up in order to receive the City Guards. At 12 o'clock, this company, headed by the City Band playing Yankee Doodle, marched up in front of the depot, where they were addressed by Mayor Parker, who pledged the Company the faith of the City that those whom they left behind should be faithfully cared for during the term of their absence. Rev. Dr. Brinsmade on behalf of the American Bible Society presented to each member of the Company a copy of the Bible, accompanying the presentation to Capt. Clark with a few appropriate remarks, which were followed with prayer.

The time for the departure of the train having arrived the Company was ordered aboard, and hasty words of parting were exchanged between husbands and wives, mothers and sons, sisters and brothers.

The scene at this moment was most touching and solemn. Stout hearts melted, and eyes "unused to weep" were suffused with tears. Never before had the dire exigencies of war been brought home to the people of this city in such sad earnest, and a deeper desire was begotten in every heart to strike down the traitors who had brought this evil upon the land.

As the train moved off three mighty cheers were given for the departing troops, and the multitude dispersed. Vol. 1, p. 1

THE PARTING.

One parting scene we must not fail to chronicle. A husband, a stalwart man, was taking the last leave of his wife;—a hasty kiss was exchanged—a warm grasp of the hand, and the soldier, as he was about turning away, stooped to kiss his child, a little girl of three summers. The child put her arms about the father's neck, clasped them tightly, and sobbed most piteously. She would not let him go, and he was forced to unclasp her hands with his own strong arms, and hand her back to her weeping mother, while the big tears rolled down his manly cheeks,—still he faltered not, but bravely resumed his place in the ranks. Incidents such as this try the reins and test the courage of a man more than facing the storm of lead and iron hail from the ranks of the enemy. . . .

In a few moments the volunteers were all aboard, and amid the booming of cannon, and the rolling of drums, the train whizzed away, and the Delavan Guards were lost to our sight. Thus closed one of the saddest days of the year. Vol. 6, pp. 165–66

A soldier corresponding for the Wisconsin Daily Argus *took pen in hand to write a lengthy description of Camp Randall, which would be the primary training ground for Wisconsin's Civil War soldiers.*

Camp Randall,
Madison, Dec. 15, 1861.

EDS ARGUS:—This Camp to which has been given the name of the best of Wisconsin Governors, was fitted up in 1860 for the annual fair of the Wisconsin State Agricultural Society. It is some 10 acres in extent, in nearly a square form, being somewhat the longest from north to south, and is surrounded by a board fence eight feet in height. The fence is constructed by setting posts in the usual manner, placing the cross-scantling as if for picket fence, then nailing on the eight-feet boards perpendicularly, making a fence which is almost proof against climbing from the outside, but one which is quite easily scaled from the inside, owing to the scantling placed horizontaly for the support of the boards, which make convenient steps for the feet of any person who desires to use them as such. This fact renders it necessary to place a strong guard around the inside of the Camp, to prevent the exit of truant soldiers, which are quite plenty here as you can imagine.

There was originally a row of pens put up on the north, east, and south sides of the ground for the accommodation of the cattle brought here for the exhibition at the fair. These have been remodeled, good roofs put on, well sheeted and battened on each side, the interstices between the sheeting and the outside boards being filled with straw to break the force of the blasts of Old Boreas, and render them warm and tenable in cold weather. In these pens now termed "barracks," are placed bunks, three high, about 4½ feet wide and 6½ feet long in which we lodge. With a goodly quantity of straw in these, three men can make themselves a comfortable lodging place, by spreading one man's blanket upon the straw upon which to lie, and placing those of the other two over the lodgers. Our company occupies one of these barracks of about 8 rods in length. We have three stoves, and a bountiful supply of dry wood, so that we are able to keep out the cold when we have any. Myself and partner are sleeping in one of these bunks, with a bed-quilt (which we purchased,) to spread over the straw to keep it from our bodies, with our two blankets over us, and we have no difficulty in keeping warm thus far. We have two overcoats each, which we are calculating will contribute somewhat to keep us warm when the cold nights of January are upon us, which are not far distant.

The building formerly occupied by the exhibition of the arts, and known as "The Fine Art Hall," which is situated upon quite an eminence on the western side of the grounds, is now partitioned off into apartments and used as Hospitals for the 15th and 16th Regiments, Quartermasters offices, and store rooms. I visited the Hospital of our regiment the other day, and found it roomy and comfortable; and as the building is situated some little distance from the turmoil of the parade ground, I see no good reason why a sick soldier here should not be as favorably situated to regain his health as he would be in the house of any stranger. . . .

Coming down from the eminence upon which the Hospital is situated, and walking about 30 rods toward the north, and we come to a large building sporting the sign of "Operative Machinery." This is the shrine at which hungry soldiers worship. It is a building of about 240 feet in length by about 150 in breadth. Entering we find it filled with tables 130 feet in length, each of which is calculated to accommodate a company of soldiers. In this building *three thousand soldiers* sit down to their meals at once, I have visited nearly all of the departments of the establishment, and I have luckily found a former acquaintance in every department I have visited. The first department which I visited was the butcher's shop. Here we found a friend slicing up pork for breakfast the following morning. He had in the neighborhood of 7 bushels of slices of pork. He informed us it required over *three barrels* of pork for a "fry" each morning. In the "bread room" we found about *ten cords* of the "staff of life" corded up on one side of the room. The superintendent informed us that it would be all exhausted by the end of supper on the evening of the following day. *Eighty five* pounds of [coffee] are required for a single drawing. Tea we are not troubled with. We usually have molasses for supper. In the department where this was dealt out, we saw men filling the pots (almost 300 in number,) in which it is placed upon the table. Probably you can imagine the amount of patience a man must exhibit, and the time required to fill all of these pots on a cold day. At all events I think you could appreciate the force of the old adage "as slow as molasses in the winter." I can after seeing some 25 of them filled by the "Job" who deals to us our small allowance of "the sweets of this life." I will not attempt a description of any of the departments of this establishment, especially the cooking department. You can, however, imagine the magnitude necessary to fry *three barrels* of pork at once. The apparatus for cooking the potatoes and applesauce for the vast multitude who board here can be better imagined than the amount of "frying surface" necessary to the frying [of] this amount of meat. It requires a small army of cooks and waiters to perform the labor necessary to the proper conducting of this establishment. The State pays the proprietor of this establishment 30 cents per day for our rations. I understand that the proprietor clears, over and above the expenses of the concern, over one hundred dollars per day. If this is the case, I am of the opinion that he ought to give the boys a Christmas dinner of the good old fashioned kind. Whether he does or not we shall soon know. . . .

The more I see of a soldier's life, the more I like it. I have the satisfaction of becoming healthy, strong and fat—having gained five pounds since I arrived here. This to me speaks favorably of the [r]ough fare and accommodations of a soldier. Quite a number of our boys are visiting your village, and a number of others will soon follow, most of whom, I presume, will give you a call, and furnish you with any little items of information which I may forget. The arms for our regiment are now here, and will soon be put into our hands. They are Belgian Rifles, and are a splendid arm—said to be the best in the service. Vol. 5, pp. 205–6

Soldiers performing artillery drills at Camp Randall, 1861   WHi Image ID 4225

Becoming Soldiers

It did not take long for Wisconsin soldiers to become disgusted with the uniforms the government provided and to weary of the drill to which they were subjected daily.

Head Quarters 1st Regiment
Wisconsin State Active Militia.
Camp Scott, Milwaukee, May 12th, 1861.

DEAR GAZETTE.—I have but little of interest to communicate this week. Camp life has but few variations and ours is not an exception to the general rule. The regiment is mustered twice a day as usual, and the men are fast becoming proficient in the drill. Our arms have not arrived yet, but the entire regiment is now fully uniformed—after a fashion—but to our eye it is anything else but uniform. The cloth is of all varieties of what is styled grey, from a light drab to a dark brown. The fact is, the uniforms and supplies for the regiment thus far, have been one complete swindle—a regular sham. The haversacks are the most miserably constructed things I ever saw, and the clothing is a regular botch.

The cloth is good enough but *such* sewing—it is almost enough to make a man swear to look at it. The shoes, too, are utterly worthless. Many of them came to pieces within two days after they were put on. . . .

Yours Truly,

P——.   Vol. 1, pp. 5–6

The gray uniforms provided to soldiers by the state of Wisconsin at the outset of the war proved impractical when the South adopted that color for its troops.

Cairo, Ill., Feb. 11, 1862.

Editors of State Journal:— . . . Our friends in Wisconsin will probably wonder why we are still in Cairo and not in the forward movement as we expected to be when we left Missouri. I do not pretend to be acquainted with all the reasons for this, but will mention one. When we came here, we had the same uniform, we received from the State of Wisconsin, and which is said to be almost exactly like that of the rebels. Indeed the day we came into Cairo, it is said that a little girl, who had seen the uniform of some of the rebel prisoners here, ran into the house clapping her bands and crying, "O, Ma! here comes a whole regiment of secessionists." It was not thought safe to send us where we would be likely to go into battle, with this uniform, as it would expose us the danger of being shot by our own men. Had it not been for this, we should probably have gone with the first troops which left here for the Tennessee river. Recently we have received the Regulation uniform, but in the meantime we have become so useful to the authorities here that they do not seem willing to let us go.   Vol. 4, p. 45

Corporal Charles Stewart (b. 1832), Company B, 8th Wisconsin Infantry, wearing one of the original gray Wisconsin uniforms given out until October 1861, when blue became the official Union color. Stewart was mustered out in 1865 as a captain.   WHi Image ID 70154

Camp Harvey,
Kenosha, Feb. 6th, '62.

. . . But few persons, who have not had experience know the *trials* or *duty* of soldiers. I find it very different from a "free fight." It is drill and discipline; discipline and drill, day in and day out. Men who have been *educated* as soldiers, think discipline indispensible to success, hence the delay in our great army. . . .

Very Truly Yours,
HIRAM CALKINS.   Vol. 7, p. 92

Mischief

Camp life was not always centered on drill and preparation for army life. Before they gained fame as part of the noted Iron Brigade, the 2nd Wisconsin achieved dubious notoriety for raising mischief in downtown Madison by various unseemly acts, in this case doing battle with a Madison brewer in the dead of night.

We regret we have to record a disgraceful affair which occurred in this city last night. Last evening, as we are informed, Col. Coon granted leave of absence to a number of the members of the second regiment to visit their friends before their departure for active service. Some of these volunteers remained in the city, and a party of nine went to Voigt's, the brewer in the first ward, and attempted to get into his saloon at two or three o'clock this morning. The saloon is in the basement of a two story brick building, the upper portion of which is occupied by Mr. Voigt as a residence. He refused to open his saloon for them. They then broke open, or let down a window opening into the bar of the saloon, and got out several bottles of liquor. Mr. Voigt, from a window above, fired a shot-gun over their heads with a view of driving them off, not intending to injure any one. Upon this they fired upon the house with revolvers, and threw stones into the windows, breaking glass, sash, and blinds. Mr. Voigt fired several times over their heads with a revolver, and finally discharged his shot gun, aiming at their legs as nearly as he could, upon which they decamped. Nearly a wheel-barrow load of stones, we are told, were thrown into the house, and the walls in several places are chipped with bullets. Blood was found upon the sidewalk leading towards the camp, and we understand that a member of the Belle City (Racine) Rifles has a wounded hand and leg this morning. A soldier was found near the Brewery dead drunk lying upon the ground; a member of the Randall Guard, it is reported. He was taken to the Guard House, the first instance we believe where any member of that company has been found guilty of ill-conduct.

In the Third Ward, also we hear that some handsome shade trees in front of Mr. Hinrich's residence were cut down or mutilated. This is attributed to the soldiers, but without any satisfactory evidence, as we learn, that they are the guilty parties.

We have been disposed to allow a good deal for exaggerations in regard to the conduct of the soldiers of the Second Regiment, but it is evident that there are some hard cases among them. The great mass of them, we believe to be sterling men, who feel as keenly as any one, how much the regiment is disgraced by the few insubordinates, and who have no sympathy with them in their riotous conduct. These wild fellows who disturb the peace of the city are but few in numbers, and ought not, by their unseemly acts, to be permitted to involve the whole regiment in disgrace. They should be sharply looked after by the officers.   Vol. 1, p. 81

Pinckney Street in downtown Madison, ca. 1859   WHi Image ID 11701

Volunteers at Camp Scott in Milwaukee, named after General Winfield Scott, apparently found plenty of time to enjoy themselves with pantomime shows, hangings in effigy, and dancing.

Camp Scott, May 31, 1861.

ED. GAZETTE:—Probably there is no mode of life in which are combined so many discomforts and privations, with so many pleasures, and so much to interest and amuse, as does the soldier's life. You have heard much about the disagreeable incidents attending our life here. I propose to give you a few glimpses at some of the fun that goes on here, and which is of course enjoyed with the keenest relish.

Let me first make note of the capital joke which is told at the expense of the gallant Capt. Michael, of the Union Rifles, Co. B. As you are doubtless aware, Capt. M. at the commencement of the war resigned his charge of a revenue cutter, to take command of the Rifle Company. For a few days he was of course a much better sailor than a solider, although he is now as accomplished a soldier as any on the ground. At one of the earliest parades, he wished his company to "file right," but could not think of the proper word of command; so he sang out, in sailor language, "Go to starboard! I don't know what you call it on land!" Fortunately the file leader understood the command, and acted accordingly. It was quite a joke on Capt. M., and no one enjoys a laugh at it better than the worthy and jovial Captain himself.

Since we commenced our tent-life on the Camp Ground "the mirth and fun grows fast and furious." Every pleasant evening witnesses some scene of sport. Two or three mock court-martials have been held, at one of which the victim was an Orderly Sergeant, who actually became much frightened at the prospect of being shot! We have often a pantomimic or burlesque show; a tall and well proportioned ostrich goes flapping his wings around the camp; or a huge snake winds here and there among the crowd; or a fat negro wench travels around with a man on her back; or some enterprising showman conducts a fine elephant with a monkey riding on his back.—The Germans of the regiment are very ready and cunning at such pantomines.

One fine afternoon, "Tangle" McCracken of the Light Guard, well known in Milwaukee, got a large crowd of "the boys" together, to have an indignation meeting about the poor fare which we have had for a portion of the time, at the "Newhall House No. 2," on the Camp Ground. But he just then received orders from headquarters to the effect that such meetings wouldn't do "not at all! no, not at all." Opportunely at the moment arrived a package of tracks and religious papers. So when "the boys" began to be clamorous for the great "Tangle" to come and open the indignation meeting, he appeared on the ground, and distributed the tracts among the crowd, accompanying them with some sober and consoling remarks, at which every one who hears of the shrewd act, exclaims, "Bully for the versatile Tangle!"

One fine evening last week, we all received notice to attend at dark on another street in the camp, and witness some fun. So we went. There was a gallows erected, and a grand marching around it. Shortly the Band came up the street, playing a dirge; and two officers followed, dragging along an effigy of the notorious Jeff. Davis. It was but a short task to hang the traitor, and pronounce him dead.—A fire was then kindled under him, and the body was burnt, the glare lighting up the whole Camp Ground.—The ashes were now buried at the head of the street, and over them stands a slab, with the inscription,

"HERE LIES
JEFF. DAVIS,
THE TRAITOR,
Or any other man"

Dancing is of late a favorite amusement at the Camp. On every pleasant evening one can hear the lively notes of the "fiddle"—(there isn't a violin on the ground.) When the ladies are not on hand, their places are filled by some of "the boys," who turn their caps wrong side before, to distinguish themselves from their gentlemen partners. Even now I hear the sound of a fiddle and bones, down on Buy-out street. . . .

Adieu for the present. If any more "good things" transpire, worthy of note, I will send them to you.

Yours, for

FUN.   Vol. 1, pp. 9–10

Going to War

After receiving drill and being equipped with their rifles and uniforms in Wisconsin, it was time for the volunteers to make their way to the front lines. As the 7th Wisconsin left the state, its train made several stops along the way, receiving a celebratory sendoff from crowds throughout southern Wisconsin.

The boys of the 7th Regiment seemed to rejoice exceedingly when fairly under way, after so many little delays, which prolonged the time of starting so long after the appointed time.

A considerable number of people were collected at McFarland, to see the train pass, but there was no time to exchange greetings.

The first stop was made at Stoughton, where almost the entire population appeared to have come out to bid their boys good bye. Such hand-shakings, and varied adieus, and parting admonitions, gave evidence that those who went forth left warm and loving hearts behind them. Tears there were, not alone on the cheeks of wives, and mothers, and sisters, but in the eyes of strong and brave men, who were leaving that which was most dear, and from which nothing but their country's call could have separated them. And some, who had bid farewell to their friends elsewhere, showed that these scenes had brought that parting afresh to their minds. Several boquets were bestowed on the boys, and two or three fair girls passed along the side of the car, shaking hands with their "brothers all," and occasionally some bold soldier boy, with a spice of fun or tenderness in his heart, would bring the face near enough to imprint a chaste salute, in memory, perhaps, of a sister elsewhere.

The ladies, we heard, had made a line banner to present to the Stoughton company, but finding that under the regulations it would be only an encumbrance if carried, did not present it.

As the train moved off, one of the soldiers made rather a hard hit at a group of young men standing on the platform, telling them to "be good boys, and stay at home."

At Edgerton and Milton Junction a large crowd variously manifested their interest in the flying train.

At Janesville there was a great crowd to welcome the boys, with something more substantial than buzzes and waving of handkerchiefs, though these were not lacking. The two trains were drawn up along side of each other, and pails of coffee and bucket of sandwiches, pies, cakes and apples were distributed. There was something for all, and the rear car, as your reporter can testify, was most liberally supplied. A good deal of curiosity was manifested to inspect the muskets, and a few were disposed to complain that the sentinels so strictly guarded the doors of the cars. The Janesville people did themselves great credit by the warmth of their reception. There came on board here a member of Capt. Ely's company, of the 2d Regiment, who had been at home on account of a wounded arm, but was returning to

active duty, one of the gayest of the gay. Indeed, there was life enough in all
the members of the 2d who were going on.   Vol. 1, pp. 271–72

*As they moved farther south, Wisconsin's soldiers found their welcome less warm.
For one Wisconsin regiment, a tense situation almost led to gunfire on the streets
of Baltimore.*

                                                        Washington, June 23, 1861
Here we are in Washington, safe and sound. It has been a hard, tedious
journey, all the boys were exhausted when we arrived, but we are all satisfied
with the result. Our journey from Chicago to Pittsburg was one perfect ova-
tion—no language of mine can describe it. Every city, every village, along
the route turned out its entire population to greet us; bands of music were
playing at the stations, cannon were fired, flags waved and boquets showered
upon us by thousands. . . .

We anticipated trouble in Baltimore, as we should be obliged to pass
through that city in the night, and the boys were accordingly ordered to load
and cap their muskets before starting. We left Harrisburgh in four trains,
at intervals of half an hour. Companies A., D. and F. (our boys) were in the
first train and reached Baltimore just at twilight—got out of the cars and
formed in line, to wait for the other 7 companies to come up; and there we
had to wait till nearly 12 o'clock, owing to some slight accident to the engine
of the train next behind us. It was rather exciting I can assure you, as well
as fatiguing, standing there with our knapsacks on our backs, 40 rounds of
ammunition in our cartridge boxes, cap box, bayonet scabbard, two day's
rations in our haversacks besides knife, fork, spoon and plate. But there we
stood not daring to sit down or be off our guard for a moment, surrounded
by thousands of the roughs of Baltimore, who were armed to the teeth with
pistols and knives. These rascals would cheer Jeff. Davis and then groan for
the Wisconsin volunteers. It looked many times as though we were bound
to have a fight, but they dared not commence the cotillion. The boys stood
in double file with their muskets on the half cock, and always at a support or
carry arms, ready and eager for the word. It was evident that some accident
had happened to the other trains, and of course we could form no idea of
how long a time we should have to stand there.

Between 11 and 12 o'clock the other trains came in and were soon on

At the time of the Civil War, mailing envelopes often included illustrations. This envelope humorously highlights the rebellious reputation of Baltimore.　WHi Image ID 76777

the ground with us. Lieut. Col. Peck broke us into sections, closed columns by sections, and thus we march through Baltimore at midnight. We all expected to have a brush, and once I really thought the ball had opened. As we were passing through the street in which the 7th Mass. Regiment was fired into some six weeks ago, a huge ruffian stepped out on the right flank of our company, with a revolver in his hand, and proposed three cheers for Jeff. Davis and three groans for Col. Coon and the Wisconsin Volunteers, which were repeated by the crowd; not satisfied with this, he raised his pistol and fired one barrel. Capt. Strong was carrying his revolver ready cocked and watching the fellow's motions very much as he would his fancy *dorge,* when prairie chickens were to be found in the wheat stubble; and there is no reason to doubt that he would have reached the scamp's heart with a blue pill had any injury been done; as it was the ball rolled between two of our platoons, and instantly brought every musket to a full cock, the *click, click,* going down the line and dying away in the distance.

In many of the streets we were received with great enthusiasm; the side walks were lined and the house tops covered with people. Boquets were showered upon us by the ladies, and the stars and stripes were waved over us. In other streets we were hissed and insulted. It was 2½ miles from one depot to the other, but we finally got seated in the cars ready for our journey to Washington, which place we reached this morning at 5 o'clock. . . .

Yours, as ever,

[unreadable]   Vol. 1, pp. 84–85

The Fight at Home

The wife of a soldier in the 10th Wisconsin shares the pain of being separated from her husband.

O, I never can be reconciled to this cruel separation. How long, O how long shall the *Tocsin of war* resound through our valleys and through our mountains? How long must we hear the drum reveille and the bugle's shrill call *to arms?*

My country! O, my country! What a sacrifice thy daughters offer at thy shrine.—Fathers, brothers, husbands, sons, and lovers, (these no more, but soldiers) we lay upon thy holy altar. How patriotic the heart, how weak the flesh.

How wisely it is denied us to raise the impenetrable curtain that hangs between the present and the beyond. Thus hearts may be happy to-day that will break to-morrow. Yet, though I shrink shiveringly from what the future may have in store for me. No! no! Persevere, and may you win laurels beneath the banner of your country. Then come to your waiting one. Come—. . . .

But the night wanes and I must hasten.—For two weeks the weather has been like May, all but the birds and buds. But this morning was cold, cold, ugh? and the sun glittered like the flashing of precious jems upon the waters of the creek. Please tell me of your new camp, and the country about you. Also all that pertains to your present prospects, and believe me as ever,

Yours faithfully

ELIZA.
TO DELMONT. Vol. 4, p. 169

Camp of Gibbon's Brigade,
Opposite Fredericksburg, Va., July 2d, 1862.

Editors Patriot:— . . . The President has called for 300,000 more troops, and I wish to say a word to the people of Wisconsin on the subject. I know that harvest hands will be scarce, and for that reason farmers will use their influence against filling up the ranks with rapidity. This should not be. There are a great many men in Wisconsin yet, and now is the time for them to lend their country a helping hand. That there is work to be done, should keep no man at home. There are thousands who cannot possibly go to war, and they must work all the harder, besides I very much mistake the character and patriotism of my countrywomen if they will not turn out and with their white hands reap, bind, thrash, and carry to market the wheat crop of 1862, if necessary, that the men may go to war. Our revolutionary mothers did not shrink from toil and privation, and their fair daughters have not all degenerated. The women of Wisconsin are loyal and brave, not afraid of the rain nor the sun, and should it be necessary for them to till the ground that their friends may go to the defense of the old flag, their bright eyes will be all the brighter and their sunbrowned cheeks more beautiful, at least to those of us who live to return from the war.

At this critical moment, when our nation is struggling for existence against traitors at home and despots abroad, when all the friends of earth and hell seem leagued against us, when nothing but the uprising of the freemen of the North, *to a man,* can save us from the dark abyss that is yawning before us. Any man that can possibly leave home for a year or two and will not, is unworthy of being called an American; and any man that will prevent another from enlisting because he fears he will lose a few bushels of wheat, or that his house will cost him more than it otherwise would, is no better than a traitor; and any man or woman that will not say to their best and dearest friends go and return not till our country is no longer in danger, is a dishonor to the American name. But I close for a while to join in the sports of the day. . . .

R. K. B. Vol. 2, pp. 271

Arlington Heights, Nov. 3, '61.

Editors of Patriot:—I am pleased in some respects to learn of the patriotism existing among the worthy sons of the famous little village of L—, in Wisconsin. There are some who staked their all in their country's defence when this wicked rebellion first broke out, and are now in the grand army of the Potomac, devoting their all to crush out this rebellion that has already brought disgrace upon our national escutcheon. There are some of L—'s brave sons, who have gone through not only the troubled scenes and hardships of camp life, and fatigues of long weary marches, but they have gone through the bloody siege of Manassas, where they were obliged to contend against great odds. Shortly after these enlistments, another call was made, and again the worthy sons of L— rallied to their country's call. These last enlistments have been accepted, and the young patriots are at Arlington Heights, nearly 1,500 miles from friends and relations. Some have left aged parents, and others have left their dearest wives and little one, some scarcely three months old. A year since these worthy sons of L— were enjoying all the pleasures of married life, and who could at their leisure sit down with their loved ones and talk over things that had passed and gone, and the bright hopes and prospects of the future. "What a change!" Now L—'s brave sons are cut off from all family intercourse and parental enjoyments, and involved in one common war, not knowing what moment they will be called upon to trudge through rivers of blood, and to meet their brethren in one great bloody conflict. I would not infer, however, that all people are alike in respect to humanity, for there are a few in *all* communities who haven't a heart as large as a peanut. I am sorry to say of those of our friends who plead for the young patriots of said town to enlist immediately and crush out this wicked rebellion, some said that if they hadn't a family to support they would certainly go. No sooner had these sentiments left their lips, they were responded to by those who dare not risk their lives in this, our nation's hour of peril, in this wise: "If you will enlist, I will see that your families are properly cared for; they will never want as long as *I* have one red left. You need not borrow any trouble, for as long as *I* have a house and home, your families shall also."

Well, they began to believe that they were in human earnest. So, after mature deliberation of matters and things, knowing well their wives and little ones would be cared for, and thinking "all well," they hastened to enlist.

No sooner had they arrived on the "sacred soil," pleas came for assistance for the soldiers' wives.—They hear of J., the P. M., abusing the wives of the departed, merely for wanting her just dues from the P. O.; and one Mr. L., who, thinking himself quite shrewd and expert in law, took advantage of one of the soldiers' wives who had no one to look to for assistance, and used his "learning" to turn out of house and home one Mrs. P. This same L. was one of the first to put on patriotic airs—assuring the soldiers that their wives would never want, and promising that so far as he could assist them in his profession, he would do so without charge. Such cunning reptiles are more poisonous than the secesh fangs that seek the overthrow of the best government on earth. And one J. M. C., one of the wealthiest of L—, keeper of a large dry goods, grocery and medicine establishment, who was one of those sugar mouths who were to keep an eye out for the needy, refused to let one of the soldiers' wives have a drop of medicine for her sick child.—She informed him that she would pay him as soon as her husband sent her some money from the war, but through an air of dignity was refused, although he had bound himself never to see her in want, saying that the fool had better remained at home and taken care of his own family.

"What a disgrace." The wife immediately repaired to the office of Dr. I., and made known her wants, which was promptly replied to by administering to her wants, and saying, "if she wanted any assistance at his hands, he would do all in his power to make her comfortable, without pay. He had promised to divide to the last cent with them, and that he meant [to] live up to all agreements." What a contrast between the former and last named gent. However among the many of L—'s sons there are some who are gentlemen in every respect; among whom are Judge P., Dr. I. and Mr. A. These latter named gents have done more than they ever agreed to do, and have shown themselves worthy sons of Wisconsin, and are deserving of a great deal of praise, and will long be remembered with grateful recollections by husbands of those women whom they have tendered their kind hospitalities from truly patriotic motives, and if these husbands should ever return, they will be doubly rewarded for their kindness.

Of these gents soldiers do not ask for favors, but do wish that they will not hear any more complaints and grievances from their abused wives and families. They wish and sincerely hope that their friends and once patriotic citizens of the beautiful and wealthy village of L— will not cause such grievances among the wives and families of the far distant soldiers, who are winning laurels not only for themselves and their beloved and insulted country, but for those of their friends who *dare not* take up arms and do battle. Friends, please do not stand idle with your unsoiled hands folded, and witness these ladies cut and haul their own wood, day after day and week after week, as you have already done, after urging their husbands to leave them in a state of utter helplessness, promising, and that surely, to care for their wants; and also, that you would furnish them with comfortable homes and wearing apparel. Please do your duty at home, if you will not on the bloody battle field.

O. S. H.   Vol. 1, pp. 153–54

Resorting to the Draft

As the realities of a brutal civil war hit home, fewer and fewer men felt compelled to enlist in the army. By the summer of 1862 bounties were being paid to entice volunteers to join, ultimately with some success. But the contentious militia act, in addition to giving President Lincoln authority to call militias from the states into federal service for up to nine months, also gave the president the power to use the draft in cases in which volunteering was inadequate. This new power solicited a variety of opinions from Wisconsin's soldiers, many of whom had spent the better part of a year in the army.

Humboldt, Tenn.
Aug. 14th 1862.

. . . It is humiliating to us, who have been in the service for nearly a year, some considerably more—to think that the state of Wisconsin.—Our own state should be compelled to resort to the *draft* to fill up her quota of troops. Can it be that all the patriotism has left the state in the nineteen regiments of Infantry, and the Cavalry and Artillery which have marched from it. I can scarcely credit it. And yet it must be so, for what else on earth could prevent our ranks from being filled with *men* who are worthy of the name. If our Wisconsin public only felt upon this subject with the same intensity— with the same *realizing sense*, with which the people of the south feel, there

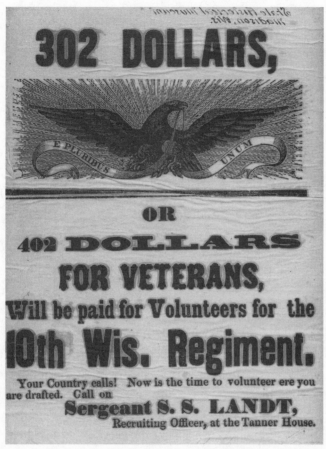

302 DOLLARS,

OR

402 DOLLARS FOR VETERANS,

Will be paid for Volunteers for the

10th Wis. Regiment.

Your Country calls! Now is the time to volunteer ere you are drafted. Call on

Sergeant S. S. LANDT,

Recruiting Officer, at the Tanner House.

A recruitment poster from early in the war, showing the enticements of enlisting   WHi Image ID 2978

would be no need of even talking of a draft. . . . It seems very strange indeed that men whose every interest is identical with the preservation of the Government, should require the strong hand of military power to drag them out of the miserable indolence and apathy into which they have fallen.

I recollect very well that a year ago Wisconsin was all ablaze—men were patriotic then. Then they said and *felt* too that the "Union must and shall be preserved." Is it of any less value now than it was then? Now that almost every family in the land, has some representative in the army of the Union, whose life may be imperiled by their delay and inaction. Is it worth any *less* sacrifices now than it was then. How have the sentiments of the people become so changed. But it is no use to write or talk about the matter. I suppose that each one has his own little ax to grind—has some business to attend to, which to him is more important than the preservation of the Government under which he is enabled to attend to that business. . . .

Respectfully Yours,

C.   Vol. 5, p. 59

                                                    Camp Gibbon, Aug. 6th, 1862.

FRIEND PEASE:— . . . I can assure them, that as *drafted militia* they will have anything but a pleasant time among the volunteers, who, although they are very *good boys in their way*, have as supreme contempt for a drafted man as an "old salt" for a marine, and would take as much delight in showing it.

Yours,

C.   Vol. 4, p. 8

                                            Headquarters 12th Reg. Wis. Vol.
                                              Humboldt, Tenn. Aug 14, 1862.

EDITORS ADVOCATE.— . . . We are very glad that the President has concluded to draft for soldiers; we wish it had been done long ago, and for a million instead of three hundred thousand. Now we shall see all those men who have been so loud in their professions of patriotism, urging others to fight for their country, marching under the folds of the starry flag, keeping "step to the music of the Union." We shall see those men who have been boasting what they would do, if they were soldiers, have a chance to show their skill and bravery, and those who have been berating others for not going, while excusing themselves, praying most heartily that no draft would be needed, that they might stay at home, enjoying its pleasures, while others no better able to leave home and families, but having more patriotism and courage, now can have a chance to get a personal acquaintance with the "pomp and circumstance of war." . . .

Yours truly,

W.   Vol. 5, p. 58

The draft met with significant resistance in Wisconsin. On draft day, November 10 and 11, 1862, riots broke out in several communities, including Green Bay and Port Washington; additionally, many draftees attempted to escape conscription, and troops were sent to hunt them down.

Camp Randall, Dec. 17th, 1862.

FRIEND SAM:—I take this opportunity to give you a few items of the doings of Company A, and the details of a trip to enforce the draft in Brown county. A sergeant and four men had been sent to the town of Morrison to bring in nine drafted men, but returned without accomplishing their object. Some had fled to Canada, and others could not be found, and others would not own their names, so the squad returned without a man. This was not satisfactory, and Capt. HARRIMAN determined to make one more attempt. Accordingly, on Wednesday December 10th, orders were given to eleven of us to pack up and be ready to move. The next morning we started out. We marched eighteen miles that day over muddy roads, and such mud! the good Lord deliver us from ever seeing again. Our plan was to surprise the "conscripts" and so we did not allow any traveller to pass us on the road. We stopped two females and although they had heavy loads to carry they managed to keep up with us, showing that the women in "these parts" know how to travel.

Gaining the vicinity of the town we stopped a short distance outside while our Sergeant went on ahead to reconnoitre. He found a loyal German that led us around to the back of his house, where we entered, and were concealed in his chamber, and who furnished us with a good warm supper. Here we rested about four hours. As the evening advanced the moon rose and shone brightly, and we quietly moved on to prosecute our search. We could not procure a guide from among the settlers, they being afraid of the consequences of serving as such when they should be left without protection, so we had to do the best we could without one.

We marched thirty miles that night, through timber and swamps, over bad roads, and sometimes nothing but foot trails, and searched twenty-two houses from top to bottom. We found but one drafted man, and he was hid in a potato bin.

The country through which we have marched is very poor. The roads where there are any, are very miserable, the swamps and marshes corduroyed without being covered or leveled, and on the whole are as much worse than the poorest road in Polk county as one can imagine. The inhabitants are all foreigners and are mostly Irish, good fighting men but not very patriotic.

We got back to our German friend's house on the morning of the 12th, about nine o'clock, where we were supplied with a warm breakfast.

It now began to rain and we concluded to remain until the next morning. We all got well rested and the next morning we took an early start for Fort Howard, our head-quarters, which place we reached at dark, tired and foot sore. The next day being Sunday, we were allowed to rest.

On Monday the 15th we bid good bye to Fort Howard, taking the cars for Madison, where we arrived the next morning at six o'clock, and went into our old barracks, having been absent just one month from the time we left them. . . .

I remain yours, a POLK CO. BOY.   Vol. 7, pp. 11–12

> Camp Lewis, Ozaukee,
> Nov. 19th, 1862

FRIEND RANN:—Since writing my last we have had stirring times here. Every day scouting parties go out into the country from three to ten miles after the rioters, and they seldom come back without bringing in a fresh bunch of prisoners.

Our Provost Marshal McIndoe holds his courts daily for the examination of those arrested, and about every day we ship off to Camp Washburn a fresh lot who are soon after re-shipped to Madison. In this way we are depleting this county of its excess of disloyalty, and teaching the stubborn Dutch that the way of the transgressor is hard.

We find, what everybody well-knew all along, that the democrats were abstaining from enlisting, so as to be at home to vote at the fall elections, and so determined and reckless were their leaders in this county that they resorted to the lowest and basest means to secure votes. . . .

And now after voting the straight ticket with the express understanding that they had done all that was required to escape the dreaded draft, to have the drafting still go on was too much to be submitted to, and they revolted. "Why," said they, "you can't draft; this is a free country, and if you draft this is no free country; it must stop."

So they took counsel together and determined to put an end to all drafting in Ozaukee county. Some two hundred collected together at a given signal, the firing of the cannon, and marched with horns and clubs and stones, and with banners flying, to the court house, seized upon and broke up the boxes and destroyed the papers and clubbed and stoned the officers till they were obliged to flee for their lives.

The most bitter and vindictive spirit of the mob was shown by the women, many of whom were foremost, and carried the banners, and shouted for Jeff. Davis, and used their clubs mercilessly on the heads of the officers. . . .

To-day (Monday 17th) our force, with the exception of two companies, will leave here for Milwaukee to attend to matters there connected with the draft. . . .   Vol. 6, pp. 313–14

Camp McIndoe, West Bend, Washington Co., Wis.,
Nov. 24, 1862.

All is well and we are comfortably quartered in the court house and town hall, and everything is going on as merry as a marriage ball. Last Thursday we tried our guns, and found them good shooters, but had no opportunity to shoot any one in Milwaukee, for the rebels *caved* as soon as they saw our bayonets gleaming in the sunlight, and the city is all quiet, as we knew it would be, there not being half the difficulty to enforce the draft that some of the democrats would have us believe. On Friday we received orders to prepare four days rations, without telling when or where we should march. . . . Our way led through a district similar to parts of Ohio and Michigan, it being very uneven and heavy timbered with oak, maple, lin, beech, walnut, elm, tamarac and cedar swamps, together with a general variety of under-brush, and stone in places, without stint, equal to anything I ever saw. . . . I am not in favor of enforcing the draft on many in this country; for improving such land as this, ought to exempt any man from any farther duty. . . . The drafting is now going on, and all quiet. The commissioner, who two weeks ago had to escape through the windows, and flee for his life, to-day, with his little daughter blindfolded to draw the names, is performing his duty as quietly as in church, and the sheriff, a noble looking Teutonic with stentorian lungs, cries off the names as fast as the recorders can write them down. I may not attempt to describe the scene, for while the lot performs some strange freaks, as the drawing of one 70 years of age, or blind, or dead for months, or incurably sick, or just married, or an unknown name, &c. &c., yet it is exhibited more in the looks, or expression of countenance than in words, and must be seen to be realized, some sad, others joyful, some crying, others laughing, some like the Dutchman, who hearing a certain name announced, remarked, dats my nearest neighbor up de road; the next name drawn, dats my nearest neighbor down de road; the next, dats my neighbor across de road; and the next, Oh mine Got! dats me, and sloped. But in a large majority of cases it evidently makes a good hit, taking "a bully secesh." There are present, a fair representation from every town in the county, of men, women and children, and when the draft of a town is ended, those drawn, gather in groups, drawn together by a fresh tie, as they must go to the war, and in deepest sympathy with each other, shake hands like long parted friends, and then away to the tavern to treat resolution; and those not drawn, also gathering and shaking hands in great ecstasy, hie away to the saloon to take a drink on their good fortune; and when well beered, Uncle Sam and his best friends, get particular fits. Poor fellows, they are ignorant, led on by wicked designing men, too many of whom, for the present, escape retribution; but particular judgments await them. The usual price for a substitute, is from $300 to $500. . . .

VAN.   Vol. 7, pp. 8–9

A receipt for three hundred dollars paid by Abraham Gilman of Yorkville to avoid military duty. Until 1864, drafted men could exempt themselves by paying a fee.   WHi Image ID 71927

A correspondent at Camp Randall, where draft resisters were being held, wrote to dispel some myths about the drafted militia, noting the physical and economic hardship that had prevented many from enlisting.

Camp Randall, Madison, Dec. 30, 1862.
. . . I wish to speak of the Drafted Militia of Wisconsin, and dispel, if I may, certain foolish ideas nourished by some of those who have never seen a

company of "drafted" men, and who seem to look upon them as a set of men different from all other mortals. . . .

The draft-rioters are closely confined in the large building formerly used during the State Fairs. When they wish they can enlist, and as soon as they get tired of their prison life, they do so.

But few of them are left, and those who remain will soon repent of their sins.

The draft in this State, you are aware, was made on the 10th of November, the drafted ones reporting in Racine, Madison and Milwaukee. The counties of Racine, Kenosha and Sheboygan reported at Camp Utley, Racine. They remained there until the 7th of December, and there no longer being quarters for them, they were sent to Madison, where they are now organized in companies.

In a draft of 5,000 men, many cases of peculiar hardship must of course have been made known, over which the Commissioner had no power to act. But had they rejected all who should have been exempt, these cases would have been far less numerous. To tell the plain truth, the draft was a one-sided concern in many counties; and while many disabled men were drafted, many able-bodied ones were exempt. For this the Draft Commissioners ought, in justice, to be held responsible, so far as possible.

Soon after the men reported in Racine no less than *forty* were discharged in one day for sufficient reasons, some of them having injured limbs, heart disease and other complaints, which even a half-way doctor should have known would have rendered a man unfit to endure the hardships of camp-life. The companies now in camp here are entirely free from all kinds of physical disability.

But there are or were cases of a different nature, and no less painful. Sometimes from one family *all* the male members would be drafted, leaving families at home entirely destitute of means for their support, and having only the consolation of waiting till "pay day," subsisting till then as best they might. One man was drafted who had *three* families to support, and *all* of them poor. Another was drafted who had two brothers in the army, and whose father was dead. He was anxious to enlist with his brothers, but it being impossible for all three to go, and being the youngest, they induced him to remain at home with his mother and sisters. A truer patriot does not live. And I might mention numerous other cases that were made known when they come into camp. Many of the worst of them, however, by order of Governor, directing that officers should substitute themselves, have been released.

Many of those who were able procured substitutes, the price at first being as high as three hundred dollars, but falling as low as one hundred and twenty-five. . . .

N. W. S.   Vol. 6, pp. 274–75

Mutiny at Camp Randall

Yet another difficulty seen in Wisconsin was the mutiny of the 17th Wisconsin, one half of which refused to go to the front until they had received their pay.

Madison, March 24th, 1862.

Dear Advocate:—During the most of last week this quiet City of Madison was considerably disturbed by the mutiny among the soldiers in Camp Randall. The only Regiment remaining in Camp after the departure of the 15th and 16th some two weeks ago, was the 17th known as the Irish Regiment. Nearly or quite all the men in it being Irishmen, excepting the Company from Oconto and Green Bay called the French Mountaineers.

Since the Governor received orders from Gen. HALLECK, two weeks ago, to forward on all the volunteers in the State just as fast as transportation could be provided, this regiment being the last one mustered in, has been getting ready to move, and when their turn came on Wednesday last to pack up for a start they had not been paid, and most of them declared that they would not move until the demand for pay had been complied with. But there was no money here and the order to move on was imperative, therefore go they must, as all good soldiers were bound to do. The paymaster telegraphed that the money would not be on in time to pay them here, but that they would be paid in St. Louis. But they were stubborn, and nothing would satisfy them but the money, no reasoning could reach them, and the officers, one and all, from the Colonel down seemed to be as little inclined to obey orders as the men. The truth was all had been running up bills in town, the officers at the hotels and the men at the saloons, and their creditors were secretly urging them to stand out to the last. The consequence was a most disgraceful and cowardly neglect of duty on the part of the officers, and complete disorganization of the men. During Wednesday night and Thursday, the excitement ran high. The Governor could do nothing, because he had no force to back him up, and the thing had to take its course. Finally about one half the regiment were persuaded to go, and accordingly left about 4 o'clock P. M. In the meantime the Governor had telegraphed to Col. MULLIGAN at Chicago for a force sufficient to quell the riot and enforce obedience, but the great snow storm had so blocked up the roads that nothing could get through. On Friday morning about two hundred more changed their minds, and followed their companions, leaving about three hundred of the worst and most desperate behind, threatening everybody generally, and the City particularly.

On Friday about midnight a detachment of Col. MULLIGAN's men, of Lexington notoriety, with several officers, arrived, well armed; and every soldier, remaining in camp, about two hundred, suddenly awoke at early dawn, with a bayonet, not his own, at his breast. Such a surprise party you never saw. They were all disarmed, marched to quarters and kept under strong guard till put on board the cars. In the mean time pickets, piloted by police officers, patrolled the city during the night and morning, and before 8 o'clock had bagged 60 in the Court House and jail. Thus in time for the 10:30 train, having been in town but eleven hours, the officers and men who knew their duty and had courage to inforce it, had caught nearly three hundred men of this rebellious crew, and had them safely in the cars and on their way to join their Regiment, and the town was rid of a dangerous mob. There was one instance of soldier-like Conduct that ougt to be recorded. Capt. ——, of a company from Milwaukee, during the worst of the excitement, and before any had consented to go on Thursday morning, called out his company and told them that he was as much in want of his money as any of them, and would be as glad to have it, but he had got orders to get to the war and he was going, and, now, says he, Boys: I want ye to vote; and every one of ye that will go with me, will signify the same by presenting arms, and I will shoot every d—d coward of ye that don't present arms when I tell him. You had better believe that every man of that company shouldered arms and marched off to the cars. An instance of good pluck in an Orderly sergeant, who fearlessly, in the absence of the cowardly officers, compelled his company to "fall in" and obey orders, was rewarded by a Lieutenant's commission by the Governor on the spot.

I am glad to say that our friend "Dave," as a good "Orderly" should do, with over half his company as good soldiers, were among the most quiet, and left with the first part of the regiment. Some of the remainder held out to the last and were caught and forced away with the last installment, and some are still behind, who as they give themselves up or are caught, will be transferred to the 19th Regiment, now at Milwaukee. . . .

Yours, truly,

INSIDER.   Vol. 6, p. 28

Confederate Prisoners

Military success in Tennessee brought a glut of Confederate prisoners north with little room to house them. From April to June 1862, Camp Randall became a prison camp for Confederates captured at Island No. 10, a battle fought on the Mississippi River from February through April in 1862.

Matters at Camp Randall.

THREE HUNDRED MORE PRISONERS.—About 4 o'clock yesterday afternoon, three hundred more prisoners, from Island No. 10, arrived at Camp Randall. A large crowd awaited their arrival, and when they came, regarded their removal from the cars to the camp, with curious interest. They were received by a guard of the 19th regiment, accompanied by a fife and drum band playing lively airs. They passed between the files to the camp—many of them heavily laden with baggage. They all looked tired and jaded, and the pale faces of some of them showed that they were more seriously affected. When they were nearly inside the camp, the band struck up the tune of "Dixie" and the steps of the prisoners were at once made firmer and their eyes brighter. There were about 60 sick prisoners, and the removal of these afforded a painful spectacle. Its sadness was relieved, though, by the tender manner in which the soldiers of the 19th supported their tottering steps while helping them to the stretchers. One lady accompanied the prisoners, in attendance on a sick brother, and we hear that her husband died on the way from Cairo, as also ten other sick prisoners, whose bodies were buried at Prairie du Chien. When inside the camp some of the prisoners sat down on their baggage and, with heads in hands, seemed to be thinking of "the sunny south." One middle aged man with a ruddy face, and substantially dressed as a civilian said, with a strong Kentuckian accent, as he passed a group of bystanders in the camp, "come and see me, gentlemen, I am a Kentuckian." The sight afforded one of the dull horrors of war, and it must have been depressing to every well wisher of humanity. Oh! humanity, thy name is weakness, and, as Ecclesiastes truly writes, "thy days are vanity."

The prisoners who came first, have got settled in their new quarters. They cook their own rations, and express themselves satisfied with their quantity and quality, although some miss very much the corn bread that they have been accustomed to. Lt. Col. Whipple tells us that some of them have written excellent letters to their friends at home, in which their satisfactory treatment is commented on in the most grateful terms. Several prisoners expressed gratitude for papers given them by visitors, and we found a prevailing anxiety for a supply of reading matter. This should be a sufficient hint for all practical philanthropists. We heard two or three of the prisoners say that they would like the chance to work with some of the surrounding farmers, thinking it would be better for their health. The impression that they were sold out at Island No. 10 seems to be general amongst them. Amongst the late arrival of prisoners, we noticed a little, fair-faced black-eyed boy. He looked barely 14 years old, and bore along baggage like his elder comrades. The wavy black hair that escaped from his military cap made us think of the fond and anxious mother that may be mourning his absence.—*April 25th.*

Vol. 6, p. 90

In late April, two prisoners escaped Camp Randall, while rumors circulated that a handful more had escaped or were planning to.

ESCAPE OF THREE PRISONERS.—This morning a person who had seen and closely scanned the prisoners at Camp Randall, met two individuals heading for the country, which from their attire, he was sure belonged to Camp Randall. He named the circumstance, and it became noised around that *eight* prisoners had escaped from Camp Randall. We understand that the commanding officers have discovered that three of the prisoners are missing. This discovery has caused extra strictness in granting admission to the Camp, and the old passes are cancelled.—*April 29.*   Vol. 6, p. 91

THE RECAPTURE.—The two prisoners who escaped from Camp Randall yesterday were promptly recaptured by Lieut. Col. Whipple, assisted by P. B. Fields, of this city. They were first seen and noticed by Mr. Philo Dunning, and it was heard that they had inquired for Waterloo, in Jefferson county. This afforded a complete scent which was ably and successfully taken advantage of by the Lieut. Colonel. Enveloped in a buffalo robe he rode along in a buggy with Mr. Fields until they came to a wagon in which the escaping prisoners were riding. The Lieut. Colonel speedily brought them to a standstill and while Mr. Fields returned to the city for a team he walked them before him only armed with a club and telling them that they ought to be ashamed of themselves, after he had treated them so humanely, to thus abuse his confidence and trouble him. They passed a house where they had taken dinner but had neither paid for it nor offered to do so. Col. Whipple asked them if they had any money and upon one of them producing 10 cts., he called the woman of the house to receive it from him. The two prisoners walked through the city tied together with a rope, presenting a miserable appearance. They will be set to digging under a guard as a punishment for the attempt, and from what we hear it is probable that they will be kept busy during their stay in camp. Both of them are of Northern birth, one hailing from Waterloo, in Jefferson county, Wis., and the other from Canada. The Waterloo man's name is Laing, and he worked for a time on a farm at Aztalan, Jefferson county. They escaped from a portion of the hospital near the fence, which it is supposed they entered under pretence of seeing some friends.   Vol. 6, p. 91

A TRAITOROUS GUARD.—Several days since it will be remembered that two prisoners escaped from Camp Randall, who were subsequently retaken. Yesterday it was ascertained that they escaped through the complicity of a private named Carr, in Capt. Grady's Co., from Milwaukee, Nineteenth Regiment. They had bribed him with what loose change they had left, and some Southern bank notes. It was also ascertained that a plot had been formed by which a large number were to be released through his agency the next time he should be placed on guard, which would have been last night. His trunk was searched and money and Southern bank notes found in it, which he had received for his infidelity.

CARR has been placed under arrest, and will doubtless be made an example of. The punishment for his offence, by military regulations, is death.

Vol. 6, p. 92

Tension between prisoners and guards at Camp Randall eventually boiled over.

—The Madison Journal says: One of the rebel prisoners at Camp Randall was shot on Friday the 10th inst, by Private Wicks, of Capt. Bennett's company, who was acting as one of the sentries. The circumstances as we hear them were briefly as follows: One of the prisoners was intruding in a certain nameless respect upon the sentry's beat. The sentry ordered him off. Upon this, another prisoner, a brother of the first mentioned, stepped forward and commenced abusing the sentry in the foulest language he was capable of using, applying the most opprobrious epithets to him. Whereupon Wicks raised his musket and shot the offender dead on the spot.

We hear that some of the prisoners have been quite insolent of late. The sentries have been ordered, we are told, to fire upon prisoners who assail them in this manner, and the prisoners duly notified accordingly. This is the first instance where the order has been carried into effect, though we hear that a sentry several days ago upon being called a "Bull Run son of a bitch" by a prisoner, snapped his musket at him, which missed fire on account of a defective cap.

Vol. 6, p. 87

In late May the Confederate prisoners started being shuffled to other camps in the North, and Camp Randall's use as a prisoner of war camp came to an end.

—The secesh prisoners for some weeks quartered at Camp Randall, have mainly left for Chicago. They took their departure a little before 11 o'clock to-day, under guard of company A, 19th Regiment, Captain Tucker, of LaCrosse, and Co. B, Captain Strong, of Sauk County.

The train consisted of 23 freight cars fitted up with seats, for the prisoners, and three passenger cars for the 19th, guarding them. The prisoners had a good deal of plunder, and it took some time to get them on board. They were reluctant to leave, as they liked their location, their camp, the water, and their treatment. They were in first rate spirits, however, singing and cheering as they started. Quite a crowd was down to see them off.

About 40 sick were taken along, straw being provided for them to lie on, and 130 were left behind as too seriously ill to move.

> ☞ Ninety-eight of the rebel prisoners at Camp Randall, Madison, Wis., have died, up to May 23d. This is a very large percentage—more than double that in Camp Douglas.—*Chicago Tribune.*

The case of the large per centage of mortality here results from the fact that the desperately, hopelessly sick among the rebels taken at Island number 10 were brought to this place instead of Chicago, probably for the reason that the Mississippi furnished conveyance by steamer to within one hundred miles of this point.

The mortality has not been among the prisoners brought here by way of Chicago, and whose sanitary condition was similar to those at Camp Douglas. These experienced great benefit in getting away from the raw air of Lake Michigan, and we doubt if a single man of the 800 or more of their class has died of disease.—The deaths have been among those who came via Prairie du Chien; men utterly broken down by disease and exposure.—The physicians predicted when they first arrived here that a large proportion of them would unavoidably die.

The item quoted above would seem to indicate, without this explanation, that the prisoners at Camp Douglas received superior care, or that Chicago is a healthier city than this. It is not probable that the former is the case, while in regard to the latter we may safely challenge comparison with any town, either East or West.   Vol. 6, p. 87

Indian Scare

In August 1862, military matters hit home in Minnesota and Wisconsin when rumors of Indian troubles began to circulate. Although no conflict erupted in Wisconsin, in Minnesota a Sioux uprising left several hundred Minnesotans dead and displaced thousands more. Instead of heading south, the 25th Wisconsin was sent west to help restore peace while Minnesotans harbored thoughts of vengeance against the Sioux.

Camp by the Wayside,
Dec. 6th, 1862.

FRIEND BRICK: On the 4th Col. Montgomery and staff left Mankato for Winona. Two companies remained until yesterday, the 5th, when we all left, not however without witnessing the long expected outbreak of the citizens, to massacre the captured Indians, who were kept in Col. Miller's camp, one mile from Mankato. It has been known for a long time that organizations were being made throughout the country for the purpose of lynching the Indians, should the President not authorize the hanging [of] them. On the evening of the 4th, some Germans from St. Peter and vicinity arrived in town bringing the intelligence that they had come to take vengeance on the Indians, that they were to be joined by citizens from New Ulm, and other towns, and that they were about eight hundred strong.

Col. Miller immediately dispatched messengers to the various posts for reinforcements. The troops, both cavalry and infantry began to come in by nine o'clock, while the Germans were lagering up and talking over the matter with their friends in Mankato. The camp had been heavily reinforced. About 11 o'clock, the people, mostly Germans, numbering perhaps seventy five, started for camp, in squads of a dozen or so, armed visibly with clubs and axes, and invisibly with bayonets, butcher knives and other instruments of slaughter. Some of them bought new jack knives and exhibiting them said, "This night that knife takes an Indian's scalp," etc., etc. On their arrival near the camp, instead of meeting their comrades from New Ulm, they were surrounded by the cavalry and taken into camp, and after promising to behave themselves they were released. The bridge across the Blue Earth, near camp, where the New Ulm delegation would have to cross to join them, was guarded by a large body of infantry, so that they could not come to their aid. They went back very much disappointed.

There is no doubt of a secret organization, composed of the best citizens of the country, ready at a moment's notice, as soon as it is ascertained that the President does not intend to give them their just deserts, to take vengeance into their own hands, and God knows it its hoped they will. To see the devastation of the country, the homes made desolate, etc., by these Indians, is horrible to think of.

On the morning of the 5th, Col. Miller ordered the Indians brought down to the new quarters, which have been built for them in Mankato. About 10 o'clock they came in, guarded on all sides by double files of soldiers. They presented an imposing cavalcade, over four hundred of them marched in couples, as they were chained together. Their heads were uncovered and as they passed through the streets almost everyone was recognized by some of the spectators as being engaged in the massacres. Some men recognized those who had murdered their families, and women recognized those who had massacred their little children. Who can blame the poor creatures for wishing to inflict summary vengeance, when there is a prospect of the demons being let loose again? Had they used more discretion, they could have killed every Indian before the guard could have been reinforced. Yours, in haste,

A. W. GRIPPEN.   Vol. 7, p. 10

The 1st Wisconsin Comes Home

After only ten weeks in the South, the 1st Wisconsin, a ninety-day regiment whose term had expired, came home to Milwaukee. Though the men had been in the field only a short time, they had visibly changed.

On Saturday, Aug. 17th, the "gallant first" of Wisconsin arrived in Milwaukee. After a campaign of ten weeks in the enemy's country, they have returned—all, with the exception of two are living—some probably will enlist again, while the greater part of them will follow other pursuits. It is estimated that there were at least 15,000 people at the depot to welcome them back again to their friends.

At a little past one o'clock, as the train appeared in sight, the Artillery Company of Capt. Herzberg fired a salute of thirty-four guns.

As soon as the soldiers were out of the cars, and once fairly in Milwaukee, the multitude charged them, and then commenced a tumultuous scene of congratulating, hand shaking and interrogating. Mothers and sisters were there, and the metamorphose that had taken place in the appearance of many of the men, from light complexioned and trim youth to weather browned and sinewy soldiers with odd moustaches and dusty whiskers, and many of them with Mexican Sombreros that had been made by ebony fingers in the land of contraband—all made up such strange *ensemble* that mothers even hesitated before kissing their own sons.

But despite the darkened skins, the faded uniforms and weary limbs, the boys looked healthy and cheerful, and responded to the congratulations of their friends with vigor.

As they passed along the streets the wildest enthusiasm filled the entire city. Cheer after cheer greeted them as they passed along. House tops and every place where there was any probability of catching the first sight of the gallant fellows, was filled long before they started from the depot.

The following was the line of march laid down:

Up South Water across Walker's Point Bridge; up East Water to Detroit; up Detroit to Main; up Main to Mason; up Mason to Cass; up Cass to Division; down Division to Chestnut Street Bridge; across the Bridge and up Chestnut Street to Ninth; down Ninth to Spring; up Spring Street to Camp Ground.

Arriving at their old mess house a splendid dinner was in waiting for the hungry and tired soldiers. The reception of the 1st by the Milwaukeans is an occasion that they may well feel proud of.

After the soldiers had finished their repast, they repaired to the South of the mess house and listened to an eloquent address delivered by Mat. H. Carpenter, Esq.   Vol. 1, pp. 49–50

CHAPTER 2

Camp Life

T HE LION'S share of a soldier's time was spent not in battle or on campaign, but in camp. Camp life offered a dramatic change from the routines the young men had heretofore known. Their rising and times of repose were no longer dictated by farm chores or a storekeeper's clock, but by the beating of reveille and taps; the labor or learning they were used to was replaced by drill and picket duty; houses were exchanged for tents or log huts in the winter, and sometimes nothing but a blanket and the southern sky over their heads.

Wisconsin's boys in blue were not shy about sharing their thoughts on their situation in the army, and their accounts of camp life reveal a range of moods—from ennui and exhaustion to a spirit of adventure and excitement—as they struggled to adapt to their new way of life. Oblique references, sometimes ironic, sometimes bitter, to the causes of the war show us how ideals could be tested even before the soldiers faced bullets or bayonets.

Daily Life

Early in the war, a Wisconsin soldier condensed army life to three activities: reading, sleeping, and drill—which left plenty of time to imagine the as-yet-unknown ordeal of battle and to long for home.

August 16, 1861.
We are on the Maryland side of the Potomac, on Rock Creek, about one mile from the city of Washington, and are entirely surrounded by troops. We are in a good healthy position. Our rapid improvement in drilling is quite noticeable. The drilling of Co. A consists chiefly in skirmishing now. The discipline is necessarily rigid: the soldiers not being allowed to pass

the guard either night or day—nor are the commissioned officers much more privileged. Our little army from Sauk County hold out nobly as far as health, hope and courage are concerned. The most of them are young and have left good comfortable homes, yet they seem to endure fatigue as well and even better than some companies composed more of pinery and river men, who have been accustomed to harder usage.

We spend our time principally, when not drilling or sleeping, in reading, as many of us brought books with us, and have also the daily papers printed in Washington and Baltimore brought into camp. But the most welcome sheet we receive is the *Baraboo Republic*, for which we are very grateful to your kindness Mr. Editor, in sending us some copies.—It is like an intimate friend from home, and talks of things familiar and people with whom we are acquainted. Some of the boys have maps also of the seat of war, which they study and they think they can plan a campaign as well as any one.

We do not notice much difference between the climate here and that of home. The nights have been quite cool since we came here. The boys are more eager than ever to get into action. They say they would like to do up the fighting and go home; but it is improbable and I think I may safely say *impossible* that all of us shall see home again. Each one is confident that some of us must die, but he rather thinks that he, himself, will not be one of the unfortunate victims. I think, however, that none would cling to life if it was demanded to gain a single victory. Though the camp is not a congenial place for a person that would be of a dreamy or reflective turn of mind, it does not serve to diminish the fond memory of those relatives and kind friends that we left in Sauk County. The usual excitement of such a place if allayed at times would, under such circumstances, naturally be succeeded by pleasant yet almost painful recollections.

Last night it seemed as if all were irresistibly and collectively reminded of home. It was a beautiful moon-light evening and Kalorama Heights, although not so very rude or wild, appeared grand and impressive last night. The camp was quiet and all seemed to be enjoying the silent beauties of the scene with the greatest admiration. But the most touching feature of all was a silver band, a little way distant, commenced playing "Sweet Home." This was almost unendurable. The gentle strains of that familiar tune had greater significance and more effect than ever before. But let me not get wearisome. The more we think of home the more determined and anxious we feel to protect them from a traitors domineering hand, and preserve their sacred relation to the government under which they have prospered and been made beautiful.

Yours in sincerity,

H. J. H. Vol. 1, pp. 245–46

Camp Jefferson, Bacon Creek, Ky.,
February, 1st., 1862.

Eds. Sentinel:—Bacon Creek still keeps on in the uneven tenor of its way, sometimes being a rapid rolling river, and at other times a pleasant meandering stream, such as poets delight to describe, and lovers to wander beside, whispering soft nonsense each to each by the soft silver light of the moon, or listening to the dulcet strains of the nightingale or bullfrog.

We read in the Holy Writ that the evening and morning were the first day; just here with a slight variation; reveille and tatoo being not only the first day but all the other days, and the performances of one day are so similar to that of all the others, that a description of one would answer for all; six o'clock being reveille, when every man must tumble out and give good advice to the deaf by saying *hear*, after which the bedding (one blanket for each man) is folded and every knapsack is packed as though for a march, the straw placed in one corner of the tent and the tent swept (we have a broom in our company). By this time it is breakfast and each man gathers himself around the mess table and takes his due proportion of hog, hominy, hard bread hocks, or their equivalent as the case may be; then comes guard mounting, where each strives to be the cleanest man, to be color guard for the day. Nine o'clock brings company drill, when for two hours the gallant defenders of their country's flag are marched, remarched, and countermarched, formed, reformed (?) and sometimes misinformed, arms are shouldered, ordered, supported, carried, right shoulder shifted, ported, secured, reversed, loaded, primed, aimed, recovered, stacked, &c., &c., until eleven o'clock, when the men go to their tents and amuse themselves as they please until two, except that they are required to partake of the dainties which they are called upon to enjoy when the sun is supposed to have reached his meridian height. (This is all supposition as we never know from observation.) At two o'clock, p. m., "the bugle again calls to arms," the battalion is formed, and the tread of armed men is heard on the hills and in the valleys near our house. After being marched forward, backward, sideways and endways until four p. m., there is a cessation of drill for a time and then comes dress parade, supper, and eight o'clock, which brings tatoo, then taps, and the day is done, and the tired soldier falls asleep to dream of the dear friends or wife and children, or sweetheart he has left behind, or perhaps of those halcyon days when he had milk in his coffee; or peaceful nights in times gone by, when a feather pillow was not so much of a luxury as now; or his truant thoughts may return to childhood's happy hours, when he could eat at a table with a knife and fork, and have butter on his bread; but hark! there is a gun, the morning signal, and, gentle reader, it brings ditto, or a repetition of what you have just read. . . .

Your growling friend,

AGAWAM.   Vol. 4, pp. 174–75

Camp of the 4th Wisconsin Cavalry, Baton Rouge, Louisiana, October 25, 1864   WHi Image ID 33529

The sheer number of troops amassed into the armies produced makeshift cities brimming with activity, large enough that men could get lost in the mazes of their streets. Returning from guard duty, a soldier of the 8th Wisconsin viewed the camp and marveled at its size and the logistics involved in taking care of such a conglomeration of men.

Hamburg, Tenn., April 25, 1862.

MESSRS. EDITORS:—My company with five others, have just returned from grand guard, four miles in advance of the main body. Our chain of sentinels on our outposts extend 13 miles in length, covering the whole front of the army. Here we deploy the men as skirmishers; they stand from 15 to 20 yards apart just as the ground will permit. They are called masked sentinels and are stationed behind trees, logs, and such things as come near. On the main roads strong detachments of infantry are stationed beyond us, and still further cavalry pickets. Just as we were relieved last evening a squad of rebel cavalry made their appearance, and our cavalry pickets started in pursuit of them. They fled to the woods, and as our pickets entered the woods a party of infantry fired on them, but no one was hurt. Our five companies were then ordered forward at once; we proceeded to the spot where the skirmish took place, but were too late to get a shot, the rebels having fled to the woods. Night coming on, and our commander not wishing to provoke a fight just now, we were ordered back to camp.

It would be impossible for me to let you how many troops there are here, even if I should try to find out. All I can say is the ground we cover extends 13 miles in length, and three miles in width, all one entire camp, and the river is lined with transports, for miles each way, loaded with troops. You would imagine yourself in some great city to see the men going to and fro, troops moving constantly. In one direction you would see a battery of guns moving out to find a camping ground; in another direction you would see a regiment of cavalry; in another you would see infantry, till you are bewildered with the exciting scene. Sights are to be seen here that will never be forgotten by those that witness them.

Besides the troops here, Gen Mitchell is south of us with 25,000 men. Our lines will soon meet his. This is the army of the war. Men get lost in the camps, and it is almost impossible to find the way back if one goes far from home. All that I wonder at is how the government manages to get the feed around as regular as it comes. . . . We keep two day's rations cooked on hand all the while, and ready to move at any minute. . . .

Wisconsin is well represented in this army, and I think every Wisconsin regiment has some one in it from Rock county, for there is not a day but some one comes to see some of my men. Lieut. King is sick in hospital here, with the fever. The rest of my men are well and in good spirits. They think after this fight the war will soon be over, and they say they will fight "for keeps," and I think they will. We have had no news from the north for the last seven days. Send the mail to Cairo.

Yours & c., W. B. BRITTON,

Capt. Co. G, 8th Reg. W. V.   Vol. 4, p. 71

The soldier's life could be rather pleasant, according to a soldier of the 1st Wisconsin, who wrote of days spent berry picking, foraging, and skirmishing with Southern pickets.

Camp near Conrad's Ferry,

Maryland, Aug. —.

Dear Journal:—This is a great country to stay in. We can live here with a perfect contempt of danger, and with all the sovereign independence characteristic of the genuine Badger. We amuse ourselves by eating blackberries and hoecake, swimming in the canal, shooting across the river at the rebel pickets, reading secession papers and the Bible, and chasing runaway niggers. What time is not thus occupied, is agreeably consumed in sleeping, playing poker, standing on guard, calling on the country belles, and thinking of the time when we shall reach our friends at home. . . .

"Picket" duty is decidedly pleasant, especially that part which consists in *picking* berries, or rather disposing of them after they are picked. To be the one forty-thousandth part of a great army is to be reduced to a very small fraction of a unit, and materially lessens ones chances for getting his share of the good things of earth. Hence, while we are unable to do Uncle Sam any greater service, we are content to be diffused along the Potomac, feast our eyes on its mountain scenery, and look zealously after our bodily comforts, on the pretext of our "detached duty." Since the appearance of new potatoes, fresh butter, hoe-cake, pies, cakes, and green apples, in camp, pilot bread, (sometimes called cast iron pies,) fat pork and burnt rice are taken at a large discount.

Incidents of note are not numerous. It is the same dull round every day, with nothing to relieve the monotony of camp life. . . .

A handsome little feat was performed a day or two since by Langworthy and three or four others from Co. E, who crossed the river, drove out a rebel picket of 10 or 12 men, who were concealed behind a pig pen, killed 2 of them, burnt a house in which the rebels were in the habit of concealing themselves and firing upon our men, and returned safely with the exception of Langworthy, who was slightly wounded in the left side. . . .

C. Vol. 1, pp. 48–49

> Headquarters 27th Reg't, Wis. Vol's.,
> Little Rock, Ark., Dec., 22d, 1863.

EDITOR TIMES:— . . . We passed several deserted plantations, the fields overgrown with weeds and brush, showing plainly the foot prints of rebellion, which has left the deluded people of Arkansas in such a miserable condition. The first day we marched 20 miles and camped for the night under the open canopy of heaven. I never saw a more lovely night, nor ever slept sounder; with the dry leaves for our matrass and knapsacks for pillows, the bright stars peeped down upon us through the overhanging branches of the trees, and as we sat around our camp fires it seemed more like a band of Gypsies than a lot of Uncle Sam's soldiers. . . .

S. M. Vol. 10, p. 337

Camps often became semipermanent in the winter. These soldiers have Sibley, or bell, tents with log bases and outdoor cooking stoves. WHi Image ID 10841

On the Picket Line

Picket duty offered some men, like this soldier of the 5th Wisconsin, time to read, write letters, or sew up holes in their uniforms with a "housewife," a sewing kit often given to soldiers when they left for the front.

I am sitting by one of the picket fires at the "Big Reserve" near Camp Griffin. I have just finished "The Jew's Daughter"—(don't misunderstand me—"The Jew's Daughter" is not a woman, but a story that I have been reading). It is,—let me see,—a quarter of twelve,—and what shall I do next? The hours tarry too long without something to occupy one's mind, and it is almost too cold to sleep. Here is my knapsack; let's see what is in it. My "housewife," presented by a little girl in Berlin. I might mend that hole in my knee, for here is the material—thread, needles and cloth—but that would not be amusement. Here, too, is my portfolio with pencil and paper. "Peleg" has gone home, and I might write a letter to the *Courant*. I'll do it.

It is supposed that a soldier "on picket" has something to tend to more "in his trade" than reading and writing. Well, so he has, but though this is called so, it *is not* properly a picket guard. Pickets are stationed in squads, and, if possible, concealed where they can see and not be observed themselves. We are stationed as sentinels, one in a place, have our beats to walk, and are relieved at regular intervals.

This Brigade furnishes, each morning, for picket duly, one hundred and forty-four men, officers included. This column of men upon arriving at the outposts is divided into the first and second relief, each relief having an equal number of men. The first relief starts immediately to relieve the sentinels; the second remains here at the "Big Reserve" until 9 o'clock P. M., and are free to spend their time as they please until that hour, when they take the place of the first, and these come into the "Big Reserve."

This is called the "Big Reserve" because further out and more in the immediate vicinity of the sentinels, are three smaller ones. At each of these twenty-two privates are posted, eleven to go on and a like number to relieve these in due time. These "Little Reserves" are known as the "Right," "Center" and "Left."—The Right is commanded by a Captain, the Left by a Lieutenant, and a Sergeant takes charge of the Center. The whole is in command of an officer, who may be a Colonel, Lieut. Colonel or Major, and who is called the "Field Officer of the Day."

At 7 o'clock A. M., the details for picket from each regiment begin to assemble on their regimental color lines, and having all "fell in" are marched thence to the Brigade parade ground to be put through the ceremony of "guard mounting." Those who arrive first have the first relief, which is much better than the second, because it stays at the Big Reserve at night, being relieved from further watch at 9 o'clock P. M.

Now the Wisconsin boys get up early, and ain't afraid of a little cold weather, so they always get the first relief, and when night comes they can sit by a pleasant fire, chat, sing songs, smoke their pipes, read novels, write letters, or, if it is not too cold, spread their blankets and take a nap. Talking about the latter luxury reminds me, as, no doubt my letter will you, that I would like to have some; so I will put up my writing and
To the "land of Nod," like wicked Cain,
Where until morning I remain
Yours, &c.,
KNAPSACK   Vol. 3, p. 148

Being in close proximity to one another, Union and Confederate pickets spent a healthy amount of time shooting at one another, while also arranging a truce from time to time to exchange small talk and trade food or tobacco.

Camp No. 21. In the field six miles from Richmond,
June 19, 1862.

EDITORS STATE JOURNAL: . . . No day passes without some exciting incident in camp, or on the line. A narrow belt of timber separates the camp of the Union men from that of the rebels.—In this timber both parties station pickets and from behind his cover, each watches the opportunity to shoot into his foe.

Sometimes the pickets get tired of this out of sight business while within hearing distance of each other, and seeming friendly colloquies take place.

While on duty last week I listened to the following:
Secesh—"Hallo! over there, got any terbacker?"
Union—"Of course I have, come over and get some."

S.—"Can't spare the time, very busy here."

Both were quiet a moment when Secesh called out. "Now don't you shoot and I won't."

U.—"I'll not shoot, come out. What reg't is that making such a noise behind the wood?"

S.—"Oh that's the relief, and I'm d—n glad of it too. Do you get all you want to eat in your army."

U.—"Plenty of beef, hard crackers and coffee."

S.—"God! We ain't had coffee for two months. Got any newspapers over there?"

U.—"New York *Herald*."

S.—"Come half way, and I'll exchange papers."

U.—"No shooting, old boy."

S.—"All right, leave guns behind."

Secesh boldly advanced, and met Porter's man half way, received his paper and piece of tobacco, gave the Richmond *Enquirer* of an equally late date, shook hands, said "good bye," and each repaired to his respective station.

The Union man was called to account for this breach of order, but I think, soon dismissed with a gentle reprimand. . . .

Yours truly,

E. C. H.   Vol. 3, p. 221

In the following missive, a writer identifying himself as "Stew" manages to impress upon his readers the importance of picket duty while at the same time casting serious doubts on the efficacy of the job Stew did while on picket. By the time his thoughts meander from practical information to daydreams, sidetracking through a solitary confessional, and back again to picket duty, it is time for him to be relieved and return to camp.

Camp Griffin, Va., March. 3d, 1862.

. . . Perhaps there is nothing has such a thorough fascination for the true soldier, as the picket service. It is a complete break up of camp life. He is thrown on his own resources for 24 or more hours. He eats when he can, sleeps on the dryest grass-plot, sometimes on a fence, or in a tree. He spends 6 or 8 hours of the twenty-four on his solitary post, without cover or shelter from the wildest storms. It is now 9 o'clock at night; the "taps" has just been beaten, after which all lights are put out in camp. Let us go forth to the picket line. Pile on all your overcoats and blankets, as the night is rather raw. The darkness is so intense, you might bottle it up. The clouds hang like a pall over the earth, portending one of those rain and sleet storms which overwhelm us every fourth day. The wind comes in moaning gusts from the south-west, opening a vista of blue in the sky at that point, "With one star peeping through it like an eye." Our way is encumbered with stumps, and brush, the debris of the pine, oak, and chestnut forests that have disappeared before the sturdy arms of our Wisconsin woodmen. After half an hours walk, through marshes, worn out tobacco fields, and over stony hills, we suddenly come out on an open space where the glare of fires and the sheen of burnished arms, stacked in long rows, dazzle our eyes. We soon get accustomed to the light, however, and look around. Men in scores are thrown in every imaginable shape on the ground, around blazing pine knots, that cast flickering shadows far into the woods. Some are sleeping rolled up in their blankets; some are chatting merrily, many are playing cards, and not a few are *cussing*. That is the picket "reserve," by whom the men now on post a mile farther out are relieved every 12 hours, and on whom they must retreat in case of an attack. No one who is not a soldier could believe, that those light-hearted, careless young men, are the guardians of the unconscious sleeping thousands we left in yonder camps a short time ago. But let us pass through. Now we enter the dark woods. Keep close to me friend. I know every track here; many a long hour have I spent on those bleak hills. Many a time have I traced those winding paths in storm and darkness. Often when on my lonely beat have I heard steps on the frozen snow, and watched with intense eagerness for the coming of, I knew not what, but they died away and were lost in their own echo. I have seen a rebel walk through that fence and glide towards me with stealthy step, and when I looked up after seeing that my gun was capped, prepared to send a bullet through his heart, he had vanished and nothing remained but that ceder bush, its arms swaying in the night wind. On them open fields beyond I have seen mighty hosts debouch from the dark forests, march and countermarch, form square and column, and all without a word of command, and in the deepest silence, but in a moment they had disappeared,

"Like the baseless fabric of a vision,

Leaving not a wreck behind,"

for they had no existence, save in my own imagination; they were but the clouds flitting across the face of the moon, or the tall, broad armed pines, casting their shadows upon the brown sward. Here, to, I have watched the stars circling in their mighty courses, and I was carried back in spirit to the lovely Mystic river, where, in the shadow of Bunker Hill, I long ago learned their names from books, and tried to become familiar with and find them on the blue map of heaven. And on the upper Mississippi, far away towards the sources of the "father of waters," I have seen and loved them in their beauty, and called their names in extasy, as persons do old and well-beloved friends; for they were associated in my mind with persons whom I knew in the happiest part of an otherwise short but troubled life. Here, while peering into their bright depths, I have dreamed and thought of the unknown future; and visions of a no less dim but ill spent past, rose up to chide me for knowledge (little as it was) misused, and opportunities lost. Here the nauseous thoughts of sinful indulgence, of unholy pleasures; the spectres of dead sins—dead as the vicious passions from which they sprung have passed before my mind's eye. And here also, resolves have been made to gain the better life, to which the stars only were witness. But they were broken as soon as made; for men's souls cannot be washed clean with the sponge of human fortitude, soaked in the waters of human frailty. But—*Hark!* I heard a step. There is a picket. Let us sit here and watch him. There is another, and yet another, and if you could see them, that line of muffled silent figures extends on either side to the extreme limits of our army. That is the guard who watch with sleepless eyes that no spy enter, or traitor leave the lines. Every one of them have a pass-word, a countersign, and certain signals by which they know even at a distance a friend from an enemy. All have their beat of about twenty or thirty paces, a stump, a tree, a rock, or a creek, as the case may be, marking where one end, and another begin. . . . Think of it, a line extending sixty or more miles in length, without a single break. On both sides of us, on every hill top, along the valleys, through water courses, in dingle and dell; among the oak and chestnut groves, and shaded by the stunted pines, that long line of armed men, that living chain of patriot hearts, extending from Mount Vernon, the home of Washington, to the Gauley river in the Virginia mountains, peer for ever in the black night, and watch, while their comrades sleep in full security. But the relief is coming, and we must return to camp. Good night.

STEW.   Vol. 3, pp. 161–62

A Union army post office   WHi Image ID 10893

The Lighter Side

Perhaps some of Wisconsin's soldiers were in the habit of saying their prayers after lights out; Charlie Dow of the 2nd Wisconsin shared his amended version of the Lord's Prayer.

Our Father which art in Washington, Uncle Abram is thy name; Thy victories won, Thy will be done in the South as it is in the North; Give us this day our daily pork and crackers, And forgive us our short-comings, as we forgive our Quartermaster, And lead us not by traitors but deliver us from skedaddlers; For thine is the power over the "nigger" and the soldier "for the period of three years or during the war."

Respectfully,

CHARLIE DOW.   Vol. 8, p. 157

Sometimes printing blocks, rather than bullets, were used against the enemy in a form of economic warfare.

Headquarters Seventh Regiment,
Wis. Vol., Camp No. 11, near Fredericksburg, Va., April 28, 1862.
. . . The Union feeling is faint in Falmouth. They prefer Confederate notes to U. S. Treasury notes. To punish them for such neutrality, the boys have flooded the town and bought up all their eggs, corn meal, bread, &c., with *fac similies* of their currency. Corporation notes of the city of Fredericksburg, are much in vogue. Thus Confederate notes will not be worth much in a short time. . . .
Yours truly,
W. D. W.   Vol. 3, p. 293

Soldiers stationed on Ship Island on the Gulf Coast of Mississippi had a surprise addition to their ranks.

April 8th, 1862.
A rather interesting and unprecedented incident occurred here a day or two ago. Modesty forbids my mentioning it, but it is so extremely ludicrous I cannot refrain. It is that the handsome and sprightly waiter-*boy*, in the employ of Lieut. Latham, Adjutant of the 21st Indiana reg., has just been *delivered of a child!!* I have seen and heard of many strange things happening since I first entered the service, but this is the most astonishing of all. This may be a natural phenomena here on Ship Island, and therefore I have no comments to make on the affair. Strange and thrilling events happen in this vicinity, and nothing startles our equanimity. I really believe, that if a large whale was to be seen off the Island singing, "I can read my title clear," etc., not one would wonder at it. . . .
Yours &c.,
HIGH PRIVATE.   Vol. 3, pp. 90–91

Not long since, while our army were resting at Corinth, one of our brave soldiers, (who for short we will call, yankee Myron) took a stroll into the country, and becoming thirsty, he called in at a farmers house, for a drink of water. After he had swallowed the cooling draught, with his back to the wall against which his gun was leaning, in sliped the master of the house, and placing himself between our hero and his gun, with his hand upon the latter, exclaimed: Sir, I shall be under the necessity of taking you prisoner. "Not so fast," said our yankee, and as quick as thought he drew a revolver from his pocket, and held it in such fearful proximity to the breast of Mr Secesh, that he suddenly found himself a prisoner of war. Our Yankee Myron, then ordered him "Right about face out door" march, double quick, and on arriving in the read opposite the house, our Myron discovered a fine, fat yoke of oxen, attached to a wagon, which the man had just drove up—"A fine yoke of oxen you have here, my good fellow, now by thunder while I think of it, we are out of beef down to our camp. Now I'll just jump in there and I'll be d—d if won't ride down with you.["] Thereupon secesh was obliged to drive to camp. What became of him, history does not say; but in an incredible short space of time, the nasal organs of our soldiers, were greeted with the fumes of boiling beef, supposed to be fat and luscious portions of Buck and Bright, seething in the camp kettles of the brave boys, of the noble sixteenth.

Vol. 5, p. 273

Camp Tillinghast, Virginia
March 5th, 1862.

Editors TRIBUNE:— . . . The monotony of camp life was somewhat enlivened by a fall of snow this morning. In the afternoon one of Co. "I," received an impression on the left cheek from a snow ball thrown by a member of Co. "C," (this Company is from Platteville,) which laid our young corporal *hors' du combat.* This warranted Co. "I," in turning out to resent the indignity thrown upon said corporal. No sooner was Co. "I" in line of battle, armed with a plenty of snow ball ammunition, than Co. "C" was on hand to meet the fierce onslaught of the infuriated Shake Raggers.[1] The battle began, the air was filled with missles, and shout upon shout rent the air, as here and there sat a hero, with his proboscis smashed, and suffering from the effects of a nasal hemorrhage. At this stage an armistice was asked for, as the left

---

1 "Shake Raggers" here refers to the soldiers of Company I of the 2nd Wisconsin Infantry, many of whom were from Mineral Point. The term derives from the custom of miners' wives signaling meal-times by shaking rags toward the ridge where the miners were working.

wing of the battalion wished to try the right wing on a skirmish. The two wings formed a battle array, under the walls of the adjacent fort, upon the parapets of which stood the good natured Lieut. Col. After all due preliminary arrangements, the battle again opened with increased fury, and many a poor hero wears a dark memento in the vicinity of the occular organ. At the suggestion of the Lieut. Colonel, the left wing, under command of Gen. CARY, Co. "E" was ordered to deploy a portion of the forces around the fort, and attack the right wing in the rear, but the quick eye of General BUDLONG, Col. "I," commanding the right wing, detected this strategic movement, and was prepared to foil the foe in that attempt. On came the left wing, with their colors flying, rending the air with their madened yells, while Gen. BUDLONG headed in person a detachment of his forces, and met the fierce onslaught. The fight now became terrific, and the troops of Gen. CARY's detachment became disorganized, and were now an easy prey to the excellent soldiers of BUDLONG. He captured the full detachment with the flag, and then wheeled his forces into line and made a charge upon Gen. CARY's forces, driving them into their quarters.—The six foot seven general, flushed with victory, then marched his forces from the field to the tune of Dixie, and drawing them up in line at the Colonel's quarters, presented the flag, as a trophy of war, to the Lieut. Col. The Colonel's speech on this occasion was most eloquent indeed, and so appropriate to the occasion, that I doubt not the propriety of publishing it in full. The Col. intimated that in his next dispatches to the war department, he would make a favorable mention of Gen. BUDLONG. LATER—Some difficulty having arisen as to the rightful owner of the flag, and the Col. being called upon to decide the matter, said that if the snow remained, the first opportunity should be given all hands to have a general set-to for the possession of the flag. Thus ended the matter with the two wings. The number killed and wounded on both sides is as follows:

    Left wing—killed 0,000
       "   "   wounded 250
    Right wing—killed 0,000
       "   "   wounded 50
       "   "   Missing 1
    Total killed, wounded and missing . . . 0,301

[NOTE.—Those killed are supposed to be dead, and those wounded are mostly harmed about the smeller and peepers.] . . .

Yours,

JUDGE.   Vol. 2, p. 240

Wisconsin's Lucky 13th

The 13th Wisconsin Regiment had the distinct privilege of never once being involved in a major battle. The regiment did gain a certain reputation, as the next two accounts attest, as builders and foragers.

Camp Lyon, near Ft. Henry, Tenn.,

Sunday, Nov. 30, 1862.

The 13th has fairly won the cognomen of the "Shanty Regiment." It leaves a village capable of accommodating a thousand inhabitants at every stopping place. For the past two weeks shanties and cabins have multiplied and been replenished. Now they are almost as thick as contrabands. The 13th, chafing to do that fighting which it is not allowed to do, expends its restrained fervor in building log cabins and plastered them with mud. . . . It is gratifying to see our men exercising their ingenuity and their muscles in thus making themselves more comfortable and secure for the winter, or whatever part of it they spend here. Swinging a maul or an ax is better than day after day at euchre, and riving shingles then reading "Claude Melnotte,"[2] besides both exercises save much to the government in the way physic. . . .

VID.   Vol. 5, p. 123

Fort Henry, Nov. 14, 1862.

FRIEND RANN: . . . Gen. Ransom made a short speech to our regiment, in which he complimented us for our bravery and readiness for duty at all times, and expressed a strong desire to lead us on at any time, as he should not be compelled to look back to see if we were coming. Among his many compliments he said he believed the 13th would steal the Lord's Supper and then go back for the table cloth, judging from the large amount of chickens,

---

2   Claude Melnotte is a character in the play *The Lady of Lyons* by Edward Bulwer-Lytton, used here as a representative of popular literature.

turkeys, geese, hogs and sheep which came into camp every night. . . .
Yours truly,

G. H. BECKWITH.   Vol. 5, pp. 121–22

Pinery Boys Tell a Tall Tale

Camp Griffin, Va.,
Feb. 22nd, 1862.

DEAR RECORD:— . . . It was one of those stormy unpleasant nights of which
we have had so many lately, and all who were on the "Reserve" were gathered around a little fire endeavoring to keep warm, and amusing themselves
by telling stories. One of the men of the "49th Pennsylvania," had been telling a hunting story, which looked rather large to one of our Pinery boys, and
he, as an off-sett told one to match it.

"Speaking of dangerous animals," he said, "the Gopher is the most dangerous animal we have in Wisconsin." "Pennsylvania" asked how large they
were. "Well," he said, "the largest of them are about the size of a "two year
old," but the smaller ones are not larger than a "yearling." "When I first went
to Wisconsin," said he, "I went to live with my uncle; and shortly after I went
there, I yoked up the oxen to go for some wood. I had never heard anything
about these Gophers. I started with the team for the grove which was about
a mile from the house. When I had got about half way to the timber, the
oxen stopped in the road and began to bellow and snort. I looked and could
see nothing; and tried to drive the team along, but could'nt get them to go.
I looked again: pretty soon, just a little ways ahead of the team, *out popped
two large sized Gophers!* The oxen wheeled, and started for the house, as fast
as they could run; and seeing the Gophers coming towards where I was, *I*
started and run as fast as *I* could for the house, and hurrying the oxen all I
could. The oxen did'nt run more than fifteen or twenty rods before they run
straddle of a stump and could'nt go any further. I looked back and saw that
the Gophers were gaining on me so much that I had'nt time to get the team
loose from the stump; so I run for my life until I got to the house. When I
went in my uncle asked me what was the matter. I told him what I had seen,
and that I expected that the oxen would be killed by them." "Well," said he,

(my uncle is a very precise man in his speech,) "well Pres, I am thankful that you escaped with your life. I have had several cattle destroyed by Gophers, and I ought to have told you about them before you started." "I did not go to look for the oxen for three or four days, but when I did go, there was nothing to be found but the yoke and chains, and they were badly mangled."

"I declare!" said Pennsylvania, "that beats anything I ever heard of. I should think they would give a large bounty to such animals as that."

"Well," said Wisconsin, "they do, but they are so hard to kill, a common rifle ball won't make any impression on them, their hide is so tough. They have guns made on purpose to hunt Gophers with. And then it ain't safe for one man to go out alone to hunt them. We sometime have what we call "Gopher hunts" out in Wisconsin, and all the neighborhood turns out, and we surround a large piece of country where they live and drive them all into the center and kill what we can of them.

When we have these "hunts" we leave all other animals out but the Gopher—Catamounts, Wolves, Lynx, and every other kind of animals but the Gopher."

Here the officer of the Picket cried out, "Second Relief, fall in!" and we were obliged to leave for several posts and thus ended the Gopher story for the night.

Semi-OCCASIONAL.   Vol. 3, pp. 158–59

A Soldier Scientist

Missouri proved fertile ground for fossils in addition to secessionists.

Camp Curtis, Sulphur Springs Mo., Dec. 21st, 1861. . . . Near here are many beds of fossil, I have visited them several times, armed and equipped with a pick-axe. A few days since Lieut. Benham and I went out in search of some fossils; we clambered up the side of a steep, even abrupt bluff, and dug into the rocky earth; we found many curious specimens, occasionally a shell fish, then perhaps a snail, or the bones or vertebra and fins of a fish, or a clam or muscle shell, and all as solid as the rocky hills around us. In the center of a huge rock which had been blasted and some

fifteen feet from the surface we found the bones and fins of a fish. . . .
Yours, &c.,
THE CHIP   Vol. 2, pp. 46–47

Holidays Away from Home

Headquarters, Camp Curtis,
Sulphur Springs, Mo., Dec 23rd, 1861.
Editors Patriot:—Yesterday it snowed and blowed furiously; all the live
long day the storm raged pre-eminent—high winds and chilling blasts. No
dress parade, no battalion drill, and the boys are trying to keep comfortable
around their fire places, which, by the way, are a very grand institution in
cold weather.—With the exception of a few days we have had most delightful weather since we came here.—Snow fell yesterday to the depth of three
inches, and it was a very tedious day; but the storm has abated to-day, the
sun is out warm, the snow is thawing some, and everything without again
wears a summer aspect. . . .

We are wondering how you are enjoying yourselves to-day in Madison.
Plenty of sleighing I presume, and the boys are out enjoying it. This is a
luxury that the Southern people don't have, but I prefer the Southern climate after all. Give me sunshine and summer to the freezing, chilly blasts
of the North. The summers are delightful in the North, but the winters are
horrid cold. "Santa Claus" did not visit us last night, but we heard from him.
He passed down the river this morning, but he could not get in through
our pickets, so he went on. I hung up my stockings last night over the fire
place, but found in them nothing but *holes!* If you have any old clothes laying
around your sanctum that will hold together in coming to us, send them,
and if you have any patriotic old ladies in your part of the country, for *peace*
sake and the Union, set them to knitting stockings.

A nice little cake of fresh butter rolled up in a piece of clean white cloth,
and labeled "A merry Christmas, from the women of Wisconsin," (butter on
a rag!) found its way into our tent this noon. It is quite a luxury; tho' simple,
it shows that the hearts of the women of Wisconsin are with us. May they
accept our sincere thanks for these kind remembrances, and while fighting

against the traitors of our country, our affections for them are strong. Long
may they live, an ornament to society. . . .
Devotedly, Benevolently, Seriously, Critically and Truly Yours,
"G. W. D." Vol. 4, pp. 33–34

Officers of the 2nd Wisconsin with some visiting women   WHi Image ID 33489

Camp Tillinghast, Jan. 2, 1862.

DEAR FATHER AND MOTHER.—I suppose you would like to know how I
spent New Year's, and I thought I would improve the present opportunity in
telling you. It is evening, and we have just come in from picket. We have to
travel ten miles to do picket duty. We started on Tuesday morning on this
business, and arrived there about noon, relieving the 19th Indiana regiment.
Two companies were left as a reserve, and our company took one road and
relieved the pickets that were on it, and the remainder of the company went
on other roads. We got posted by the middle of the afternoon—four men on
a post—one man on the look-out, all the while, while the other three would
keep secreted a few rods off in the woods; we relieved each other every hour.

The post to which I belonged was on the edge of some big pine woods, being the third from the last on the right wing of our picket lines. As it happened, I was on foot from half past eleven to half past twelve, so I watched the old year out and the new one in, standing behind a large pine tree, right in the edge of the woods, with my old musket by my side, looking out for secesh.

In the morning we were relieved by the reserve, and we then acted as a reserve ourselves. We remained there all New Year's day, the next night and part of next day, when the 7th regiment came out and took our places. We had no roast turkey, mince pies, nor any of those nice fixings for New Year's, which I suppose you had out there in Wisconsin. We don't get much of that fancy kind of living, I can tell you. But our New Year's will come pretty soon, for we are to get our pay next week, when I shall go over to Washington, and will have a time.

We have been fixing up our tents, so as to be comfortable, although we have had no cold weather yet. A man is comfortable here with his coat off, while you are freezing with all the clothes you can get on. I like Virginia on that account, but for nothing else. We have our tents logged up five feet inside, with a door in front, so if cold weather comes we shall be prepared for it. The officers all have blockhouses which the boys built for them. We are all in good health and in good spirits, and everything goes smoothly and nice. There is not much drilling now, but we go on picket once in three weeks. There is not much prospect of our moving forward this winter.

At three o'clock, on New Year's night, we received orders from Gen. McDowell to double the pickets, as he thought the secesh would make a break that night, but did not dare to come. They fired on the pickets on the Potomac, but were driven back. It takes twenty regiments to do picket duty; this is, 20,000 men for picket, every day, so large is our army, and so extended are its lines. Our pickets extend further than they ever did, and we keep advancing all the time. "Mac" will keep crowding until the secesh will think that the Yankees, as they call us, are imposing on them, when they will pitch into us, and try to drive us back; but that will be a job for Jeff and his "gentlemen," as he styles them. This driving back is played out; McClellan says we have made our last retreat, and we all have confidence in him. We are waiting patiently for him to lead on, for they think the more fighting they do, the sooner the war will be ended.

We are pretty near neighbors to the secesh, the pickets being about two miles apart, and like some other neighbors, we don't agree very well. They have heavy entrenchments around Centerville, and when the battle does take place, it will be the greatest one ever fought.

But I will bring my letter to a close, as it is getting almost time for tattoo. I wish you would send me a few Janesville papers, and I hope you will write soon.

From your son,

C. H. CHENEY.   Vol. 2, pp. 210–11

Dealing with the Elements

In the summer of 1862, the 8th Wisconsin found itself stationed in northern Mississippi, enduring heat and insects the likes of which they did not normally see in Wisconsin. In a letter to the Wisconsin Patriot, *a soldier identified only as G. W. D. relates his method of doing battle against southern insects.*

Headquarters 2d Brigade, 2d Division,
Camp Clear Creek, Army of the Miss., July 10th, '62.
Editors Patriot:—After several weeks of uninterrupted silence, I again write you from the land of Secession and Rebellion—of lizards, snakes and varmints, by the million. . . .

Our muskets are hanging on our cabin walls, and the excessive heat of the past week has compelled us to retire for a while from the busy scenes of life, and seek some shady nook, where, free from toil and care, the swarming multitude of flies cannot annoy us. These are the only enemies we have to contend with at the present writing, and if the secesh army possessed half the pluck and courage these infernal flies do, they might soon gain their independence. So formidable an array of these unwelcome visitors is enough to mar the patience of Job. But it is said that "one evil follows another," and that "misery likes company." This assertion I verily believe to be true, for when the heat is almost insufferable, you are tormented continually with flies buzzing around your ears, and with bugs crawling up your boot leg, or something worse. Of all the vexations incident to the life of a soldier in this climate, *these* cap the climax—their torture is excruciating, and the only method we can adopt, to spare even our bones, is to act on the defensive, when they come out to make an attack upon us in force. The plan which I have devised for my own special safety, is found to work admirably, is to place a drop of molasses on the end of your nose, lie down in the sun, and await the arrival of the enemy. The molasses will draw them out—they attack you in your front, you then immediately throw out your arms and flank them on the right and left wings, thus drawing their main force to the centre, when they will immediately make a desperate break for your nasal organ, whereupon, it is the imperative duty of every soldier to understand the next movement, and to keep an eye single to the glory attending his success—just as the enemy are about to make their last, final dash to capture the prize, you suddenly throw open wide your mouth, and the day is yours! They have such a horrible dread of *masked batteries*, they will turn in wild confusion, leaving you "monarch of all you survey!" . . . When the supply of molasses is exhausted, nothing can be resorted to but humble submission, with the conviction in your mind that its all for your beloved country and the indomitable nigger you are compelled to endure all these trials and perplexities.

I am studying *Bugology*—have quite a collection of various kinds of varmints of all colors, sizes and formation, which I intend sending you at the earliest possible moment. Think they will be very attractive in your Sanctum Sanctorum; and admired by the "big bugs" who call to see the editor. . . .
G. W. D.   Vol. 4, pp. 100–101

Camp Griffith, Washington, D. C.,
March 18, 1862.

"There is a gracefulness in the picture of the youthful warrior." So says a certain author; and, if I mistake not, the fellow thought twice before giving utterance to the idea, else it would scarcely have occurred to him that the picture deserved a compliment not due to the original. Certain it is that whatever of gracefulness Nature may have endowed a man with, little of it is likely to remain after a good "knapsack drill," or a day's march *through* the "sacred soil;" and whatever coloring of romance the "youthful warrior" chose to give the dream-picture of his newly welded life might, I think, be effectually erased by a few nights' bivouac in the rain with the soil of Virginia for a bed, though, in truth, no feathers could be softer.

I am on picket to-day, and I think I can safely say, for myself and my companions here, that picketing in this kind of weather is one of the sternest kind of realities, and not much of an institution. A dense fog is settled all around us, and, as if in forcing its way through this each drop was divided into a thousand parts, the rain comes drizzling down while our little fire hisses and crackles in the repugnant embrace of the watery element.

You are, I believe, an "antimudsillist," that is, you don't believe in the "mudsill" doctrine. I believe you could be converted if you were here to see our little party—(the "Leftinint" calls it *"squad"*)—as we sit couched around the fire. 'Twould take an "ould hand" to tell the original color of our pantaloons so perfect is the coating of mud. When I first stepped out of the tent yesterday morning, I got my shoes full, and haven't lost any of it yet. We might have dry feet if we were allowed to wear boots; but that's "contrary to regulations," and the shoes we get are a very poor affair. The pair which I have on my feet are out at the toes, and I have not worn them quite two weeks yet. My neighbor on the opposite side of the fire has just finished a lecture upon "the proper method of preserving boots and shoes." "First," he says, "put on a coat of grease and then a coat of mud, and continue to apply alternately a coat of each." "Poke," who is making a cup of coffee, and claims to be something of a shoe doctor, recommends "first a coat of mud and next a coat of *mud*." But "Poke" has a pair of patients on his feet, which get no better too fast, to recommend his system. . . .

But here comes the relief, and I must "pack up" my

KNAPSACK.   Vol. 3, pp. 164–65

The mud apparently got the best of "Stew," a soldier of the 5th Wisconsin, who was ready to "damn everything but the Union" after the mud had decisively spoiled his mood.

Lewinsville, Fairfax Co., Va.,
January 30, 1862.

There is nothing here to write about but mud. Anything else but mud is a rarity. Everything is covered with mud. Men and horses, soldiers and teamsters, tents and wagons, food and raiment, are covered with mud. Hoses sink to their knees and wagons to the hubs, from Chain Bridge to Langley's, and from there to this place is, if possible, worse. The days are dark and gloomy, and the fogs are so dense and murky, that some of your Berlin citizens with whom I am acquainted, could not see the end of their long noses, were it not for the fiery glow that rests on the top.

It is raining now as if it never rained before. If it keeps on much longer, we must see about building an ark. Can't move outside the tents, as five seconds would put any one in a way that they would be squeezed out of their clothes. If we moved now, we would carry the whole of the "sacred soil" on our boots. Through the fog you can see nothing but a sea of dirty water. We haven't seen the sun for a fortnight; some think he has lost his way in the fog, or gone west to winter. Mud, gloom, rain, dirt, cold coffee, leaky tents, salt junk, hard crackers, want of exercise, *enui,* blues, blue devils—damn—yes, damn everything; the army, the rations, the rebels, and the mucilaginous mud.—(There, I knew I'd cough up something)—the Generals who don't fight, and the Cabinet who won't make them fight, the Congress who keep talking about proclamations of emancipation; when the only proclamation needed, and the one that will do all the work they keep jabbering about, is an order to march. Yes, I say again, damn everything but the Union, but GOD bless the Union, mud and all; for at present, it would be as difficult for it to prosper with the "mud" of incapables it has clinging to its back, as for the army of the Potomac to move with the mud of the "sacred soil" hanging to its boots. Then hurrah for the Union, mud and all. Let us have a song boys; come go on "Thingumbob," give it to us

> "The union of lakes, the union of lands,
> The union of States who can sever;
> The union of hearts, the union of hands,
> The flag of our Union forever."

Oh! shut up, you can sing no more than a crow; the mud is in your throat—damn the mud. . . .

STEW.   Vol. 3, p. 155

A soldier of the 5th Wisconsin, writing under the biblical name Peleg, *of whom it was said "in his days the earth was divided," mused on a number of facets of camp life, including sickness and living conditions.*

Camp No. 20, in the Field,
June 10th, 1862.

We are delightfully situated among the tall oaks, pines and hickories, about one mile west of the ugly Chickahominy, and seven or eight miles east of that coveted city, Richmond.

Our camp first was in an open field front of the woods we now occupy; but somehow the "rebs" got range, and dropped shell and "hard heads" rather near to warrant our stay; so we fell back by order of Brig. Hancock. Almost four weeks have spun away since we appeared on the bluffs of the "Chicken." The time has been consumed building bridges, fighting, reconnoitering, and playing the artillery "hoop de doodle do." A few showers which generally sprinkle away for three days has softened the roads, washed down rail road embankments, lifted bridges, and been very unkind, take their actions in most any way we will.

These misfortunes are nothing, however, compared with the terrible increase of sickness. I have no heart to tell you the sad tale. But I will say the last month has thinned the Union army to a very serious extent. I do not know any other cause than that these rains have meted this out to us. Our regiment has less by 250 men than it had when we started from Lee's Mills. I dare say all other regiments have suffered equally. I have been on the sick list for three weeks. Fever and diarrhœa are the prevailing diseases. Yesterday Lieut. Strong went on the same glorious list, so when an alarm came, and the whole army was drawn up in a line of battle, company G had no commissioned officer to lead it on had a fight occurred. I buckled on my sword and went as far as the line of battle, and had to back down and go to my quarters. It seems that one can never get his strength after the fever and diarrhœa have pulled him down. I am gaining, however, every day. Lieut. Strong is improving fast, and Co. G will have one commissioned officer to lead it I know if ever the fight comes on. . . .

The suttler has just arrived with two loads of trash from the White House.—Those who regularly attend the sick call, are the first to crowd around his tent.—From the surgeon's tent to the suttler's they waddle, where is dealt out that which, if they survive the war, will destroy their constitutions, and which now keeps them under the doctor's paw. They are building a little red earth-work at the end of which a piece of board will be posted, on which will be written or roughly carved—

"PETER SOMEBODY, DIED 15TH OF JUNE, 5TH
WISCONSIN VOLUNTEERS."

Yet you cannot make these men believe this. They always know more than any one else about it. With a big piece of rancid cheese you may see them sitting at the foot of a big tree, and gorging themselves to an awful extent. I got one of company G to do an errand for me, and gave him some money for his trouble.—Away he went to the sutler's, and the next day he was sick and has been on the sick list for two weeks. I am tired and sick of seeing these things. An order issued a few days since has shut suttler's from selling cheese to soldier's. A good thing. Now if they would order the whisky stopped the sick list would grow less every day. . . .

This army is wild for the great battle.—It is curious that men will be so anxious to fight when they must know 10,000 dead will be stretched upon this coming field. But it is after the battle that horror comes—not the beginning. We have better artillery, better muskets, and better food than they; so we need not despair. . . .

I suppose my next will be written either in Richmond or on the other side of the Chickahominy.

Yours,

PELEG.   Vol. 3, pp. 221–22

Camp near Black River,

December 16, 1862.

Messrs Editors:— . . . It rained hard all Sunday, and the water rose rapidly during the night. I was on picket and had taken possession of an old log house which I supposed was above "high water mark." We were cut off from camp before nine o'clock, and at three I could hear them shouting in camp. At daylight the pickets had been driven in and we were surrounded. The water came into the house and was a foot and a half deep, when it commenced falling at eleven o'clock. We had put some rails on the rafters and resolved to hold out until *reinforcements* should come. A part of the guard which had been sent to the ford were entirely surrounded. They commenced firing guns to let us know that they were in distress. They were taken off on a pontoon Monday forenoon, and Monday night they landed us on a bluff. We were not long in getting into camp, where we found the boys rejoicing over their escape.

They were not alarmed in camp till three o'clock in the morning, when the water commenced running through camp. Some of the companies had not time to remove their tents. Lieut. Freeman was across a ravine, and could not get on the high ground by Col. Harris' tent for several hours, when they swam horses over after them.

The scene at daylight was beyond all description. Groups of men had collected around the Colonel's tent. Some had got up on the high corn crib, and others were at work falling trees toward the bluffs, hoping to escape in that way. They stood in water three feet deep, and worked with a will. When they thought the water was falling, it commenced rising again. The pontoons from the bridge train were brought up, and they commenced crossing on them. I believe the water had then risen about fifteen feet.—Our brigade got over without losing a man. Some tents and baggage were carried down the river. The boys laugh about their experience that night, as though it was fun to wade rivers in December.

Capt. Miller was sent with his company (D) to Morris Ferry, five miles from camp, with orders to repair the Ferry boat and hold it. They camped on the bank of the River Sunday night, but were compelled to move in the night. They found they were surrounded by water, and their only hope of getting off was in keeping the boat. Thirty of the men got on the highest ground and built them a platform of rails, while the others went back after their things. The boat turned over, throwing eleven men, including Capt. M. and Lieut. Chamberlain, into the water. They swam to the trees, and Lieut. C. succeeded in getting to a house soon after daylight, where he got assistance, and in the afternoon they took a wagon box and rescued the men on the trees. Two of the men who were in the boat had been drowned. Their names were George Rhinehart and John Beichly. The men who were left on the rails could not be taken off until Tuesday noon, after having been there two nights. Some of the men are suffering from the effects of the exposure. They lost everything, guns, knapsacks and camp equipage. Some of it they may recover. Lieut. Chamberlain was up after rations to-day. Capt. M. says he shall hold that ferry until further orders and the Captain will do it if any one can.

Gen. Davidson went out with a cavalry brigade and a battery before the storm, and has not returned. The First Wisconsin Cavalry was with him. They must have a rough experience. Our bridge across the river was washed away. The knowing ones say we cannot go to Little Rock this way. . . .

OTIS.   Vol. 5, pp. 3–4

As if floods weren't bad enough, soldiers of the 11th Wisconsin also dealt with falling trees.

Steamer Sunshine, off Cape Girardeau, Sept. 28, '62.
. . . In my last I mentioned I a propensity the ground of our camp had for earthquakes, since then a more serious danger has manifested itself in the brittle character of the trees, some of which come crushing down every little blow that sweeps over us. One evening I was contemplating retiring to my sleeping tent, when the arrival of a friend caused me to postpone my interview with Morpheus long enough for a tree to fall and cut the tent in which I had slept in two, my cot was cut short off in such a position as to lead to the opinion that if I had occupied it as usual, I should have varied the monotone of camp life with amputation of both limbs below the knee. I remarked that "a miss was as good as a mile," as was felicitating myself upon a narrow escape, but several others of the same evening arising from similar causes were of so much more serious character that mine sank into oblivion. It is remarkable trees have in a few instances fallen right across a tent full of men, and yet no one has been seriously injured. . . .
Yours,
CHARLIE.   Vol. 4, p. 313

Bridge Building and Trench Digging

Not all of Wisconsin's men fought in the war. One A. J. Sexton described a busy stretch he spent working as an engineer, building and repairing railroad bridges in Virginia.

Shenandoah Valley, June 5, 1862.
Dear Father: I wrote you some time since, and should have written again before this, but for the past month I have not had time to write to any one—in fact Sundays and week days are all one to me. Perhaps you would like to know what makes me so busy; I will tell you: About a month ago while we were at Fredericksburg, I was detailed from the regiment and put into McDowell's Construction Corps. They consist of two hundred picked

men from McDowell's whole army and divided into squads of twenty, and each squad is under charge of commissioned officers so in all there are 10 commanding officers. I am detailed as an engineer. We built the big railroad bridge across the Rappahannock river at Fredericksburg; it was 700 feet long and 58 feet high; also built a side track at Fredericksburg; built a bridge on the railroad six miles beyond the latter place, and when Gen. Banks retreated the rebels burnt all the railroad bridges. Gen. McDowell sent for me immediately; we took the cars and went to Acquia Creek, a distance of 15 miles, then took the boat up the Potomac to Alexandria, a distance of 45 miles, then took the Manassas Gap railroad, got about 25 miles Friday noon, and found seven bridges burned within five miles of each other, then we rebuilt two of them that afternoon, and built the other 5 the next day. Then we went on about ten miles and found three quarters of a mile of track torn up, we put that down on short notice, then came on Shenandoah river and found the bridge across there had been cut in several places and burnt in six places. The bridge is about 500 feet long and 40 feet high. It only took us one day to rebuild it so that the cars could cross. . . .

We are a gay set, have our own transportation boat and cars, have large Sibley tents, live high and work hard; this will be our occupation during the war. I must explain how the squads are regulated. We have three squads of framers, two of hoisters, two of hewers, one of picks and shovelers, one to get out ties and one of track layers they are all soldiers. I am the only engineer in the corps. . . .

A. J. Sexton. Vol. 3, p. 35

A soldier explains how the men were able to dig trenches in sight of the enemy without suffering great losses.

It may be a puzzle to conceive how our men can throw up fortifications in the face and in plain sight of the enemy without being seriously disturbed by them. A brief description may be interesting, as the work is done right under the noses of the rebels:

A working party is detailed for night duty; with muskets slung on their backs and shovels and picks on their shoulders they proceed to the selected ground. The white tape marks the line of excavation. The dark lanterns are "faced to the rear;" the muskets are carefully laid aside; the shovels are in

William H. Pomeroy, Company G, 13th Wisconsin Infantry   WHi Image ID 70227

hand, and each man silently commences to dig. Not a word is spoken; not one spade clicks against another; each man first digs a hole sufficient to cover himself; he then turns and digs to his right-hand neighbor; then the ditch deepens and widens, and the parapet rises. Yet all is silent; the relief comes and the weary ones retire; the words and jests of the enemy are often plainly heard, while no noise from our men disturbs the stillness save the dull rattle of the earth as each spadeful is thrown to the top. At daylight a long line of earthwork, affording complete protection to our men, greets the astonished eyes of the enemy, while the sharpshooters' bullets greet their ears. Frequently this work is done in open daylight, the pickets and sharp-shooters keeping the enemy from annoying our men.   Vol. 3, p. 275

Breaking Camp

Charlestown, Va.

March 1st, '62

. . . Now we are in the field in earnest. Now we must go days without a washed face, a combed head, or a decent meal partaken in that serenity which promotes digestion. Now we lie down to sleep in our uniform with an eye open, and [are] haunted by the expectancy of the "long roll." Now we are on that perpetual tension that wears and wearies the nerve, but the cry of the spirit is "Onward to Winchester." Thence Southward.

E. E. B.   Vol. 3, p. 7

CHAPTER 3

Battle

ALTHOUGH INITIALLY eager to put down the rebellion on glorious fields of battle, Wisconsin soldiers learned soon enough that civil war was a terrible and terrifying ordeal, waged by individuals amassed in soon-to-be-famous fields and forests attempting to inflict maximum harm on their own countrymen. All but a few were underprepared to experience battle, to see their friends and comrades shot and die next to them, or to take in the sights of the field after the battle where thousands lay broken and dismembered, while the wounded cried out in pain or begged for water. Wisconsin's soldiers also found that battle was a confused affair, with harm awaiting them from infernal machines like mines and grenades, or even from the hands of women pointing revolvers out of windows as they retreated through a Southern town.

Fame did await some of Wisconsin's men on the battlefield. Most notably, the Iron Brigade, consisting of the 2nd, 6th, and 7th Wisconsin, as well as the 19th Indiana, gained a reputation in the fall of 1862 as a hard-fighting unit after defeating Stonewall Jackson's famous brigade. Within a month, the Iron Brigade fought two more major engagements, at South Mountain and Antietam, where its reputation increased. All of this came at a fearful cost, however, as thousands of men in these regiments were killed and wounded.

Wisconsin soldiers participated in the most famous and difficult battles of the Civil War, from Bull Run to Appomattox, and shared their stories of these fights in letters to friends and family, and, of course, to the local newspapers. Their accounts of battle teem with energy and shock, pride and regret. The death of friends is sometimes treated unemotionally, while the death of a good horse is depicted movingly. And much is left unsaid. As Dr. George Conant wrote after the Battle of Cedar Mountain, "the horrors of war and battle are truly indescribable." This fact, however, did not stop Wisconsin boys from doing their best to put into words their experiences in battle.

Bull Run

While many in the North thought that one great battle would end the rebellion, the First Battle of Bull Run, or Manassas, fought on July 21, 1861, proved otherwise. A Wisconsin boy who fought in the battle wrote to his mother just two days later, giving a picture of the confusion that reigned among the inexperienced troops.

Washington, July 23, 1861.

DEAR MOTHER: * * * * * * You must have heard that our Regiment was in battle near Manassas on Sunday last. Saturday night we were encamped a mile beyond Centreville and were told in the evening to hold ourselves in readiness to march at two o'clock the next morning; that we were to have an engagement with the rebels. Two days' rations were put in our haversacks, and with this and our canteens of water and cups, rubber and woolen blankets, gun, cartridge box with 40 rounds in it, we commenced our march at about half past three o'clock in the morning. At seven o'clock we came in sight of the enemy, but as their batteries were masked we could not ascertain their position, and were drawn up in line of battle and our batteries commenced firing to find the place where the rebels were entrenched. Our Brigade of four regiments, was then on the east of the enemy; about 10 o'clock we could see from our position, that one of our batteries, had gained a position, to the northwest of them, and was driving them back. During all this time their batteries had not fired a cannon, but were in such a position that we could not tell where they were. About half past eleven we were marched around to the place where our battery was planted, a distance of 2 miles; on the way we threw off our blankets, and run a good share of the distance, at double quick time, under oppressive heat. At one time in this march I had such excessive pain in my side I could scarce keep up with the company, but I was determined not to give out.

When we reached the place where our batteries had driven the enemy back, there were about 10,000 men drawn up in the line.—Here the masked battery was opened upon us; it was situated on a hill to the east of us and surround on the north, east and south by woods. We were on an elevation to the west of them and a small brook ran between the two hills.

Three or four of our Regiments were across the brook on the other side attacking the battery, and our Colonel ordered us forward to help them. As we were going down the west side of the hill, a cannon ball went thro' the center of our company, taking off the arm of poor Humes, of Beloit, and a gun out of Henry Gintey's hands bruising his right hand so that he could not use it. Amos Botsford and Seneca Flint fell out of the ranks and carried Humes back to the house where the wounded lay. Gintey came on and told the Captain that he could use his left hand and would fight with us, but Capt. Strong told him he had better fall back.

We marched up the south side of the hill behind a rail fence, we were then about twenty rods from the battery, our Lieut. Colonel was on our right and gave the order to charge. We got over the fence and were marching up to the battery, when a Regiment behind us that had broken and scattered back of us, commenced firing right through our ranks, and they were hallooing all around us not to fire, that we were killing our own men, and we had to lie down to keep from getting shot from behind.

After the order to charge was given we had no orders given us. I did not see one of the Field officers after we commenced firing, so we had no one to give us orders; no one to rally us together, the enemy were just re-inforced in large numbers, and no regiments coming up to help us.

We then fell back over the fence, still firing, and a heavy fire pouring in on us. Here Charlie Filer was shot a little below the neck and while some of the Company were carrying him away he died. A moment after, Willie Upham was shot through his side near his elbow. I saw the boys carrying him away. I cannot say whether he lived or not, at least he must be in the hands of the enemy, and there can be little hope for him. James Anderson another of our boys from Canada, was shot here. Our Regiment was now scattered, with nobody to command us and all falling back. I went back about ten rods and stopped; seven or eight others were near me, among them Walter Stone and Lincoln from Union Grove. While we were falling back a ball passed through my coat sleeve and took the skin off my arm. We staid here firing till I had fired 20 rounds; my gun had got so dirty that for the

The tattered battle flag of Company F, 2nd Wisconsin Volunteer Infantry, also known as the "Belle City Rifles"   WHi Image ID 70831

last five or six rounds I had to take hold of the butt of the gun and strike the ramrod against a tree to get the charge down.

The rebels had been firing all the time from the woods, and they now received a strong reinforcement; while nearly all of our men had retreated. The rebels were coming out of the woods to the south-east and from the battery to the north-east of us. LINCOLN and HINTON from Waukesha who had been sun struck and could hardly walk were the only ones of our Regiment that were near me. LINCOLN and I took HINTON's gun and helped him off the field; we gave him some water, and put some on his head and got him back to Fairfax, where he laid down; I think he must be safe now.

We retreated with our division all broke up, different Regiments all mixed together. The rebel cavalry charged on the rear killing the stragglers and some say stabbed our wounded that could not stir. It must have been half past two when we came off the battle field and we kept on the retreat till 11 o'clock Monday morning. SENECA FLINT, JOHN WILSON and I of our company reached Arlington Heights scarcely able to walk after being on the march and on the battle field *thirty-three hours*. Probably about 8 of our company were killed; we are not together yet and cannot tell who they are.

* * * *   Vol. 1, pp. 101–2

Shiloh

The 18th Wisconsin had the misfortune to join General Ulysses S. Grant's army the day before the Battle of Shiloh. One week later, Sergeant Calvin Morley from Company C of the 18th Wisconsin wrote to his family, giving a few details of the battle, but also relating more pleasant details about the weather and the plants in bloom.

Headquarters 18th Regiment,
Pittsburg Landing, Tenn., April 13, 1862.
DEAR WIFE AND CHILDREN:—One week ago to-day I dropped you a line from here. At that time our company was in good health and spirits, but one short week has produced a sad change. Our company was then 81 strong besides the officers. Now we have not more than half that number. This morning we have but *seven* reported for duty. There are a few waiting on the wounded and the balance are unwell. I believe there are about 36 missing. I presume some are taken prisoners. Some wounded and taken in at other camps and died, and many living insensible. It will never be known what became of them. Some of the wounded laid on the field from Sunday morning until Tuesday, in the rain. Some of our company who were wounded in the first of the battle have not been found. We only found two of the Tigers dead. Benj. F. Rantz and Samuel Fish are severely wounded—others badly but not dangerously. Capt. Layne, Mr. Fretwell, Samuel McMichael, Peter Campbell and enough to make the aggregate about 36, are missing. The wounded are generously taken on the boats. Those who die during the night are brought on shore and laid on the bank in rows. The carts for carrying

the dead, are constantly running, and hundreds and thousands will thus be disposed of and their friends never know what became of them. Hundreds would recover if they had proper treatment and care. A bandage and cold water is all they get.

I suppose you get the accounts of the battle, and I will not attempt a description of it. It is an awful sight to see the ground covered with dead and dying—mangled in all shapes—some with an arm off, some with severed heads and others with both legs cut off! In one place I saw five rebels killed with a cannon ball. I saw many of them with broken limbs, left to linger out a few days of pain and die for want of medical aid. Our heavy Belgian balls smash the bones so that amputation is the only remedy. We have a large army here, and lost a great many men, but the rebels left dead on the field about five to one of ours.

A word about myself. I am not very well, but keep about. The day is beautiful and we appreciate it, for the past week we have had rain every day. From the night before the battle until last Friday night we slept in the mud and rain without any shelter whatever. It appears now about like our June month in Wisconsin. Everything is in full bloom, and one tree in particular, is completely covered with large white blossoms.—There are also some splendid climbing-roses growing spontaneously, but not yet in bloom. This is a great country for fruit, and if it was not for slavery would be a delightful country to live in. I have not had an opportunity of getting a "contraband" yet. I have not seen the first one since we landed. They have all fled to the back country. Tell the little ones to be good children. Good bye.
CALVIN MORLEY.
P.S. I write this on the battle field sitting on a tree that was cut off by a cannon ball, and a lime-stone for a writing desk.   C. M.   Vol. 6, p. 56

The knife of the surgeon is busy at work, and amputated arms and legs lie in every direction. The cries of the suffering victim and the groans of those who patiently await for medical attendance, are most distressing to any one who has any sympathy with his fellow man. . . . I hope my eyes may never again look upon such sights. Men with their entrails protruding, others with bullets in their breasts or shoulders, and one poor wretch I found whose eyes had been shot entirely away. All kinds of conceivable wounds are to be seen, in all parts of the body, from all varieties of weapons.   Vol. 5, p. 229

A correspondent identified only as "B." described the scene one hour after the Battle of Shiloh, while the dead and wounded still lay on the field.

Pittsburg Landing, April 14, '62.
One hour after the enemy had retreated from the main battle ground, I was surveying the same, alone and unattended.— . . .

While surveying the killed and wounded in a thickly wooded locality, but where trunks of large trees lay about in a half-rotten state, I stepped upon one to look about the ground, and, hearing something move at my feet, looked down upon what was evidently the figure of a man, covered up by a blanket, and lying up alongside the log. The ground was thickly strewn about with bodies, many of whom I found to be only wounded. Lifting the blanket from the wounded man's face, as I dismounted from the log, he immediately faltered out, "Oh, sir, I'm wounded; don't hurt me, my leg is broken and I'm so cold and wet."

Within three feet of this wounded Secessionist, lay a dead Unionist, with his hair and whiskers burnt off. Just at this moment two or three of our men came up, and observing the horrid spectacle of their dead companions in arms, with his hair whiskers and clothes burned, addressed the wounded man referred to in violent terms, accusing him of aiding in setting fire to their comrade.

For a moment I felt apprehensive that they might retaliate, but upon his assuring them that many on both sides were burned in a similar manner, quiet was soon restored. I soon learned that the leaves and dead undergrowth had been fired in various places by the explosion of shells, and also by burning wads,[1] the fire communicating to the bodies, burning them shockingly. Some of the wounded must have been burned to death, as I observed one or two lying upon their backs, with their hands crossed upon their faces, as a person naturally does when smoke or heat becomes annoying.

Replacing the blanket over the face of the wounded man, I proceeded to step over another log near by, and was considerably startled by a loud exclamation of pain from another wounded rebel. Having stepped on a small stick that hurt a wounded limb of his by its sudden movement, he was compelled to cry out. He, too, was snugly laid up in ordinary, close alongside of a fallen

---

1   A wad was a piece of crumpled paper placed between the powder and the bullet when loading the rifles used by both armies. The explosion of the powder often set the wadded paper on fire.

tree. His wound was serious, and the poor man begged for some assistance. The only thing I could do was to get him a little water and promise that he should soon have relief. I do not think he received any however, before the following day, as it was more than we could do to attend to our own suffering men, night being near. "What will you do with us?" said the wounded man to me. "Take you, dress your wounds, give you plenty to eat, and in all probability when you are able, require you to take the oath of allegiance, and then send you home to your family, if you have one."

"Oh god!" replied the suffering man; "I have a family sir, and that's just what my old woman told me. She said if the Northern men was so ugly and bad as our General says, they must ha' changed a heap." Occasionally there was a pause, accompanied by a distorted countenance, that showed the painful character of his wound. "Stranger," continued the prostrate man, "I've got six little boys at home, and the biggest just goes of errands. I live on —— river, in Alabama, (the name sounded so peculiar that I was not able to recollect it;) 'taint further than that cottonwood from the bank, where my house stands." "What has your wife to maintain the family with, or does the State help them?" said I. "O, she's "shifty," my wife is, stranger, she's mighty "shifty;" she's a Northern born woman, and her father lives in Wisconsin now. I never was north before; I married my wife in Alabama."

I was obliged to leave this man, who possessed an undercurrent of nobility, although his superficial knowledge had allowed him to follow the fortunes of his base leaders. He persisted in saying, as I left him, that he was certain he never had killed a man. . . .

In the cleared field fronting the peach orchard, before referred to, a variety of bullets might have been gathered—and even the following day—as they were lying about on the ground like fruit from a heavily leaden tree after a storm.

B.   Vol. 5, pp. 245–46

Retreat through Winchester

As the gateway to the Shenandoah Valley and an important railway center, the embattled town of Winchester, Virginia, changed hands over seventy times during the war. A soldier of the 3rd Wisconsin described the disarray as the Union army retreated through the town in the spring of 1862.

WILLIAMSPORT, Md., April 29th, 1862.
J. C. Cover—*Dear Sir:*— . . . Overpowered by such an overwhelming force, orders were given for a retreat; on we went pell mell through the streets of Winchester, in such a confused mass, we hope never to witness again: wagons, ambulances, soldiers, horses and mules in a pile together, making big tracks for the Potomac, then 37 miles distant. Soldiers throwing off knapsacks, guns, accoutrements, clothing and in fact everything to accelerate their speed—the last hope left. Astonished we was, though not unexpectedly, did citizens of the city, including women and all, fire at our troops from their windows, which killed and wounded quite a number. Several "*ladies*" while taking deliberate aim at our troops were knocked down with muskets, by observers passing, in time to save the life of many intended victims. More to aid the excitement, were some three or 4,000 cavalry dashing through the streets killing and capturing large numbers who couldn't keep up with the main body.

Laughable instances occurred which I cannot here enumerate; however, I will give one because it is too good to be lost: Lieut. Bently seeing a number of his company behind, resolved to go back a short distance to inform them that they would surely be cut off, if they remained there any longer; but in going, was cut off himself by two citizens, behind some shrubbery, one armed with a formidable club and the other with a musket. He was struck in the back with the club, but the musket was not true to the desires of the possessor, the cap only snapped. The Lieut. made his way through a gate (badly hurt) but was captured by a cavalier, who handed him over to a couple of women to guard him, under instructions to keep him, of the strictest character. Bently not liking his new habitation much, still more, guarded by two women, concluded to leave. An idea struck him, that he "was dry," asked one of them if she would "bring him some water." She assented, and when *she* went out, *he* followed her, bidding her "good bye," to her utter astonishment and indignation. He then took "double-quick" for the railroad track, and again captured; but with all his sad misfortunes of the day, badly hurt, etc., he arrived in camp on the Potomac, at an early hour in the evening.

A great many were taken prisoners and we hear the sick and wounded were shot or smitten down with the sabre, as *they* use the term "don't want to be bothered with the d—d Yankees!" Some of the "Third" and Second Mass., did their best to fire the city, by setting the ordnance and magazine department on fire, which was accomplished. We heard the explosion of the shells and saw streets on fire, but have not learned to what extent the flames raged. The supposition is that much of the "traitorous hole" is in ashes. All is, if it isn't, it will be at our next coming, and halters also prepared for swarms of men and women, should they remain. . . .

Yours Respectfully,

C. N. [unreadable]   Vol. 3, pp. 20–21

Dealing with the Dead and Wounded

Mead Holmes Jr. of the 21st Wisconsin described the work of the burial detail after the Battle of Perryville.

Near Perryeville [*sic*], Ky., Oct. 12th, 1862.
DEAR FRIENDS AT HOME: . . . The night of the 9th the dead were buried: thirty-three of our regiments were trenched—no coffin or marks, except sometimes a rail or stone. . . .

It seems hard to throw the men all in together, and heap dirt right on their faces, but it is better than to have them lay moldering in the hot sun. Oh! to see the dead rebels in the woods! From one point I counted thirty-one; in a fence corner twenty-four; everywhere, the eye fell on one, and this was not on the *field* proper; in our short march we passed at least two hundred, of horses I made no count. It was a fearful sight, and to think of all those soldiers having friends who would give anything for their bloated, putrefying bodies, laying there crows and hogs tearing their flesh; Oh! it was hard! . . .

Yours ever

MEAD HOLMES jr.   Vol. 6, pp. 145–46

Like many young men who joined the Union army, George E. Conant, assistant surgeon with the 3rd Wisconsin, went to war wanting to see battle; after treating the wounded during the Battle of Cedar Mountain, he had seen enough.

In Camp near Culpepper, August 13, 1862.
Within the last two or three days I have seen what I hope never to see again. I have often said that if there were to be a battle I should like, or be willing to be near and witness it, and I have been gratified to my full desire. The battle that was fought last Saturday took place in my hearing and most of the firing within plain sight, and such a roar of cannon and musketry was truly awful. Banks division was ordered to move early in the morning towards the enemy, and by eleven o'clock we arrived upon the battle field. Our division left the main road and filed off to the right. The ambulances belonging to our regiment and other portions of the division, were left in the road by a stream difficult to pass. Our regiment had got almost out of site when I told the drivers that we must in some way follow. I turned them off and got through the fields about half a mile, to a house that was near by our regiment. I went to see the colonel to see if I should advance and farther, and he said no, for I was now near where the centre of battle would be, and in fact it had already commenced. I went into the house and took possession of it for the purpose of a hospital. The women was considerably alarmed, but I told them to be quiet, the house and yard we must have if anybody was hurt. The battle by 3 o'clock P. M., began to rage, and the position of the enemy's fire was such that we began to suspect the safety of the house, for the purpose we wanted it. I informed the medical director of the position of an other house about half a mile off, and he sent me to see if it would be a good site for a hospital. I went and found it to be an excellent one and sent him word to that effect. I then soon returned and followed my regiment into the field. I had not gone far before I met a wounded man. I kept on, often meeting them and those that bled much I put something on and around to stop the bleeding. I still kept on, meeting numbers until I entered the woods, the musketry roaring with incessant shots, and I passing on until I could smell the gunpowder with distinctness. By this time I met long files of men coming back, and to my sight, a short distance off, the firing was awful. I was told a retreat was ordered, and I fell back with the rest and stationed myself by a deep creek, to which place the ambulance came, and then stopped and helped dress the wounded until dark. I then went back to the house where the first hospital had been established, and such a revolting sight is seldom found. A large yard was completely strewn with the wounded, and I was the only Surgeon the boys knew of in the regiment, and there was a continual cry of "doctor, do dress my wound first," or "do come and see me," or "do

give me some water," &c. I took off my coat and went to work dressing the poor fellows wounds as fast as I could. In about an hour another Surgeon that I was acquainted with, came to me and asked what and where he should do, and I told him to pitch in where ever he was needed. I worked there until about 10 o'clock, when I was ordered to go to the other hospital where most of the wounded had been transferred, where I worked almost incessantly until the next day about 11 o'clock, when we got most of the wounded off to Culpepper and Alexandria, and then left, more dead than alive for our own camp, which was about two miles off, since which time I have done but little, and have but little inclination to do that. What I had to do in particular I need not tell you at this time, but the horrors of war and battle are truly indescribable. How many lay dead and wounded on the left we knew not, for we supposed the enemy occupied it and could not go back that night, and it remained so all the next day and night, expecting every hour the fight would again be opened. Early next morning a flag of truce was sent onto the field asking the privilege of burying the dead and getting off the wounded that had remained there during the whole time. I went with the flag, and when I got where the battle had raged the hardest—O, my God! how the ground did look. Dead bodies with swollen and distorted faces, lay thickly upon the ground in all directions while mingling in and close around, we found the wounded that had been left. We found one of our best captains mortally wounded and robbed. He was placed upon a stretcher and carried off the field, but soon died. He asked me what I thought. I told him after I saw where the bullet had entered his body that his case was a fatal one. The wounded that were left were close up to the enemy's front and were shot so near night and so badly, that they could not go off the field. The dead were almost all of them robbed. All of their money, some of their shoes, some of their pants, coats, and generally of their guns. Those that were alive we took away, and the dead were buried mostly in one common grave. The enemy having the possession of the field, had buried their dead first, but when ours were buried, the same earth in a near locality held, in quiet silence, those who but a short time before had been exerting their utmost skill and bravery in the destruction of each others lives. Now all is quiet upon that battle field, and the south west base of Cedar Mountain will be a place that will long remain vivid in my recollection. The papers will give you a better account of the battle and its particulars than I can.

I feel almost worn out, but shall be able to do duty again in a few days. You ask me what I think of the termination of the war, &c. I think we shall come off all right at last, but at how great a sacrifice and how soon, I cannot tell better than I could when I left home. The policy that is now adopted is more satisfactory to the army, as far as I can hear and better determination is felt.   Vol. 3 p. 59

The "Infernal Machines" of War

The Civil War saw the use of many ingenious gadgets designed to kill or maim from a distance. Two Wisconsin soldiers described the mines and torpedoes Confederates used to fortify the town of Columbus, Kentucky.

> Headquarters 12th Wis. Reg't
> Columbus, Ky.,
> June 4th, '62.

Dear Pioneer:— ... We are finally in the land of cotton if not in Dixie. Old Kentuck hung on the fence some time, but came over to the right side at last. We can see rebel marks to the hearts content. Columbus was, and is yet, a strongly fortified place, and as the rebels had it arranged, 10,000 determined men could have defended it against one hundred thousand invaders. To prevent boats from approaching, there was a large ship cable, made of two inch iron, stretched across the river, which is a quarter of a mile wide at this point, and strung with torpedoes made in all manner of shapes, and filled with combustibles. A fuse of submarine telegraph wire connected with the part with a galvanic battery attached. Any boat could have been blown up that attempted to run down the river. This cable and the torpedoes lay in piles along the levee, with two large anchors weighing some eight thousand pounds each. The town originally, I should think, did not contain more than one thousand inhabitants before the rebellion, and is situated on a flat that overflows in high water.—The fortifications are built on the bluffs back of the town. The bluffs are from one to two hundred feet above the river. The fortifications consist of earth works, rifle pits, stockades, &c., extending for five miles. It has been heavy timbered close to the bluffs, but it is now cut down for a mile back, mines, torpedoes, and all kinds of infernal machines being buried in the ground, with fuse attached and running to the main fortifications.—Our men have dug up hundreds of these torpedoes, and are finding more every day. The fort was supplied with water from pipes under ground connected with the river, and the water forced up with a steam engine. This work they tried to destroy, but failed. Yankee ingenuity is fast repairing it. . . . There has been great skill manifested in fortifying Columbus, but the seceshers could not stand the shells that our gun boats throw among them. . . .

W. W. D.   Vol. 5, p. 46

Camp near Columbus, June 6 [1862].

DEAR RECORD:— . . . There is a splendid specimen of secesh ingenuity displayed in their works, in the outskirts near the woods. They consist of death-dealing implements in the shape of large flat bottom pots, that will hold about one and a half bushel, which are filled with shell, shot and powder, and then buried about four feet under ground, and attached to a galvanic battery, under ground, so that in case they were attacked in their rear, they could blow up half of the country around. There has been quite a number of them dug up, also a number of different kind of infernal machines . . .

Yours,

SQUIBS.   Vol. 5, pp. 46–47

Another curious weapon was the hand grenade, which one soldier found to be an effective device.

Arlington, Jan. 16, 1862.

DEAR SENTINEL:— . . . I suppose most of your readers have heard of the hand grenade, but I will venture to say that not one in a hundred knows anything about what they are. A large number of this deadly little missile have been distributed through the forts along the line, and they may come directly under the head of "incidents of the war." The grenades now in use are called "ketchums." They are of three sizes—one, three and five pounds—and are shaped like an egg, only you must carry the big end of the egg down to a taper just as the small end does. This shell is of cast iron, and hollow. Near one end is a gun tube which connects with the chamber, and on this tube you put a common gun tube by means of a pine stick, the cap going into a hole in the end of the stick which is inserted; the cap sticking to the tube and the stick being withdrawn. The shell is then filled from the other end with fine rifle powder, and the orifice filled with another long pine stick, which is driven in closely, the outer end of which is split, and two pieces of cardboard inserted, as, boys insert them in a stick to make a dart. This is to direct the grenade, which is now loaded, but which is perfectly harmless, and can be handled at will without danger. With the grenade is a small plunger, which goes into the end over the cap, fitting in with a spring. This plunger is carried in the left hand, the grenade in the right, and just before you want to use the latter you insert the plunger. The grenade is thrown with the right hand, and the dart assists the direction of it. Upon striking any object it explodes like a shell, bursting into many pieces, and these pieces doing great damage.

I have seen pieces of the hand grenade thrown an eighth of a mile. They are used and designed to throw into a fort on approaching to storm it, and from a fort to protect it when the enemy is approaching too near it. Thrown from a fort into the ditches full of men, the slaughter would be terrible. The grenade now in use are a patent of last August and differ materially from the old grenade of which we read. The single pound ones are but little larger than an egg, the five powders [*sic*] as large as a man can throw easily even a short distance. When loaded, with the plunger in, they must be handled carefully, as it takes only a slight jar to make them do damage when it is not wanted.

C.

Vol. 2, pp. 219–20

The Making of the Iron Brigade

In the fall of 1862, John Gibbon's brigade, consisting of the 2nd, 6th, and 7th Wisconsin Infantry, along with the 19th Indiana, began to make a name for itself as a hard-fighting unit that wore distinctive black hats. In a lengthy letter to his brother, excerpted in the Portage Register, *Frank A. Haskell of the 6th Wisconsin sketched the battles that made the Iron Brigade famous: Brawner's Farm, South Mountain, and Antietam.*

Members of the Iron Brigade in their distinctive black hats   WHi Image ID 41960

THE FIGHT NEAR GAINESVILLE.

On the 29th of August, on the turnpike from Warrenton to Centerville, near Gainesville, King's Division encountered the right wing of the enemy.

I will not say now whose was the fault, but of the Division consisting of four brigades, two were not engaged at all, and one other but lightly. But Gibbons', the 2d, 6th, and 7th Wisconsin, and 19th Indiana, which the rebels have named the "Black Hat" Brigade—they wear black felt army hats—went into the fight. This was their first hard battle. As the sun was going down upon this pleasant August day, their line was formed and they stood face to face with three times their number—nowhere a hundred yards distant, and in some places not more than twenty—and for nearly an hour and a half, until entire darkness came upon the earth, the little hill whereon they stood was a roaring hell of fire. Retiring never an inch, with no confusion, now standing up, now flat upon the earth, now swaying backwards or forwards to get advantage of ground, the devoted 1800 blazed with fire. Line after line of the rebels confronted them and was swept away, or broke in confusion. Fresh regiments would again appear upon the grounds their discomfited ranks had left, and with a cheer would rush on for a charge upon the "Black Hats." But their rebel cheer was drowned in one three times louder by the Badger boys, and their lines met the fate of their predecessors. No battle was ever so fierce before—no men ever did better than did the men of Gibbon's Brigade. With the darkness came cessation of the rebel fire, and then and not till then, ours ceased. We had yielded not an inch and our pickets covered our advanced lines. Then came the taking off the dead and wounded. Then we learned the extent of our loss.

Now was the hardest part of the battle—to learn who of our friends were killed or wounded. 771 of the brigade had fallen. I cannot give the names of any; you have read them in the papers. At a little past midnight we were ordered to leave the scene of our terrible battle, and having cared for the wounded as well as we could, and taken as many as the ambulances would hold with us, we silently took up the line of march for Manassas Junction. As the daylight came on the next morning, none of us could look upon our thinned ranks, so full the night before, now so shattered, without tears. And the faces of those brave boys, as the morning sun disclosed them, no pen can describe. The men were cheerful, quiet and orderly. The dust and blackness of battle were upon their clothes, and in their hair, and on their skin. But you saw none of these; you only saw their eyes, and the shadows of the "light of battle," and the furrows plowed upon cheeks that were smooth a day before, and not now half filled up. I could not look upon them without tears, and could have hugged the necks of them all.

THE BATTLE OF SOUTH MOUNTAIN.

Our forces here, I suppose, exceeded 30,000. That of the enemy was from 30,000 to 40,000. By one or two o'clock P. M., the battle had become general. Reno first attacking on the left, and Hooker on the right; the turnpike was the center, and was guarded on our side by our numerous batteries. At about 4 o'clock P. M., Gibbons' Brigade, which belong to the bully Joe Hooker's corps, but was that day detached, got orders from Gen. Burnside to move up the turnpike towards the gorge, and attack the enemy and dislodge them. This was the hard place of the whole line, but this Brigade never falters, and amid Hooker's thunder upon the right, and Reno's upon the left, the "Black Hats" moved steadily on to their work.

At the sun an hour high in the afternoon, with its rays streaming full in their faces, they were engaged with the enemy's infantry, largely their superiors in numbers, and posted behind stone walls and in woods, the rebel batteries meantime hurling shell among us, to which our own artillery replied with interest. The rebel artillery was silenced, the brigade drove all before it up the gorge, as darkness came on, and we heard first the cheers of Reno, then of Hooker, upon our left and right, telling us that all but the center was won. Wisconsin, though commencing last, and with its work not done, could not fail to do that work well before it slept. So above the roar of the battle went up the cheers of the Wisconsin men in response to those of their friends upon the right and left, and with the coming on of night they redoubled their work.—At about 10, P. M., the battle closed.—The enemy was dislodged from the gorge, and the Brigade rested upon their arms—the 6th where they fought, the others relieved by fresh troops, who came and took their places, and they fell back a few yards, first for more ammunition, then for sleep. And the victory was won along the whole line, and the rebels were in confusion and retreat upon the other side of the mountain.

BATTLE OF ANTIETAM.

Our brigade moved out to battle a little after sunrise, and before we had moved a hundred yards toward the enemy, their second shell—the first just passed over our heads—dropped and exploded in the 6th Wisconsin, and killed or wounded thirteen men and officers—Capt. D. K. Noyes, of Baraboo, being among the latter. He has had his right foot amputated, saving the heel and ankle joint—is doing well, and will undoubtedly recover. We moved on to battle, and soon the whole ground shook at the discharges of artillery and infantry. Gainesville, Bull Run, South Mountain, were good respectable battles, but in the intensity and energy of the fight and roar of firearms, they were but skirmishes in comparison to this of Sharpsburg. The battle raged all day, with short intervals, during which, changes were being made in the disposition of troops. At night we were in occupation of almost all we had gained of ground; this was a good deal.

The enemy's dead and wounded were nearly all in our lines. The slaughter upon both sides is enormous. All hands agree that before they had never seen such a fearful battle. The loss of the brigade was in killed and wounded 380—$47\frac{1}{2}$ per cent of the men engaged. The victory was complete, but not decisive. The 18th was consumed in maneuvering and ascertaining the position of the enemy, and on that night he skedaddled out of Maryland, leaving his dead unburied, his wounded uncared for, and a large amount of arms and some guns, in our hands. About twenty stands of colors were captured by us—two by the 6th Wisconsin. The flag of the 6th received three bullets in the flagstaff and some fifteen in the flag. That of the 2d Wisconsin, three bullets in the staff and more than twenty in the flag. We are now near the field. I hope you may never have occasion to see such a sight as it is. I will not attempt to tell you of it. But amid such scenes we are all cheerful, the men were never more so—victory in two hard, great battles, and the rebels out of Maryland, made us glad.

INCIDENTS.

Through all these four battles which I have hinted at, I have been and am unharmed. I cannot tell how any one could have survived; but we are alive, and I have the belief that He who controls the destinies of nations and men, has saved me, and will, unharmed, in many more battles. I have not been afraid of anything in battle. One does not mind the bullets and shells much, but only looks to the men and the enemy to see that all is right. I saw many incidents of battle that would interest you, but cannot now tell them. One, however, I will tell. On the 17th, about 10 o'clock A. M., I was sent to Gen. Hooker with a message. I had to ride through a hailstorm of bullets from the enemy, not a hundred yards off, and was upon the gallop upon my pet horse "Joe," a fine creature, fleet as a deer, and brave as a lion, who had carried me in all the battles, when a musket bullet hit him full in the side, he jumped into the air—the blood spirted several yards from the wound, and he staggered to fall. I dismounted and patted his neck to take leave of the faithful creature. He leaned his head against me like a child. But I must leave him; I started, and he whinnied after me and tried to follow. I went to him and again stroked his neck and patted him. He seemed to know as much as a man. I again started to leave him. He again tried to follow, but his poor legs could carry him no more; be whinnied for me, feebly, and fell, and was dead in a minute. I could not help a tear for him. Captain Bachelle of the 6th Wisconsin, had a pet Newfoundland dog that he had raised, and which was always with him. Master and dog both fell dead together upon the field, shot with bullets.

Lieutenant Frank A. Haskell of the 6th Wisconsin. Before the war, Haskell practiced law in Madison. He was a close friend of General Gibbon and reached the rank of colonel before he died leading a charge at the Battle of Cold Harbor in 1864.   WHi Image ID 3343

Colonel Lucius Fairchild, future governor of Wisconsin, rejoiced when he learned that his regiment, the 2nd Wisconsin, did not run from its first major battle in August 1862.

Upton's Hill, Va., Sept. 5, 1862.
. . . When night threw her sable mantle over the bloody field, Col. Fairchild cast his eyes along our lines, and, with tears in his eyes, he asks: Where,

Good God! Where is the Second? Have they ran? Have they scattered? Tears gush unbidden from his eyes; the Major answers him. "Colonel, they are all here—all that's left—more than half lay on the battlefield!" As if a mountain's weight was lifted from his soul, he says: "Thank God the Second have not deceived their friends." We fought *Jackson's tried Division—about ten to one—and they* RAN! . . .

H. B. R. Vol. 2, p. 298

Vicksburg

A member of the 12th Wisconsin recounted for his sister in Madison the scene in Vicksburg after it surrendered to Ulysses S. Grant's army on July 4, 1863. Vicksburg's capture effectively cut the Confederacy in two as the Union gained control of the Mississippi River.

Vicksburg, July 5, 1863.

DEAR SISTER:—Our regiment has gone out to the Big Black, with the rest of the 13th army corps, to hunt up Johnston, and I am left to take care of the quartermaster stores left here by our brigade.

We had kept up a continual fire on the enemy for the past week, until the morning of the second of July, when they sent out a flag of truce by Gen. Smith, to Gen. Grant, we all supposing that it was a flag of truce to bury their dead, as we had an engagement with them on the night of the first, killing and wounding a great number of their men, leaving them lying on the ground for about six hours in the sun, and they began to smell quite bad, the reb's getting nearly the whole benefit of it. But about eleven o'clock they began to put up their heads and sing out: "Yank's don't shoot, there is a flag of truce out, and we are going to surrender." Well, we thought that was good enough, so the boys begun to pile out of their pits and works, the reb's following suit, and you can bet that it looked quite queer to see the men that had been firing at one another mingle together and play cards.

I went up when I found out what was the matter, and had a gay old talk with a Captain of a battery. He was sick, and said that he would give five dollars for one pound of coffee. I told him that if he would wait a day or two he would get plenty, but he could not see it, for he said he knew that they were not going to surrender. I remained up on the works for about three hours, the sun pouring down, and the thermometer stood 95 in the shade. The armistice continued all the rest of that day and night, during which time there was not a gun fired on either side.

I went up early on the morning of the 4th, when they (our batteries) were firing a national salute of thirty four guns. I saw the rebs come out of their works and stack their arms, then I knew that the thing was played out with them. I went back to the regiment and told the Colonel, when we both got on our horses and went over to their lines, and had quite a talk with them. One Colonel showed me the ham of a mule that he cut his breakfast out of. I asked him how it went, and he said that it tasted good enough, but that the mules had been worked so hard lately that it made them tough. I saw another fellow that was on Pemberton's staff, who said that they had some young ladies in their mess, and that they had run ashore for meat, when their cook, being a Frenchman, thought that he could get them up a good dish; so he caught some rats, and made them into soup, which he said they relished very much.

I went through the town to look at the buildings that had been injured. The lower part of the town has been all knocked down by our gunboats, but the residences have been left standing, although very much injured. There is not a house in the town but that has been bored through and through.

I got down to the river just in time to see our gunboats sail past. There was twenty of them. They went by two abreast, and were covered with flags. They have gone down to Port Hudson. Gen. McPherson's army corps went down on transports last night. Port Hudson will soon be ours.

We captured twenty-eight thousand prisoners and about two hundred cannon, four Major Generals, and I don't know how many Brigadiers; making, in all, prisoners and guns captured since we got on this side of the river, thirty-four thousand men, and about three hundred pieces of artillery— pretty good for one campaign, is it not?

I am going over to the town, again, in the morning. I think that I will get orders to move our traps over there, as they are lying out here in a ravine, unguarded, and are somewhat liable to be picked up by some of the guerillas in our rear.

Col. Poole has resigned, and is going home in a day or so. He is quite unwell but in good spirits.

The rebels have all been paroled, the officers retaining their swords and side arms.—There are quite a number of them now in our camp, picking up old clothes that our men threw away when they marched, this morning.

I have now told you all the news I can think of. When I get home I will be more explicit.

S.   Vol. 9, pp. 106–7

Chickamauga

The year 1863 saw the Union army in the west advance down the Mississippi and through the state of Tennessee. The momentum was lost in northern Georgia when, on September 19–20, the Union army was routed at the Battle of Chicka-mauga. H. J. Hoffman of Company G of the 10th Wisconsin wrote to his parents about his escape from the field and the retreat to Chattanooga.

Chattanooga, Sept. 23d, 1863.
Dear Parents:—By God's will I am spared to write to you once more. I can hardly realize the dangers and horrors I have passed through in the last week. But the worst I think is over, though the rebels are hardly willing to let us alone yet. We fell back from the position 5 miles from here, from where I last wrote you, night before last, and are now strongly intrenched at this place on the south side of the river. The rebels are in front of us, but they do not seem to like the idea of assaulting the works they built themselves before they left here. They are trying hard to cross the river above us to cut us off, but as yet have come nowhere near accomplishing their object.

We have suffered a terrible loss, but will never give up to them. I can hardly suppress the tears when I tell you that all that remains of the noble old tenth, besides our company, (which is at Stevenson) is four officers and thirty men. Col. Ely did not get the order to retreat, and while the rest of the division were falling back he rallied the regiment and charged the advancing rebels. Those that were not killed, besides the thirty that escaped, were surrounded and taken. Oh, how nobly they fought all that long terrible Sabbath day, and when their cartridge boxes were empty for the last time they charged the solid ranks of the exultant foe. There are but a few over five hundred men left out of the five regiments and battery of our brigade. Lieut. Van Pelt, commanding the battery, was killed while aiming a piece with his own eyes, and four of his guns were captured. Well may the rebels exult over the capture of such a part of the famous Loomis Battery, that has laid so many of them low.

Col. Scribner received several slight wounds, but led his brigade with heroic valor to the last, and is still with us. On Sunday every officer of his staff were cut off by the rebels, and joined us no more that day. The three that remained acted not only as staff officers for the Colonel, but also as division staff officers for Gen. Baird, commanding our division, as he had but one of his staff and not one of his escort left.—We did our duty faithfully and well. Gen. Baird called us noble boys, and said we should be remembered.

Our division occupied the centre, and was the last to leave the field. When the order came to retreat we left the same place on which we first took position in the morning. This was on the edge of a large open field. As we moved away before a heavy fire of musketry and grape, the rebels charged on us, and our retreat soon became a route in appearance. When we were half way across the field Col. Scribner's horse had one leg broken off by a shell. We were riding from right to left at the time, the Col. telling the men to keep near their colors and rally on the hill before us. I jumped off my horse and told the Col. to ride him. He told me to keep my horse, as he could go as fast as the men, and he wished to go no faster. I insisted, telling [him] he must reach the hill first to commence the rally. "God bless your brave heart, Hoffman," he said as he got on my horse.

We were under a terrible fire, but I stopped long enough to take the Col's pistols and splendid marine glass from the saddle of the wounded horse. I overtook the Col. in time to draw my saber and help him rally the brigade on the top of the hill. It was easily done, for fear had long before left the hearts of the men, and we soon had a good line formed, and began our retreat in order.

We fell back to Rossville, five miles distant, reaching there about 9 o'clock, (it was only a little before dark that we left the battle field.) We found the whole army there in perfect confusion, but the Generals were busy in reorganizing. By daylight all was right again, and we were occupying a strong position. The rebels attacked us, but were driven back. That night we fell back to this place, but the rebels did not know it till they made a furious assault late the next morning and found us gone.

Bill Darrow was shot through the leg in the Saturday's fight. Ed. Court was also wounded on the same day. I was struck by a piece of rock that was shivered to pieces near me. It struck me on the hip, and made me lame for a little while. I was only thankful it was not worse.

So far I mentioned but little of the fight on Saturday. You cannot expect me to give you the full detail of everything at present, but I must give you some idea of Saturday's work. You must know that the rebels attacked our army before we were ready for them, which caused much confusion. The infantry of our division marched down to the front, and drove the rebels from their first position. Some rebel prisoners were taken and sent to the rear. I came in shortly after in company with one of the aids, who was left to direct the battery. When I got up the Col. put a couple of rebel prisoners in my charge, to take back to the provost guard. I went back the same way we had just brought the battery in, and the road the ambulances were taking the wounded out on, but had hardly got out of sight of the brigade when a line of rebel ambushers rose up along the left of the road not ten rods from us, and ordered us to surrender. I happened to be on the right hand side of the ambulances. In the confusion that followed I made my prisoners (who were not willing to be recaptured, I think) turn, and away we went in the other direction. I reached the brigade again just as a heavy body of rebels charged on it and drove it back, capturing four pieces of the battery, which were unlimbered and not got into position.

Here is where poor Van Pelt was killed. I kept my rebels before me, and soon overtook the division provost guard with a lot of other prisoners, and delivered them up. A terrible fight ensued. The rebels were driven back, but they got our four Parrot guns out of our way. About dark we stood another heavy assault, were overpowered and driven back. That night we took the position where we fought the next day.

I could write a volume concerning this battle, but for the present you must be satisfied with what I have written, as paper is very scarce. This is some I picked up on the battlefield the first day.

Company G, I have learned just now, have returned and started back

again to Stevenson with a lot of prisoners. I will give you more particulars of
the battle when we come to another stand still.

Yours,

H.

Missionary Ridge

*Arthur MacArthur, father of General Douglas MacArthur, penned a letter to his
own father to describe the role of the 24th Wisconsin in lifting the siege of Chattanooga at the Battle of Missionary Ridge.*

> Headquarters 24th Wis. Vols.
> Camp near Chattanooga, Tenn.,
> Nov. 26th, 1863.

My Dear Father:—It is Thanksgiving evening. By the time you receive
this, you will know how many and manifold are the blessings for which
we should be thankful. I will now give you the details as nearly correct as
I remember them, of one of the most successful campaigns that the world
ever saw.

. . . About noon heavy cannonading was heard on the extreme right,
on Lookout Mountain. It proved to be Hooker storming the majestic old
mountain. He was successful, and that evening Union fires burned in the
usual position of the enemy's old camps.

The balance of the night was quiet with the exception of some slight skirmishing that Hooker had on Lookout. The next morning we moved again
about a quarter of a mile to the right, and remained in that position until
about 2 o'clock, when we were ordered to move to the front. We moved by
the flank for about one fourth of a mile, when we formed in line of battle on
the left of the 88th Ill. Vols. We did not remain here long before we received
orders that we were to charge the enemy's rifle pits. This was a very suggestive order, and set us all to thinking. We remained in our last position about
one hour and a half, when we moved to the front at common time. We had
not advanced far before the double quick was sounded, and away we went
toward the very jaws of death, as it then seemed. We carried the first line

with very little resistance. By this time both officers and men were so much exhausted, that it was impossible to move forward without resting. In about five minutes, however, the charge was continued. After passing the first pits the line of battle was not regular. The men took advantage of all obstacles in the way, and thus continued to advance steadily and surely toward the top of the ridge. In the course of the ascent the men had to rest several times. Owing to the trees, stumps and felled timber, the men were able to partially secure themselves from the deadly volleys that were being hurled at them on every step of our advance. But after about two hours steady fighting, we succeeded in reaching the top of the ridge directly in front of Brigg's head-quarters. Our brigade captured 11 pieces of artillery, and an innumerable number of prisoners. The success was complete, and the route general. The enemy were beaten on their own ground, and the glory of our little army complete. There was no drawback whatever, the charge was a complete suc-cess and no discount on it. I think this the most decisive battle of the war. At all events it was the grandest success our armies have ever known. We drove them from their own position, and that position a mountain 1,000 feet in height, crowned with batteries and filled with rifle pits swarming with enemies. If you were only here to climb the elevation on a calm, clear day, without any impediment, it would be considered a big thing. As I said before we were able to protect ourselves by getting behind trees, stumps &c., and for that reason our loss was quite small comparatively. Our loss was only 39 all killed or wounded, no missing. Among the killed are Capt. Howard Green Co. B.[,] 1st Lt. Robert Chivas Co. I, Capt. Austin and Lt. Balding both of Co. A were very severely wounded. All the boys did splendidly and I am proud of them. About half way up the hill the color sgt. became unable to carry the colors. I immediately took the colors and carried them the balance of the way, and had the honor of planting the colors of the 24th Wis., on the top of Mission Ridge, immediately in front of Bragg's old headquarters. I showed the old flag to Gen. Sheridan immediately upon his arrival upon the top of the ridge.

The regiment remained on the top of the ridge about four hours and were provided with ammunition and rations, and proceeded down the opposite side of the mountain in a southern direction as far as Chickamauga Creek, remained here a few hours and then returned to camp. Arrived in camp Thursday Evening, making the whole campaign only 3 1-2 days and 3 nights.

This is the shortest campaign on record. Old Napoleon never did anything like it.

While I was carrying the flag a whole dose of canister went through it tearing it in a frightful manner. I only received one scratch and that was through the rim of my hat.

Everything is progressing finely. Write me soon.

Accompanying you will find a list of casualties of the regiment for publication.

I remain as always, your aff'ate son,

ARTHUR MACARTHUR.   Vol. 10, pp. 297–98

Spotsylvania

When Ulysses S. Grant was promoted to lieutenant general and given command over all Union armies, he made his headquarters in the field with the Army of the Potomac. As soon as the weather permitted in the spring of 1864, Grant and the Army of the Potomac moved south and brought on a new kind of warfare—a relentless and incessant push forward toward Richmond. Alex Q. Smith of the 5th Wisconsin Infantry wrote to his sister and gave a glimpse of the frenetic new pace of warfare.

Headquarters 5th Wis. Vols.,
Near Spottsylvania C. H., Va.,
May 16, 1864.

My Dear Sister:—

I will now commence and give you a detailed account of our campaign, as near as I can.

We left our winter quarters on the 4th, at sunrise, and took our way towards Germania Ford on the Rapidan, where we crossed on pontoons at two o'clock, and marched two miles beyond, where we camped for the night. The next morning we started on the plank road towards Fredericksburg, and about eleven o'clock we came to the rebel pickets, and the right wing of our regiment, (including our Co.), were sent out as skirmishers. We drove the rebel skirmish line about two miles; it was thick woods all the

Soldiers of the 21st Wisconsin posing on Lookout Mountain, near Chattanooga, Tennessee, April 20, 1864   WHi Image ID 4489

time; it was like Indian fighting. At last the rebels were reinforced, and as we had no support, we were forced to retire, but did not retire far before we got a commanding position, and stood our ground, and took about two hundred and seventy five prisoners—more than double our own numbers. We had some wounded, and after the skirmish was over, myself and two men left our guns and took a wounded man and carried him to the rear, and while we were gone the rebels had come on to our skirmish line in force, and forced it to fall back, and as our Co. was on the extreme right, it passed us and we did not know it, and when we went back to the line we could not find it, and the first thing we knew ran on to a rebel Corp.'l with five men, and he halted us and asked where we were going. I told him that we were going back to the lines. He asked me if those two men with me were prisoners. I told him yes, for I saw when he asked me that question, that he took me to be a rebel, as I had picked up a gun and the other two men had no gun. He then asked what brigade I belonged to? I told him I belonged to Hays' Brigade. (I knew Hays Rebel Brigade was there, for some of the prisoners had told me so.) He then told me I could pass on, so we went over, a little out of sight, and there held a council of war; we came to the conclusion that we were inside of the rebel lines and must make an effort to get out. We thought a bold front would be the best, so we looked around and found two more guns and went back to the six rebs that we had just left, and commanded them to surrender, which they very reluctantly did, and we marched them in, and joined the regiment on the front line of battle. . . . The 6th commenced with a pretty brisk skirmish at daylight, but it did not last long. We dug rifle-pits in rear of our line of battle, and at night we fell back into them and the rebels followed us. We repulsed them with no loss in our Co., but there were some in the regiment. At midnight we pulled up stakes and joined the 5th Corps, which was on our left, we got there just at daylight and lay there all day. There was nothing going on except digging of riflepits, until half past eight at night when we pulled up stakes and started for Fredericksburg, the rebs having retreated that way. We marched all night and at eight o'clock on the 8th inst., we turned off the Fredericksburg road and took the road to Spottsylvania Court House, and came up to the rebs at 12 o'clock, formed line and threw up riflepits, and at five o'clock we piled up our knapsacks and prepared for a charge, but when the time come the rebs advanced on us, and we held them in check. We lay there all night, 9th we were relieved at 10 o'clock, and moved to the left and threw up riflepits, Gen. Sedgwick, our Corps General, was killed by a sharpshooter. The lines were very quiet during the day, we lay in our riflepits all night. On the morning of the 10th, the rebs opened on us with artillery at 9 o'clock and the firing became pretty general along the line, at 5 o'clock we piled up our knapsack and haversack and formed line in front of the rebs riflepits under cover of the woods, and a little before sundown we made a charge and took two lines of rifle pits with lots of prisoners, but we were not supported in time and were forced to abandon them or be taken prisoners ourselves, and we chose the former although it was running the gauntlet for the rebels had a cross fire on us from both flanks, our Color Sergt. was killed and the Colors came near falling into the rebels hands, but when I saw the man fall I ran and grabbed the flag and brought it off the field with a shower of bullets after me. But I escaped them all except one which burnt my right side a little, but not enough to draw blood, I have been acting as Color Sergt. since that night. . . . [W]e fell back to our old position and stayed during the night, the morning of the 11th we went out to the edge of the woods in front of where we made the charge and commenced to throw up riflepits, but a heavy rain storm come up and we retired to our old position, and stayed the night, and on the morning of the 12th we were routed out early, and went to the left to reinforce Hancock's Corps, they having succeeded in carrying the rebel works, we got there about 10 o'clock and was taken right into the fight, and fought until dark, gaining nor losing no ground, it rained all day by spells, and we were in an open field, and the mud, blood and water was about six inches deep. . . . We went back about a half mile and camped, and on the morning of the 13th we found the rebels had fallen back to their next line of riflepits, I went over on the field and got J. R. Williams' things, and buried him. He was the last man of the old Color guards, the rest being either killed or wounded. After the battle was over there was ten bullet holes in the flag, and one in the staff. The 13th we lay still all day and we had a chance to send off mail for the first, and last, we have had since we started. On the morning of the 14th about 3 o'clock we started after the rebels again, they having fell back. We marched about three miles and formed a line in rear of the 5th Corps and they were going to charge the rebel's works, which they did at 5 o'clock and carried them with but small loss, we supported them and had to march in line of battle through Po River, which was about three feet deep, and then had to lay all night in line of battle without any fires, but we had to dig riflepits so we managed to keep warm part of the time. We have laid in these riflepits ever since, and there has not been any fighting. There is a little cannonading on our right but not very alarming. The rebels are pretty well whipped but I don't think the campaign is over yet, but perhaps I will be able to give you an account of the rest of it before I get a chance to send this letter off.

The total loss of killed, wounded and missing of our regiment in the whole campaign is two hundred and seventy-five, but there are some missing that are stragglers and will come up so I will put our loss at two hundred and fifty, well I will finish this *short note* when I get a chance to send it.
Yours as ever,
ALEX. Q. SMITH   Vol. 10, pp. 118–19

Atlanta

After a grueling summer campaign, Atlanta fell to the Union on September 2, 1864. "U. S. S." of the 25th Wisconsin provided a sketch of the campaign.

Camp at East Point, Ga.,
September 12th, 1864.

DEAR EAGLE:— . . . Our long tedious summer's campaign is now ended. Atlanta fell into the Federal hands on the 2d inst, the enemy being forced to evacuate, from the fact that Gen. Sherman's army was pitching into their *end* pretty sharply, and succeeded in cutting their *sow belly* line in twain.

I will briefly note down a few of the most important items concerning our movement on the flank of Hood's invincibles, *i. e.* skedaddlers. It was quite evident from the lay of the country around Atlanta, and the manner in which the rebel fortifications were built, that an assault upon their front would either be attended by great sacrifice of life, or result in a complete failure. In view of these facts, Gen. Sherman displayed his military genius and ability to cope with the fighting Field Marshall of the South, by making such a brilliant movement on the enemy's left flank; and so effectually covering its designs, as to awaken no suspicion of his purpose until it was too late.

Necessary works and arrangements being completed for the withdrawal of the left centre of our lines on the 26th inst, we accordingly moved back, our skirmish lines falling back without any loss, it having kept up such a hostile demonstration for twenty-four hours, as to blind the Grey Backs of our intentions. The 25th was the last regiment to leave the lines in front of the 16th Corps; it came off in splendid style.

Marching back one mile, we took a position behind works, and protected the flank the while our left wing passed to the right.

During the day, the rebels shelled our old works, and our train, which was partly visible from one of their forts; but not till towards evening did they make an advance from their rifle pits, and then very cautiously did they sally forth. They plundered our camp of all discarded rubbish, even carrying our empty hard tack boxes to their lines; then pushed on a short distance, when they were very suddenly brought to a stand still by our pickets. They were kept at bay until midnight, when we too came up missing, and the enemy were left sole possessors of the field. . . .

Monday, the 29th, the reveille called us up at an early hour. 8 a.m. found us moving down the railroad in *light* marching order. Commencing two miles south of Fairburn, the work of destroying the railroad began in good earnest. For two miles each way, the blue coats could be seen at work tearing up the rails, piling the ties, placing the rails on top of each pile, after which they are fired, the rails become heated and softened so that they bend. Many of them are taken and bent round trees so as to either break or render them unfit for further use until manufactured over.

Company D acted their part in the work of destruction; it acted on the motto of "do what you do, quickly," and then lay in the shade. The latter we were wont to do frequently, for the day was desperately hot.

Our work occupied the whole day. At night we marched back to our camp, taking along a few stray geese, turkeys, chickens, vegetables, &c., which we had lifted on our way out.

Some fatigued with our day's labor, it was not long after reaching camp, that all were quietly reposing on Mother Earth.

Tuesday, Aug. 30th, we look up our line of march for the Macon road. All day we marched along, halting now and then for our advance to drive back a small force of the enemy, which was sent out to gobble the small cavalry force as our army was supposed to be. The different corps moved on parallels, so it was necessary to make new roads. Ours was a new one cut through the timber; stumps two foot high; rocks plenty, and worst of all, we had to travel over them until 11 o'clock at night through Egyptian darkness. May be we did not stumble any. No, not at all.

At the aforesaid hour we came to a halt, and after a short brigade drill, in order to find a suitable location, we stacked arms, and rested our legs on the ground. We were then one mile from Jonesboro, a town on the Macon & Western R. R. Our skirmishers were busy during the night with the rebel pickets. Trains were heard as they brought up reinforcements.

Wednesday, Aug. 31st, skirmishing began at an early hour pretty sharply; but not until 4 p. m. did it assume the form of battle. Our lines had then been fortified rudely but strong, and the enemy was seen to advance after their picket line, which was deployed as skirmishers. Moving quickly forward, they first encountered a line of works in which our pickets had first been thinking we still occupied it. They charged furiously forward—over the works and into the pits—but no Yanks were there.—Being out of wind, they halted, reformed their lines, and again advanced feeling confident that we had *lit out*. On they came, and soon they found our skirmishers, who gradually fell back to small pits previously dug. Coming up in sight of our lines they partly reformed again, and with a yell pushed on, when all at

The desolation of war is made clear by this photo of the deserted rebel lines outside Atlanta in 1864.   WHi Image ID 78973

once, as if ten thousand demons had lit amongst them, they were stopped by a most terrific fire from our lines; but once more they come on, when with guns double shotted with grape and canister, our batteries belched forth into their ranks, mowing mile roads, and scattering the dead and wounded all over the ground. Furiously the battle raged in front of the 14th, 15th and a part of the 16th corps, until the shades of night put a stop to further hostilities.

At this time our Division was on the right wing entrenching ourselves, and awaiting an expected attack on our lines; but none was made.

THURSDAY, Sept. 1st.—The day was very hot, and there was hard fighting on the lines all day. About noon a general order was received from Gen. Sherman, announcing the rebel army cut in two and being driven badly. This brought forth long and hearty cheers from the troops. At night all was unusually quiet, and Friday, Aug.[2] 2d, the enemy was found to have left.—Marching orders were soon issued, and we moved forward through Jonesboro and three miles south, where the enemy was again found, and some artillery fighting took place.

In the evening an Official Report of the occupation of Atlanta by the 20th Army Corps was received from Gen. Sherman, and read to each Regiment, after which cheer after cheer was given for Gen. Sherman and the victory.

During the 3d, 4th and 5th instants, a demonstration was kept up in front, our corps still lying in reserve.

Monday eve. Aug. 5th, we moved back and held a position, while the main army passed. We then formed the rear guard, and fell back to Jonesboro. From there we started on the 7th instant, and on the 9th reached this place, where we now lay undisturbed by the cannon's roar. Gen. Sherman says our work is well done, and in a general order, says that upon the Battle Flag of every regiment that participated in the campaign before Atlanta, may be inscribed, in gilded letters—ATLANTA.

Preparations are now being made for the Pay Masters, who are expected soon.

The troops here enjoy good health, and with a month's rest and some

---

2 An error. This should read September, as should the reference to "Aug. 5th" below.

G. B.'s³ can start out on another campaign in as good spirits as ever.
Yours respectfully,
U. S. S.   Vol. 10, pp. 328–29

Relics of the Past

After the armies left the field, relics of past battles remained. Coming across the
Bull Run battlefield, a correspondent found a "fair and peaceful scene," even as
only a thin layer of dirt concealed bones, bullets, and sundry accoutrements that
retold the terrible events of the battle.

On Monday night I rested with a part of the army that pitched their tents
for the night on the section of the old Bull Run battle field adjacent to the
Warrenton pike, and here alone I gathered material enough to form the subject of a long letter had I time, or you the space to admit of it. A poet might
here find in the suggestive relics of the deadly strife the theme of an epic; or
a painter might illustrate on canvas the horrors of war from the mementoes
here left of its ruthless work.

Bullets are picked up and exhibited by the handful, and soldiers who
participated in the fray are comparing at the same time their gathered
mementoes and their personal recollection of the bloody field. In the long,
luxuriant grass one strikes his foot against skulls and bones, mingled with
the deadly missiles that brought them to the earth. Hollow skulls lie con-
tiguous to hemispheres of exploded shells. The shallow graves rise here and
there above the grass, sometimes in rows, sometimes alone, or scattered at
irregular intervals.

Through the thin layer of soil that hides the nameless hero who gave his
life for his country, one sees the protruding ribs whence the rain has washed
their covering, a foot or an arm reaching out beyond its earthen bed; and
once I saw one of these long sleepers covered snugly up to the chin, but with
the entire face exposed and turned up to the passer by; one could imagine
him a soldier lying on the field wrapped up in his blanket, but that the blanket was of clay and the face was fleshless and eyeless.

---

3   Perhaps "Green Backs."

In one case a foot protruded, with the flesh still partially preserved; in another an entire skeleton lay exposed upon the surface, without any covering whatever. The tatters of what had been his uniform showed that he had been a cavalryman. The flesh was, of course, decomposed; but the tanned and shriveled skin still incased the bony framework of the body, and even the finger nails were in their places. The ligaments that fasten the joints must have been perservered, for he was lifted by the belt which was still around the waist, and not a bone fell out of its place.

When found he lay in the attitude of calm repose, like one who had fallen asleep from weariness. This was in the camp of the ninth Massachusetts regiment. He was buried, as were many more that night, who had waited a long fourteen months for their funeral rites. In fact the different pioneer corps were engaged for some time in paying the last tribute to the gallant dead, whose fragmentary remains were scattered round our camps.

The Pennsylvania Reserves bivouacked for the night on the ground where they themselves were engaged in deadly strife in the battle of fourteen months ago, and the skulls and bones of some of their former companions in arms lay around within the light of their camp fires. It may even have happened that men pitched their tents over the grave of a lost comrade, and again unwittingly rested under the same shelter with one who had often before shared their couch on the tented field.

A soldier of the 1st regiment struck his foot against a cartridge box, near his tent, and, picking it up, read on it the name of an old associate, who had been among the missing, and whose death was only known from his prolonged absence.

An officer of my acquaintance recognized the spot where his tent was located as one near which he was severely wounded, and where he lay through a long weary night by the side of a dead captain. The painful reminiscences which the place called up rendered it anything but an agreeable camping ground to him.

Yesterday morning I devoted a half hour to a slight survey of the field by daylight. As I looked around in the soft sunlight of early morn, from a point of woods where the trees were scarred by bullets or fragments of shell and the graves of the dead lie underneath, my eye wandered over a fair and peaceful scene.

A light silver mist concealed whatever the bare earth may have presented of horror or deformity; like a soft white shroud it enveloped the graves of the dead, and I saw only the pleasing, graceful contour of the fair landscape, the rising swell of a hill bathed in mist and sunlight; bright, sunny slopes bordered by a delicate arboreous fringe that almost seemed to melt away in the still atmosphere, and on another side over hill ravine and slope, a tract of woodlands, as lovely in their sweeps and undulations, their infinite variety of fretted outline, as in the matchless glory of their mingled autumnal hues, here swelling broadly out into the mellow sunshine, and there clothing the steep sides of a ravine that carries them back into realme of shadow and seclusion; and to complete the serene and peaceful aspect, cawing crows flit to and fro in short and lazy flights, or rest quietly in the tops of a few leaf-less trees that tower above their fellows, and lift them up into the cheerful warmth and light. Even in its desolation, this part of the field presents a scene of soft and gentle beauty whose present charm is in vivid contrast with the horrors it once witnessed.   Vol. 8, pp. 153–54

CHAPTER 4

Slavery, Emancipation, and African Americans

O F ALL the differences between the North and the South, probably the most provocative was the institution of slavery, about which Wisconsin soldiers had plenty to say. Letters home and to Wisconsin newspapers show Wisconsinites at their best and at their worst, as soldiers expressed a variety of emotions and attitudes toward that institution and the human beings, both masters and slaves, who were a part of it. While many rejoiced at the thought of slavery coming to an end, others proved more cautious, not wishing to interfere with Southern ways of life, and some were openly hostile and deprecating toward African Americans, slave or free. Still others saw slavery as a source of strength for the South, as forced African American labor liberated white Southerners to fight the war. Accordingly, they expressed a desire for slavery to end merely as a war measure against the South and not as a moral imperative.

Whatever their views on emancipation, as Wisconsin's soldiers observed slavery in practice, they came face-to-face with a social system more complex than they knew from their life in Wisconsin. While many slaves fled to the Union army in search of freedom, the soldiers wrote of cases in which freedom, though attainable, was deferred in order to keep families together. Several correspondents expressed surprise upon discovering that slaves who appeared as white as themselves were not uncommon. As "contrabands" came to the Union army, Wisconsin soldiers shared daily life, and eventually duty and combat, with men formerly held as slaves, noting their customs and expressions, so different from what was seen in Wisconsin. While some were overjoyed with the thought of bringing freedom to oppressed people, racism and inequality abounded, even among soldiers who eventually were fighting as much to free the slaves as to unite the Union. Yet for many of

Wisconsin's men serving in the South, the war was an opportunity to know African Americans not as slaves or contrabands, but as human beings.

Human Property

Pocahontas, Arkansas,
May 1st, 1862.

Mr. Editor:— . . . On our march I have discovered the following notice nailed to a tree, I had the curiosity to go and see it and when I read it, I had the same curiosity to tear it down. These are the words it contained:

NOTICE.

A black man to be let to the highest bidder for one year, George Edwards, he is 25 years old and weighs one hundred and eighty pounds, he is now sound, whoever gets him will have to give 2,000 dollars bond to have the said George Edwards delivered back to me in as good condition at the end of the year as he now is. The bids to be taken at the grist mill at Foreshateman, Arkansas, May the 5th 1862.

WILLIAM SHEPHARD, Prop.   Vol. 4, pp. 281–82

Camp (near no place) among the hills of
old "Kentuck," 33 miles north of Lexington,
October 17, 1862.

. . . But I must tell your children a story; of course you old-fogy Democrats won't be expected to believe it. But it is hoped you will let your children hear it.

We, part of our Regiment, were out on picket duty, Tuesday last, the day before we started for this place. . . . We, your humble servant and a squad of men from Co. G, were posted along the "Pike," and therefore had a good opportunity of seeing all the people who passed: I might tell your children that just as night closed in, an old *man* was seen to approach my post with a basket. He was halted; and upon the inquiry, "Who comes there?" he answered, "Me." I discovered my mistake, 'twas a "negro" a "slave." He continued; "I thought as how ye might be liking to buy some pie and chickens." We very naturally introduced the subject of his personal welfare. He was fifty years old. He was born and brought up where he now lived. His mister was very kind *just now,* to him. He had seen the curse of slavery in all its phases; he had seen his own children hand-cuffed and driven, together with others, in a gang, to the South, for market. He had seen the poor fellows whipped, and whipped so that their backs were covered with blood; and had seen the salt sprinkled upon them. I could not tell you *all* that he told me, now; wait till I come home. We asked him if he didn't wish to be free. "Oh," said he, "I have been waiting for the time this fifty years, but it has not yet come. I would go with you now, but I cannot leave my poor old wife and children who live with me in yon cabin. No, you fellows tell us, and massa he tell neighbor—that the thing look a little rough." He said it had never looked right to him that he should be kept down, a slave. In fact he talked just like a *man.* He was fifty years old, but had never had the chance to learn to read. He staid with us two hours, and when he parted our company, we told him that a million soldiers were now at work to set him free. The old slave gave us his hand and blessing, and turning away with a tear in his eyes, he said, "I will wait. I love the Union soldiers. I hope we shall be free."

One fact we learned; that the slave, although his master is kind to him, and he has everything comfortable to live upon, yet he wants to be *free;* they want to own themselves, and be *men;* and they have got the notion, ("as sly as ye keep it,") that ["]the kingdom's coming."

Things are growing interesting to us.—And we think if all the Northern troops go forth with a principle, and preach the doctrine of universal liberty in a practical way, that we can free the slaves without the help of a proclamation, and right speedily, too. . . .

Respects to all &c.,

C.   Vol. 6, pp. 175–76

After witnessing slavery in Missouri, one man was convinced the institution would die a natural death and was willing to let "the whites of the south" handle its demise.

Town of Union, Washington, Co., Mo.

February 6th, 1862.

EDITORS INDEPENDENT:— . . . I have seen slavery, and can truly say that I love it none the better for having seen it; for truly,

A weary lot is thine, poor slave;

A weary lot all time;
From morn of life, toil to the grave,
The doom of thee and thine.

But I must say that an intercourse with the slave's master has caused me
to like *him* better; for if I had heretofore given the inhabitants of the slave
States the credit of being as good hearted as those of the free, and deemed
that the existence of such an institution as slavery in their land was more
the result of circumstances than crime, yet it has been mere theory, founded
[more] on cosmopolitan principles than real political feeling. But with a
sight of it, and a knowledge of its owners, I am willing to leave it to them
to dispose of themselves, and at the same time, I will give my testimony to
the fact that there are as damnable masters here as ever the most bigoted
abolitionist painted, as there is evidence enough of their guilt in their own
offspring, as white as themselves, and whom they doom to toil equally with
the blackest negro, and would sell with as little remorse. Yet, I say, let whites
of the south take care of such things, for it is manifest that we cannot.
And for this reason I like the course of the administration, in steering close
by the land-marks of the Constitution, and prosecuting the war on strictly

An artist's rendering of the arrival of Union troops at a Southern plantation, from *Harper's
Weekly*, **April 4, 1863**   WHi Image ID 82138

Constitutional grounds, as on such it alone can be successful. Better let slavery die a natural death, . . . as it surely will in the advancing light of civilization, than strive to uproot it with violence, and entail on ourselves a worse evil. Already Missouri, Kentucky and other States are tired of it and will ere long abolish it, when other states will become border States, and in their turn go through the same process. It is true it will take a long time; but we must be united, at least until Europe has been revolutionized; so I say to the friends of the slave in the north—do all you can to provide for the wants of the slave when he is once freed; but let the master in the south free him in his own time. . . .

Yours, &c.,

WILL HAZARD   Vol. 4, pp. 262–63

A War for Union, or for Freedom

Some soldiers, like Captain David McKee, went to war convinced that slavery should end, while others were less zealous abolitionists, fighting only to preserve the Union.

Camp Peck, near Washington,
July 4, 1861.

FRIEND MILLS:— . . . This war must put an end to the institution of slavery. And should something[,] now by us unforeseen, happen which would cause the defeat of our arms, it still makes no difference with the ultimate destiny of this institution. I have conversed with some of the slaves I have met here. They say they expect better times after [a] while. I don't think that insur-rections among them will amount to much, from the fact that their extreme ignorance will prevent the formation of any fixed purposes or places among them, and consequently they cannot design and carry out any definite plan of operations. The negroes on the plantations seem to be ignorant, almost, of the existence of a great North; and at the present time all the knowl-edge they have is derived from rumors set afloat amongst them. The fact is, strange as it may seem, if the negroes on the plantations here were to be now freed and turned loose with full permission to go where they chose they could not, without great difficulty[,] make their way to any of the northern states.—That this deplorable state of ignorance does exist among the slaves is true. But Oh! if there is a just God, how I pity those who are responsible for this damnable and deplorable state of human degradation. The extermination of this institution, is at most, now but a question of time. You and I, if we live to the allotted days of man, will have seen it exterminated. God grant that it may be speedily accomplished. . . .

Yours very truly,

DAVID McKEE.   Vol. 1, pp. 88–89

Hospital Ward, No. 3, Newport News, Va.,
June, 1862.

ED TIMES:— . . . The legitimate results of emancipation can be seen here on a large scale. A large number of blacks are here from different parts of the state, and North Carolina. They are mostly employed in some way by the government, and considering their previous life, work pretty well. But they all have the airs, peculiar to their race, and seem to think themselves as good as the whites, and rather superior to soldiers.

On Sundays, the males are dressed in fine clothes, with starched collars and dickeys, and the wenches in great style, decked out with ribbons, boquetts, &c.—Thus at about ten o'clock, they can be seen, wending their way to their places of worship. Their fine ivory, and black shining faces, and in fact, their whole appearance, may be fascinating to an Abolitionist, but during thirteen months service, I have not seen a soldier, officer or private, but despises them and wishes them off the continent. After they have been here for a few months, they begin to be uneasy, dislike to work, and seek other means than labor to get a living. Hence they can be seen around the hospitals, peddling fish, strawberries, cherries, &c. to the invalids, at enormous prices. The idea of their being permitted to spread through the northern states, is detested by every man of the Potomac Army. . . .

Yours, &c.,

S. R. KNOWLES   Vol. 3, pp. 224–25

Altruism aside, this soldier saw a practical reason for emancipation.

Camp Rousseau, Decatur, Ala., August 8, '62.

EDITORS MOTOR:— . . . The negro question receives its full share of discussion among our soldiers, and many who were death on meddling with it in any way, would sooner see him set free than the government destroyed. They begin to see that the negro is the main stay of the South, for producing supplies for their army, and in depriving the enemy of his slaves you strike his most vital part. And the sooner it is done the better. . . .

Your humble friend,

L. C. N.   Vol. 2, p. 178

Changing Attitudes toward Slavery

Leavenworth, Feb. 17, 1862.

Dear Journal:— . . . I made the peculiar institution my study while in Missouri, and while each hour my abhorrence and detestation of the system increased, I, at the same time, found my prejudice against the race giving way. I have talked with colored men, bond and free, in the streets and in their lowly cabins, and never yet have I found one contented, and never yet seen *one* that was loyal to his master; and the stories of their careless happiness are forgeries, I firmly believe. A great grief seems to rest upon them, and a cloud is on their brows which is seldom lifted save when the prospect of freedom is held out before them. There was one exception, a quadroon named William, a wild, jovial, happy fellow as ever lived, with a good place, a chance to earn money for himself, and a wife and children as fair as any nigger, or "any other man," could wish. The day before we left Weston, I was out with some comrades scouting for apples and chickens, and met him driving his team. I stopped to talk with him, and as soon as we were alone his manner changed. We spoke of his plans for freedom, his longing to have his wife and children where he could feel that they were his own. They did not belong to the same plantation with himself, and they had "such a hard time of it." The next night he would risk everything for freedom. My feelings were aroused while I listened, and I forgot that I was only a union-saver, forgot my constitutional obligations, and exclaimed, "I

must leave Weston to-morrow, but if I can help you any way I will." "Oh! if you only *will!*" said he; but his countenance fell again and he sighed, "can't go tonight, no way. . . ."
COMSTOCK   Vol. 5, pp. 17–18

On a moonlit night near Jacinto, Mississippi, the scene of thousands of runaway slaves carrying what worldly possessions they owned and following the Union army to freedom inspired a soldier to agonize over what the future held for them.

Camp near Jacinto, Miss.,
September 23d, 1862.

Whether this will ever reach you or not seems very doubtful, as the fate of army correspondence, I discover, forms no exception to the characteristic uncertainty of all mundane affairs. . . .

On the 8th inst. the 2d brigade of the 2d division, commanded by Col. Murphy, left Tuscumbia, having previously sent off all the Government stores and cotton by railroad. Thousands of contrabands accompanied us. Thousands more had previously gone off on the cars, the tops of which, for several days, had been black with them as they started off for Corinth. These were but the rear guard who accompanied us, and who could not get away on the cars. I wish I could describe the scene I witnessed, as we marched out of Tuscumbia that moonlight evening. It will live forever in memory, though I cannot find language adequately to describe it as it appeared to me. In the advance moved the army of the Union and of Freedom, with gleaming muskets, serried ranks and steady tramp. In the rear came the army of contrabands, of all ages, sexes, and shades of complexion—from the blackest ebony to the fair Caucasian from which almost every trace of the African was effaced. Crying children, hoary age, and athletic youth were there. On foot and in wagons; mounted on horses, mules and jackasses; loaded down with burdens containing all manner of worthless traps and contrivances, being the sum total of their worldly goods; on through the moonlight came that strange procession. In spite of its ludicrous aspect and the irresistible impulse to laugh, there was to me something strangely sublime in the spectacle of these thousands of human beings fleeing from bondage to freedom. It is true these people's conceptions are not of the lofty order, nor do they describe them in the lofty language of Demosthenes or Patrick Henry.

Their ideas are low, their language rude, and their manners degraded. Yet under these black skins beat human hearts, and these hearts, in spite of the crushing effects of long years of slavery, still throb under the impulse of the imperishable instinct which makes men everywhere love liberty and hate oppression. They know little of what is before them. Many of them, no doubt, think that liberty means plenty to eat and nothing to do.—In this they are sadly mistaken as they will soon discover. Hunger, cold and nakedness, I fear, will be the portion of many of them during the coming winter, and in view of what they must suffer as the price of freedom, I could almost, from my heart, advise them to return [to] the bondage from which they are fleeing. But no! let them go. Liberty is ever a costly boon, and the path which leads from bondage to it is always through great tribulation. They have few friends here, and I am afraid they will not find many where they are going. In spite of all our boasted civilization, our people are still the slaves of caste and of the lowest and most irrational of prejudices, and the simple fact that these refugees are "niggers" still seems to many sufficient reason why they should be kicked and cuffed and trampled upon. God help them! for they will not find much help anywhere else. . . .
M. Vol. 4, p. 115

Camp Curtis, Sulphur Springs, Mo., Dec. 13 [1861]
Dear Gazette: . . . You may be surprised to hear that slavery exists even within the limits of our camp, but such is the case. A general order of Gen. Halleck forbids us interfering with slaves who may come within our lines, but it does not hinder us from putting a 'flea in their ear' occasionally. To-day I was talking with a little fellow (a slave) about 8 years old, around whose brow the hair hung in 'lint white locks,' blue eyes, and skin as white as any boy who walks the streets of Fox Lake. His brother older than himself, is of a pure African complexion, walking by his side, both cursed by the same inevitable doom, a life in bondage. Let those who live in the North and preach up slavery, only look on this unholy sight which is now witnessed by two Regt's of freemen and then say that it is right. No man with the least spark of humanity in his heart could do so. I have often wondered since I came here, why so many slaves were here with only the river between them and freedom; but in conversation last Sunday with three or four smart young men, I asked them if they would not rather be free to work where they chose, and why they

could not go across to Illinois? They told me if it were not for men on the other side they would soon be free; men who got 50 dollars a piece for every one they return. They believe that there are plenty of such men in Illinois, who live by catching fugitives with blood hounds. I do not believe half they told me about it. The fact is they are made to believe it when they are young, and they grow up with that idea till it becomes a fixed fact to them. Slavery *may* be right, but I have seen enough in this place to condemn the whole institution,—enough of slavery. . . .

Yours &c.,

S. C. Mc.   Vol. 2, pp. 28–29

One Wisconsin newspaper relates the story of an army chaplain who was changed by his time in the South.

Rev. A. C. Barry, Chaplain of the 4th regiment, has recently returned to this State. He made a few remarks at the celebration at Kenosha on the 4th. He said, when he left the regiment a few weeks ago, Col. Paine was under arrest. Two slaves came into the Federal lines, near Vicksburg, and gave much valuable information. Their owners came and demanded their "property."—The slaves were driven out of our lines. The masters then captured them, *administered* 150 *lashes to their bare backs,* as pay for giving information to the Federals. The masters also put on their necks heavy iron collars with horns sticking up into their necks. In this horrid condition the slaves again escaped, and came within the lines of the 4th Wis. The masters again demanded their property, and Col. Paine refused to give the men up. The masters appealed to the commanding General, who ordered Col. Paine to give up the slaves to those human bloodhounds! Col. Payne declined to obey, and was deprived of his command, and put under arrest for carrying out the law of Congress which provides that slaves of rebels shall not be returned to their masters. How long will such things be! Mr. Barry was a democrat when a resident of this State, and was not long ago honored with a State office by that party. He comes back now a "raving abolitionist."—Three rousing cheers were given for Col. Paine, at the conclusion of Mr. Barry's remarks.   Vol. 3, pp. 125–26

Encountering Fugitives

In the middle of hostile country, Wisconsin troops found that African Americans were reliable sources of information and encouragement.

Camp Gibbon, Va., Aug. 6 [1862].
. . . The contrabands are the only people here we can depend upon. They tell us where the Secesh are—never lie to us—wish us God speed—and are of great use to us. They leave here by car loads every day, and go to Washington. Where they go from there I know not. Probably sent off on the Underground Rail Road. . . .
Yours, &c.,

D. W.　　　　　　　　　　　　　　　　　　　　Vol. 4, pp. 7–8

Bolivar, Tenn., Oct. 28th 1862.
. . . We have been led to the hiding places of arms, ammunition &c., many times, by the slaves, when their masters and mistresses have stoutly denied all knowledge of their existence.—In fact, we have come to consider all Southerners as *liars,* and never believe what they say, unless it is confirmed by the darkies. Having had considerable experience among them, being on scouting expeditions nearly all the time for months, I know of but *one* instance where a slave told us a wilfull lie, and he had been prepared by threats and promises beforehand, by his master, so as to defraud the authorities, of a fine horse, captured from our cavalry during the summer, and left with him for safe keeping. . . .

W.　　　　　　　　　　　　　　　　　　　　Vol. 5, pp. 64–65

As the war progressed, the question of what to do with escaped slaves became pressing. Abolition-minded soldiers had a hard time reconciling their beliefs with the exigencies of war.

Camp near Fredericksburg, King's Division, May 2, '62,
EDS. SENTINEL:— . . . I would like to make public an act of cold inhumanity which was perpetrated in a company of our regiment lately. A colored boy came into the camp, bare-footed and ragged, stating that he had left a cruel

master, who kept him all Winter without shoes, and treated him cruelly in other respects. Some of the men of the Prairie du Chien company took the little fellow in their charge, intending to clothe and feed him until he could be otherwise cared for; but the Captain and Lieut. Harris ordered him out of the company at once, and threatened with severe punishment the men who should attempt to shelter him. One of the men then went to Capt. Noyes, of Co. A, who kindly took the boy in his care, and supplied his wants.

All this transaction can be well proved by various persons in the several companies of the regiment, who were eye-witnesses of the atrocious act of turning out a child of ten years in a place where, if caught by his unnatural master, nothing could save him from a brutal and barbarous flogging—such as a Western farmer would be ashamed to inflict on his horse. . . .
Yours, truly,
U. M. W.   Vol. 3, pp. 253–54

Arlington Heights, Dec. 16th '61.
. . . The Seventh at last have seen some active duty. On the 10th we started to serve on picket, and to relieve the Sixth Wisconsin guarding the line between Gen. Blenker's and Gen. Smith's Divisions, about three miles to the west of Fall's Church. . . .

Company A and F first occupied the posts on the line, while company I, D and C remained in the thicket as a reserve. We built blazing fires, boiled coffee, and took our supper, as best we could. We had gay times. Before we retired, or rather laid down, with belt and cartridge box, &c., on us, and our knapsacks for a pillow; acting Adjut. Bailey warned us, to be ready in case of an alarm. After some had gone to sleep, and while others wore bivouacing around the fires, a loud report of a gun was heard, succeeded by every gun on the line of the left wing. Fall in, fall in, was sharply echoed throughout the whole reserve, and in less than 2 minutes we were in line of battle on the hill in the advance of our reserve post. Lieut. Col. Robinson rode forward, and soon returned reporting nothing ahead, but that there might be danger in the morning if at all. In the morning we learned, and saw the cause of the alarm in the form of two negro women—a mother and a daughter, the latter was to be sold South that day, and she and her mother determined to hazard whatever fate might have in store for them within our lines. They did not choose to "bear the ills" they had, but rather courted those "they knew not of." Tis true they knew not but what they might be returned, as Gen. Stone does return fugitives to their rebel masters.—The policy of the Government on this question is as much a riddle and a mystery as the ancient oracles of Egypt. Secretary Cameron says something to please the North, which the President modifies to suit Reverdy Johnson and the Border States. So it goes. Each Commander of our volunteers follows his political predilections in regard to contrabands. The Government is afraid to assume the responsibility. Fremont was removed because he did. But the Seventh Regiment is not afraid to assume the responsibility. Every private in the ranks would assume it; and when a thousand men assume the responsibility, each one having a good musket and forty rounds of ball and three buck-shot cartridge you may be assured we were responsible. The Democrats in our regiment were fiercer than those who had been Republicans. The North Star shone pure and serene through the pine boughs, and if you looked on the countenances of these women—the daughter was nearly white, and goodlooking, the mother a mulatto—you would not surrender them back to suffer the contingencies of that system which tramples on the honor of man, and makes merchandise of the virtue of woman. . . .

Yours, very tired,

W. D. W.   Vol. 2, pp. 4–5

On July 17, 1862, Congress passed the Second Confiscation Act, which freed slaves owned by anyone serving in the Confederate army and also authorized the seizure "of all the estate and property, money, stocks, credits, and effects" held by Confederate soldiers. A soldier on picket duty outside Corinth wrote with joy about the Confiscation Act and related an encounter with a slave who gave a compelling reason not to run away from his master.

Corinth, July 27, 1862

To-day we are on picket three miles west of Corinth. I am writing in the woods with my oil cloth on the ground for a table. . . .

We are all rejoiced at the determination of our government to confiscate everything that can be used by the rebels against us. When I enlisted, I said that if I thought it was the purpose of the Government to emancipate the slaves, I would not lift a gun; but I now see the necessity of it. Down here there are thousands of plantations with large fields of corn and cotton, tilled by slaves whose masters are off in the rebel army, or indirectly assisting it all they can. The families, of course, claim to be neutral, and the property is guarded by our soldiers. . . .

Last Sunday evening, when we were eating our supper, a negro came along riding upon a mule, with a bundle of clean clothes on his arm. When he got within about four rods of us he halted, passed the time of day, and inquired if we allowed folks to pass. We replied not unless he had a pass. He presented his master's, and on the back was written permission for him to go in our lines until seven o'clock P.M. On inquiry, he said he was a slave belonging to a man living about a mile outside of our lines, and that he had permission to visit his wife every Sunday morning and return at night. His wife was the property of a man living about 30 rods from our camp, where we get our drinking water. Both the wife and husband are as black as ink, yet she is nursing a child quite white, and bearing a striking resemblance to her master.

The negro said that both his master and the master of his wife were bitter secessionists, and he could prove it; but his word would not be regarded as good for anything. His master had been in the army at Corinth; and he amused us telling with what haste his master tore off the stripes of his pants, when we took possession of Corinth. We asked him why he did not skedaddle. He said that he did attempt to run away, intending to take his wife with him; but our pickets caught and returned him to his master, who whipped him and compelled him to swear that he would not attempt to escape again. And says he:

"Gentlemen, I will not; I love my wife as well as any white man loves his. I intend to do my duty by her as well as a man in my circumstances can, and unless fate separates us, I shall remain with my master until I can take off my hat and politely bid him farewell—adieu!"

And sitting astride of his mule, with his hands extended heavenward, he said:

"Gentlemen, if you believe me, and I speak the honest sentiments of my heart, every night I pray to God to prosper your army, and make it victorious in every engagement. . . ."

More anon,

J. A. B.

Envelope illustration showing escaping slaves   WHi Image ID 75847

Cherokee, Ala., Sept. 11, 1862.

EDITORS GAZETTE:— . . . I have seen more than once, parties of more than 500 come in at one time, and at Tuscumbia, when I was officer of the provost guard, Col. Loomis and myself in one day took the job of feeding and housing not less than three thousand of all ages, sizes and colors. I see, here, every day, slaves as white as myself; and this morning I saw a child and mother at the depot—the mother had but very little of the negro features, and the child was as white as the whitest child in Janesville, with light, straight hair, and a slave. Just think that many such are here, and held and sold in bondage. But, thank God, the time has about come when all such folks can claim their freedom by just coming into our lines, and thousands are availing themselves of the blessed opportunity now afforded them. . . .

We have in our regiment nearly 100 contrabands for cooks and teamsters, it makes a great increase in the army. By receiving them in that capacity it saves just that many men to the ranks. But what is to be done with all the women and children, is a question yet to be answered. I think at Tuscumbia we shipped not less than five thousand of them towards Corinth, and every station along the road is crowded with them . . .

Respectfully yours,

W. B. BRITTON,

Capt. Co. G., 8th Regt. W. V.   Vol. 4, pp. 114–15

Camp opposite Fredericksburg, Va.,
May 19th, 1862.

Messrs. Editors:— . . . This is a most beautiful country. One could wish for no better. The crops are all in and look finely. Who will take care of

them when harvest time comes, I cannot tell, as most of the laboring class—
"contrabands"—are coming to our camps.—They come in every day, sin-
gly and in squads as large as twenty. We give them something to eat, and
some of the boys get them at very cheap rates to cook and do other things
for them. We have 12 or 15 in our company. You would laugh to see them
manœver. They do not like to work over well, and some of the boys say it
will take three or four of us to attend to them in a few months. You know
that a soldier in camp has little to do beyond cooking and keeping himself
and his arms and equipments in good order. Still he likes to be a gentleman
of leisure, and as servants are so easily procured it is handier to have them do
our work than to do it ourselves. So the officer now says, when there is any
police work to do—"Send down your man to do this or that."
When anything turns up I will let you know.
WILLS.   Vol. 3, p. 298

Officers of the 7th Wisconsin with an African American servant behind them   WHi Image ID 25588

*Even after the Second Confiscation Act, not all escaped slaves were safe, particu-
larly in the border states, and confrontations between lower-ranking soldiers and
the military command were common.*

Camp Price, near Nicholsville, Ky., Nov. 5th, 1862.

. . . I need not say that on the question of "contrabands" the 23rd is sound. Fugitives have been demanded of us, but as yet none have returned. The poor fellows are willing to do any work about the camp, and to earn their freedom by serving their country, while their masters stay at home to decry the government, or engage actively in opposing it. It is pretty generally understood here that Wisconsin soldiers cannot be relied upon to return fugitives. That is one of the things they didn't come for. . . .   Vol. 6, p. 231

Sharing their encampments with increasing numbers of escaped slaves made soldiers witnesses to heretofore unknown customs and behaviors that contrasted with the images of African Americans received from the popular culture of the day. A member of the 7th Wisconsin recorded a prayer meeting he observed one clear and starry night in Virginia.

Headquarters 7th Regiment.

Gibbon's Brigade, King's Division,

Fredericksburg, May 4th, 1862.

. . . It would astonish any one to notice the number of contrabands, which flock to this army. Every day the roads leading to our camps are lined with fresh arrivals,

"And still they come."

A few, in comparison to their aggregate number, stay with the regiments, and hire out to the officers and privates. A mess generally hires one or two. They assemble in the evening after retreat and hold prayer meetings. Imagine one of these interesting scenes, when these dusky children of the tropics address their petitions to the Throne of Grace. I have been present at revival meetings, have read Uncle Tom and Dred, and seen the drama of the Octoroon and Christy's Minstrels.[1] But nothing I ever saw or heard rivals one of these meetings, on a clear starry night, on the banks of the classic Rappa-

---

1 *Uncle Tom's Cabin,* published in 1852, and *Dred: A Tale of the Great Dismal Swamp,* published in 1856, were two novels by Harriet Beecher Stowe. Each had strong abolitionist themes that helped influence public opinion in the North. The "drama of the Octoroon" is likely a reference to *The Octoroon,* a four-act play by Dion Boucicault that premiered in New York on December 6, 1859, and told the story of a romance between a white man and an octoroon—that is, someone with one-eighth African American ancestry—in Louisiana. Christy's Minstrels was a popular antebellum singing group that performed in blackface.

hannock. The hulks of the steamers Virginia and St. Nicholas, and hosts of lesser craft, schooners, &c., submerged in the still, rising tide, having contributed their quota of tarred rope to the fires which blaze fiercely and add to the picturesque but grotesque scene. The city of Fredericksburg is quiet. The Drum Major of the Seventh has concluded his taps. A large group of every hue, surrounded by a larger multitude of whites, are assembled. One commences a hymn; that is the dusky portion. Another follows, succeeded by a third, until they are all engaged. The poetry, the very flower, the calumniating blossom of every guttural fellow, howl and dismal yell finds its echo in this concert. An Indian War Dance, our drum corps beating the double quick on the wildest wails of the Ranshee; the song of the bullfrogs, the hoot of the owl and the sorrow of the ape and wild cat would be nightingale's notes compared with it. All the representative echoes of Afric's golden sands, dismal swamps, ravines and caves, find utterance here from the uttermost Barbary States to Mozambique Bay. A cry of grief ascends from the heart of Africa, and the resounding halls of hell cannot rival it. The figures move about uneasily by the strong relief the fierce fires afford. Finally one kneels in prayer. You can hardly distinguish what he utters. He is followed by another more audible, one who does not mouth his words so much. He prays for the white man and black; asks that our camp ground be blessed; that we may win the victory; that they may not be scattered. And that all may be blessed; forgetting not to mention our enemies. They wind up with more unearthly singing. . . .

Yours, truly,

W. D. W.   Vol. 3, pp. 294–95

Emancipated slaves faced a difficult road ahead after having been denied an education. A soldier of the 13th Wisconsin who while serving in Kansas happened upon a school for contrabands run by a Wisconsin man was impressed by the desire for freedom and knowledge among runaway slaves.

> Headquarters of the Troops in Kansas,
> Department of the Mississippi,
> Fort Scott, March 24th, 1862.

MY DEAR FRIEND:— . . . At Ossawottomie I saw a novel and interesting sight in the shape of a school of "contrabands." The school in question is taught by a Wisconsin man called Elder Reed. At his solicitation I visited his school during an evening session, finding congregated there some fifty pupils of all sizes, ages and shades of black, and of both sexes. Five weeks before they were all slaves in Missouri, and scarcely one of them knew a single letter of the alphabet. When I saw them, after they had attended school some thirty days, all knew the alphabet, many were spelling words of two syllables, and a few were beginning to read.—It was a strange sight to see old gray-bearded men struggling for knowledge amid the a-b-abs of the speller, and reciting in the same class with their children, and, for aught I know, grandchildren, for men upwards of fifty and children of six were often in the same class. In one instance I observed a mother and son in the same class, the boy so small that he had to stand upon a desk behind his mother in order to look over with her. But, to give the little fellow his due, he was the brightest scholar of them all, and could even beat his mother reading. Besides spelling and reading, which are made their particular study, the whole class is occasionally united in a general exercise upon Geography or Mental Arithmetic. Their aptness at answering the promiscuous questions put them induced the remark from an officer near me, "They beat me. I never learned so fast as that." I think the most skeptical proslavery mind could hardly fail to be convinced, after visiting this school, that there is something human in the negro; that at least he possesses an intellect susceptible to cultivation. . . .

　　Running away has got to be an epidemic among the negroes of Missouri, or perhaps I should say, a *plague* among their masters. Leavenworth, Lawrence, Ossowottomie, every town, is black with contrabands. There are lots of them with the army, in the capacity of cooks. To illustrate how well the negroes all understand the issues of these times, I will relate an incident that come to my notice while at Leavenworth. There was a bright looking little negro boy who used to bring wood into my room, and once or twice for amusement I engaged him in conversation. He told me that he was ten years old, and related how he came to be in Leavenworth. His master, residing near Platte City, Mo., had joined Price, and let him out for his board and clothes to a party in the secession hot-bed mentioned. While his master was gone he lived with two families, both of which maltreated him, and was living with a third when his master returned and at the time of his own absconding. One Sunday his new master whipped him because he could not find and chop up old rails enough to keep the fires going. This was in the afternoon. In the evening the little fellow, after having formed a determination to seek liberty, went to the house of a neighbor and got another black boy, a year or two older, to engage in his plan also. Taking a couple of pails, they started for the well as if for water; but instead of getting water they set the pails down, told them to stay there till they came back, and started for the bridge over Platte River, which was guarded by a Union sentinel, and which they had an idea they must pass, though they knew not the way to Leavenworth any more than that it lay west of them. They walked up to the sentinel, and asked him if they might pass over the bridge. He told them *they might,* which having accomplished, in the language of the boy himself, they "got up an' dusted." They got lost in the woods two or three times, and finally laid down covering themselves with leaves. When lying down they heard horses' feet, but they "never said a word, but just lay still." The night was very cold, but their hopes kept them from freezing. In the morning they found themselves within sight of Leavenworth, which they reached in safety.

Does not this incident show how thoroughly diffused among the slaves is a love of freedom and a knowledge of the present crisis? They know well enough that if they but get to Kansas their masters may whistle in vain for them. Which brings me to Maj. Cloud, Provost Martial of Leavenworth. The Major is fairly worshipped by these poor runaways, for he don't allow a Missourian to lay his hand upon a black before he has him up for kidnapping. The Major advises them all to go out into the country, masters cannot find them, and go to work for the farmers for a reasonable compensation, and they generally take his advice and act upon it.

A case of kidnapping occurred while I was there. A man was working for the gentleman with whom I boarded. His master set some men upon his track—probably Leavenworth men—who managed to get in with him by degrees. They finally proposed to go some night with him to Missouri and assist him in bringing away his wife, for he was a married man. So, working with the baseness of hell upon the holiest of affection, they went with him and betrayed him into the hands of his master. He sent the poor fellow to Liberty jail. This same jail is full of such captured runaway slaves. *Liberty Jail*—a queer name, isn't it?   Vol. 5, pp. 88–89

Peter D. Thomas (1847–1925). Thomas escaped from slavery and joined the 15th Wisconsin. He served Lt. Charles B. Nelson of Co. G at Chickamauga and other battles. Eventually, Thomas would follow Wisconsin troops back to Beloit, where he attended school. He settled in Racine and was elected county coroner.   WHi Image ID 3399

Peculiarities of the Peculiar Institution

Oxford, Miss., Dec. 12, 1862.

. . . The farther we get south the whiter the negroes appear to be bleached.
. . .

W. B. BRITTON,
Eighth Wisconsin Volunteers   Vol. 4, p. 139

Camp at Davis' Mill, Miss.,

November, 24, 1862.

Editors State Journal: . . . Contrabands are plenty down here. We find them useful as cooks, teamsters and laundresses. You would be surprised at the number of "white slaves" on every plantation. Perhaps the Southern people think it is all right, but it *looks bad.* In the negro quarters of the plantation on which we are encamped, there is a mulatto woman who has half a dozen children, two of them by a white man and the rest by a black one; the first, a boy and girl, are as white as anybody need to be, with not a single negro feature about them; the others are regular "Samboes." So, on every planta-tion, there are white and black slaves, living in the same quarters, married and otherwise. The most revolting effect of this amalgamation we met with, since we have been in the South, was at Cherokee, a small railroad station in Alabama, between Tuscumbia and Iuka. While we were camping there, one day a white woman, who was a slave, with her white child a year or two old, also a slave, came into our lines for the purpose of going North. Before we left, her master came after his chattels, but of course failed to have them returned. To all outward appearances he was a fair sort of man, as intel-ligent as the ordinary run of well-to-do planters, and probably regarded in his neighborhood as a moral man; yet the incestuous scoundrel was *father to both the white slaves*—mother and child! This was told as a fact by the woman herself, and confirmed by several other slaves of the same man, who came with her into camp, one of whom was her sister; the father, in *her* case, hav-ing evidently been black-skinned, as she was a tolerably dark Dinah. Every "white slave" is a sufficient commentary on the institution—a volume—tell-ing the depth of degradation, crime, inhumanity and barbarism to which a people will sink, who make a business of trafficking in the souls and bodies of their fellow men.

G.   Vol. 4, pp. 134–35

Corinth, July 10, 1862.

. . . There is a white girl living near our picket lines, who says she is not a slave, and remembers her freedom till she was six years old. Was then car-ried off and sold. She is now 14 years old, and is now worked on the planta-tion just as a negro, but sighs for her freedom! The boys are bound she shall have it. Her mistress called on Gen. Tod yesterday morning for a guard. Of course the guard went, but he told Col. Allen "he was not going to hunt slaves for the South.["] The plan by her master is, the boys say, to save the girl from being taken away from him, to make her marry a *negro on the plantation!* . . .

Vol. 5, p. 295

Columbus, Ky., August 15, 1862.

EDITORS STATE JOURNAL:— . . . The contraband question occasionally suggests itself, even in this morally benighted district. It would please you to hear "loyal Kentuckians" expatiate on "Northern views," "negro equality" and "amalgamation." They haven't the intelligence to reflect that this same equality of races is nowhere so nearly approached as in their own door-yards, where white, black and all the intermediate shades of youths play together unrestrained, and on equal terms; but they can hardly refuse to admit that slaveholders themselves have done principally all that has ever been done toward illustrating the doctrine of amalgamation.

We have a "boy" now in camp (in spite of Grant's order,) whose history is an epitome of the whole institution. His hair is straight as mine, his cranium better developed than a majority of the white race in the south,—better than that of his own master, who is also, accidentally, his father. Having too much enterprise to endure the routine of plantation life, he hired his time and bought cotton on his own responsibility. Living near Humboldt, Tenn., and marketing his cotton there, he "informed" of the whereabouts of a guerilla band. His *half brother,* a representative of southern chivalry, suspecting his sympathy with the federals, sought excuse for a quarrel by snatching money from his hand as he was counting it, and then denying its possession. "Boy" claimed his money. Chivalry was insulted. "Did the 'boy' call him a liar!" "Not particularly, but you have my bills, I can prove it." This was followed by a blow from the lever of a cotton press in the hands of "Chivalry," which left a horrid gash in "Boy's" head, from which he may and may not recover, but which did not prevent the latter from pitching "Chivalry" headlong over a pile of cotton bales. The affair soon came to the ears of the 12th; result, two of "Chivalry's" boys were soon on the road to this place with the prospect of going still farther north. "Chivalry" is doubtless reaping the rewards of justice at the hands of Col. Bryant, and I can assure him the latter never uses gloves in handling traitors. Would we had five hundred such Colonels and a few Major Generals with similar backbones. But the signs of the times are brightening. The end only waits for the coming hosts of fresh-banded freemen.

VID.   Vol. 5, pp. 118–19

KING'S BRIGADE.

. . . During the second day's march we fell in with a group that Hogarth would have delighted to sketch.

An old negro, his gray wool contrasting thoroughly with the deep sable of his skin, was seated on a stone by the roadside, with his hands clasped fondly around a beautiful little boy, with blue eyes and flaxen hair. Never for a moment did we dream that the little fellow was not the child of wealthy parents. Judge of our surprise on learning that he was born a slave. Near him stood the mother.—"Harriet," as she informed us her name was—a fine looking yellow girl of about twenty-four. Here the beauties of the peculiar institution were amply illustrated. The old black man, his skin as black as night, was the great grandfather of the little boy—singular effect of acclimation, what is not? What a gradation from black to white, if not "from lively to serene." Who will say, henceforth, that the Ethiopian cannot change his skin, or deem it difficult for the leopard to get rid of his spots? Virginia is the land of miracles. . . .

Vol. 4, p. 4

Emancipation

Not all Wisconsin soldiers looked kindly on emancipation or African Americans. In this letter to the Wisconsin Patriot, *"G. W. D." of the 8th Wisconsin expresses his paranoid anxiety over abolition and equality.*

Headquarters, 2d Brig., 2d Div.,
Army of Mississippi, Camp Clear Creek, Miss.,
Tuesday, August 5th, 1862.

Editors Patriot:— . . . The Abolition fanatics of the North are greatly encouraged at what they may call the recent defeats before Richmond—they wish to prolong this war till niggerism is blotted from the land—

"Not that they love the Union less,
But the Nigger more!"

Yes, we are going to have a Black President, a Black Cabinet, and a Black Congress in '65. Hurrah for Nigger-Abolitionists! the twin relics of Barbarism and A(ni)malgamation.

> Will not this be supremely fine
> To kneel and bow at Nigger shrine!

This distinguished class of beings are passing through our camps daily by the hundreds on their way North. They say they are going to be colorized! I intend, for the sake of a hereafter, to court their favor a little more— no knowing what may happen in the North in the absence of Union men. When the Black Convention is called, I want you to give me due notice, for we have one of the smartest niggers cooking for us you ever saw, who wants a position in the New Government. He can eat more, sleep longer, snore louder, and endure more rest than any other Abolitionist in the country!—is blacker than a coal pit, and his hair curls so tight he cannot close his eyes when he goes to sleep. I saw him a few days ago standing up against a tree sound asleep.—His name is Sir John Bunyan, and he glories in the name. I wish to recommend him at the next Congressional Convention (by his authority and request) as a candidate for a position. He is eminently worthy the consideration of his admirers, and being a man of vast dimensions, I think, also, he would have a great weight in the halls of Congress and would *fill* a seat in that "august" body with dignity. . . .

More anon.

G. W. D.   Vol. 4, pp. 106–7

As contrabands reached Union lines, many wished to take up arms and join the fight. The Union soldiers, as usual, had mixed feelings on whether to accept former slaves into their ranks.

West Point, Harden Co., Ky.,
Camp Buell, Nov. 22, 1861.

. . . To-day three contrabands came into our camp, asking to join the Union army. They represent themselves as the property of rebels. One of them was, to all appearances, four-fifths white, and all of them were stout, able fellows. We can fight this cursed thing through without them, I believe. . . .

Vol. 1, p. 67a

Camp in Helena, Ark.,

June 3d, 1863.

Mr. Editor: . . . I care not, perhaps, as much as some about the freedom of the slave, but while we are at war with rebels, and they using all the means in their power, I think we at least should use a portion of ours.

Some people in the North clamor a great deal, saying that the soldiers are not willing to go into battle and fight with the negro by his side. When such folks have been in the service as long as we have, they will see that the soldiers are willing to cooperate with anybody to defeat the enemy and gain a victory. . . .

Yours, &c.,

J. L. O'Brien,

Co. H, 28th Reg. W. V.   Vol. 10, pp. 377–78

. . . Thus to gratify whims, prejudices and fears, the brave men who are anxiously waiting to join their arms with ours, are insultingly refused, and their places filled by white men, while the agricultural, manufacturing, and all other interests must suffer from their absence, the revenue be lessened for want of the taxes on the products of their industry, and to that extent the power of the government to sustain itself in this crisis be lessened; thousands of parents, sisters, wives and children be sorrow-stricken and brought down to the grave in misery and want, on account of what, under the circumstances, seems little short of murder of loved ones in the swamps, trenches and battle-fields of the south; and aid and comfort given to the enemies by refusing to use those against him who are best able to stand the climate, who know every by-way and hiding place in the country[,] who can point out to a certainty every one in the least compromised, who are the only ones that can search out and successfully cope with him in his chosen style of guerrilla warfare, and whose absence from the plantation will compel the enemy to detail soldiers in their stead, that the rest may have food while in the field against us. How long must we wait for the advent of a wiser policy?

Vol. 5, p. 63

On Grand Guard, Six Miles South of Corinth,

July 29th, 1862.

Messrs. Editors:— . . . There appears to be a new life in the army since the

government has decided to use the black folks to help put down the rebellion. The men are anxious to have them to do their work for them, and if need be, to shoulder the musket. The blacks appear to have learned the late laws and orders from Washington already, and they are flocking in fast. At one town that I passed through in Tennessee, on my way to the regiment, I saw about 100 blacks at the depot, waiting to be taken, wherever the government wishes to use them. They said they were willing to take the spade or musket, or whatever was given them. One nigger says, "we have now started, and we are going through, come what will; we want our liberty, and are willing to fight for it." One planter at Jackson lost 25 blacks in one day; they learned the laws before their master. He come in after them, but the commander of the post told him, according to the late orders he had no power to put the niggers outside of his lines. The learned southerner was surprised to think our government had passed any such laws, and said he might as well have lost $20,000.—He consoled himself by thinking our good government would pay him, some day, for his live property. . . .
Yours, &c.,
W. B. BRITTON
Capt. Co. G, 8th Reg. W. V.

The Emancipation Proclamation, which freed the slaves in areas not yet under Union control, was met with some approval among Wisconsin's men, but at least one soldier was upset with it.

Camp Forsyth, Mo., Feb. 14th, 1863.
. . . I tell you I am getting tired of this horrible war. I did not think when I enlisted, that I was going to fight to free the nigger, as that is against my principles, and it goes very hard with me. There is a great deal of talk about Old Abe's proclamation and Abolitionism, but one thing certain, a great many of our soldiers cannot go the nigger, and they will leave the service as soon as possible. . . .

We are of the same opinion in regard to the cause of this war, that is, that the Abolitionists of the North are alone to blame. I would rather see one of them hung than the worst Secesh that I have ever come across.
Yours, &c.,
K.

February 3rd, 1862.

. . . Emancipation affects the loyal and the disloyal alike, and will, beside dividing the public sentiment of the North, paralyzing our strength by sowing the seeds of discord in the mighty army now rallied to the defense of the Union, and driving from our support the moral and physical aid of the border states now enlisted for the maintenance of the Union, will effectually crush and obliterate the large Union sentiment, claimed still to exist in the very heart of the revolted states. The only salvation for the country now is the Constitution. Let the Administration adhere to the requirements of that instrument, and we are safe. Violate that, and the Union is forever gone.

BADGER.   Vol. 2, p. 230

Some soldiers supported the Emancipation Proclamation as a war measure against the south. "D. W." seemed to think the proclamation would both cause the South to "raise the black flag," asking for peace talks, and hasten its eventual military defeat.

In Camp Near Oak Hill O.,

Oct. 9, 1862.

MR EDITOR: . . . Well, the President has at last come around to *the* point, and in my opinion in good time too. One year—yes six months—ago would have been rather soon to have issued the proclamation.—I heard an officer from the state of Tenn. say, but a few days since—'that if that proclamation had been issued one year ago['] that he and nearly one half of his regiment would have gone with the South—but *now* he was for enforcing it to the letter, and thinks it one of the best acts of his administration. It, I think, will meet with a general support from all officers and soldiers in the army, and from a majority of Union citizens in the South. The rebels will squirm and threaten to raise the black flag, but 'twill avail them nothing. They must have something black to worship and if 'tis not the "nigger" it must be a flag. It is the general opinion of the soldiers that within 90 days from the time they raise a black flag they will be pretty effectually whipped, consequently all are rather anxious to have them try the experiment. Let the *"wolf howl,"* their existence as a confederacy is *short* at most. It is now time to take the gloves off and let *every* man show his hand.—Kid gloves and Rose water are "played out." The "dogs of war" must be let loose and be allowed to bite

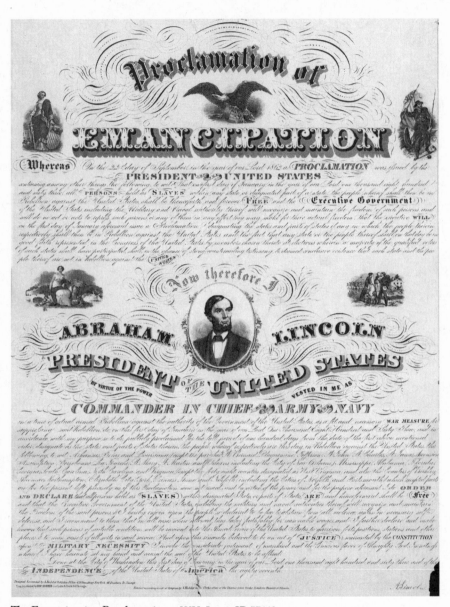

The Emancipation Proclamation   WHi Image ID 77662

wherever they can among the enemy. If the Indians of the N. W. are their allies, let us know it—let the world at large know it, and we will have the matter properly attended to. . . .[2]
Jackson Co. Ohio.
D. W.   Vol. 7, pp. 248–49

                                                                    September 25, 1862
. . . But little is to be said in camp about the emancipation proclamation, but I think it "is generally approved;" even Lieut. R., an incorrigible Democrat, acquiesces to it; but he is sadly in want of a contraband for a servant and body-guard. I somewhat suspect his motives. . . .
E. G. M.   Vol. 6, p. 117

By the spring of 1863, a growing number of former slaves were enlisting in the Union army.

                                                          Camp near Lake Providence,
                                                          Louisiana, April [10th], 1863.
. . . Adj. Gen. Thomas, direct from Washington, made us a speech and gave us the object of his mission here. It is to raise Colored Regiments along the river, and arm and equip them for actual service. There are to be officers furnished out of Gen. McArthur's Division for two Black Regiments. Non-Commissioned officers and privates who are competent, are to be promoted to officer the Colored Regiments. This plan of giving the blacks a chance to help themselves, is a great thing, and will be a great lever in helping to crush this rebellion. The General also stated that it was his intention, in a good many cases where the owners had left their plantations and taken up arms against us, to put colored men enough on the places to work the land and raise supplies for themselves, and in cases of danger there would be a guard furnished to protect them, and any officer or soldier who was caught abusing any colored man, should be punished. This announcement met with the warmest reception from officers and soldiers in the 6th Division. . . .
E. T. C.   Vol. 9, pp. 275–76

---

2 In August 1862, an uprising of the Santee Sioux in Minnesota left several hundred settlers dead and spread panic throughout Minnesota and Wisconsin, then referred to as the North West (see chapter 1).

"D. W." noted changing attitudes toward black troops and their effect on the war effort.

Milliken's Bend, La., April 24, '63.
DEAR BANNER:— . . . The soldiers, as a general thing, are well pleased with the idea of arming the negroes. Those who but a few weeks since were bitterly denouncing the arming of negroes as very wrong and unnecessary, as well as barbarous, are now strong advocates for the measure, and many are even anxious to command them. I think myself it is an excellent idea, and hope that as fast as places are captured by our forces from the rebels the negro soldiers will be used to garrison them, until the whole territory now in possession of the Confederate army is completely protected and held in subjugation by their bayonets. It will be a bitter pill to the "chivalry" indeed, but it would be the "most unkindest cut of all" to the "dear Copperheads." . . .[3]
D. W.   Vol. 10, p. 63

Union soldiers found that black troops exceeded expectations when given the chance to become soldiers.

Quartermaster's Office, 7th Division, 17th Army Corps,
Chickasaw Bayou, June 12, 1863
Dear Brother:— . . . The negroes had a fight at Milliken's Bend, and although I wrote you once from that place that I thought they would run at the first smell of powder, I must admit they fought bravely; and the fact of the matter is, that if the government will only place *good* officers over them, they will be the greatest terror to the —— rebels.—They have old scores to mend, and I assure you there will be no sympathy, or no quarter on either side. It would do you good to see them drill. They pick up the manuel much faster than white men, and O, how it *sets them up* when they receive a musket and United States uniform; and they show their approbation by making the old musket "shine like a nigger's heel." In the fight at the Bend, the negroes lost

---

3 "Copperhead" was an epithet given by Republicans to the Democrats who opposed the war against the South, likening peace Democrats to the venomous snake. Perhaps the most famous Wisconsin Copperhead was Marcus Pomeroy, editor of the *La Crosse Times Daily Democrat,* who once described Abraham Lincoln as "the fanatical tool of fanatics—the greatest widow maker God ever cursed mankind with" (*La Crosse Daily Democrat,* August, 15, 1864).

about 20 killed and 150 wounded. They used the *bayonet, stock* and *barrel*. One fellow shot one rebel, bayonetted another, and finished the *third* by knocking his brains out with the butt of his musket. Another took his old master prisoner, brought him in to his officers and introduced him as "My old massa." . . .

Thankful for past favors, I am yours,

ARCHY.   Vol. 10, p. 129

CHAPTER 5

War Is Hell

SOLDIERS FACED trials and ordeals outside of combat and camp. Capture by the enemy was an unwelcomed fate, as it meant privation and hunger in a Southern prison. While some troops were lucky enough to be paroled, many Wisconsin soldiers spent months in prison waiting for release or the chance to escape. Escape could be its own hardship, as exhausted and malnourished escapees had to travel great distances, often on foot, through enemy country to get back to Union lines. Several Wisconsin men learned that travel through the South—even those parts occupied by the Union army—could be a perilous undertaking, with bushwhackers and ambushes to contend with not infrequently.

The hospital was feared nearly as much as a rebel prison. The archaic medical technology of the time was unequal to the task of providing anything like adequate care for the sick and wounded. Infection was little understood, and drugs, some of them highly addictive like the all-too-popular morphine, were used with only an imperfect understanding of their therapeutic utility. In the end, sickness and disease would kill more soldiers than combat, and fortunate were the men who recovered their health.

In a war that saw over eleven thousand Wisconsin men killed in combat or by disease, Wisconsin's soldiers and their families had to come to terms with losing their comrades and loved ones. Though they saw death on a regular basis, soldiers struggled when they saw their friends succumb to disease or wounds, evinced by the heartfelt letters home singing the praises of the fallen. Equally difficult was the lot of families who received a letter from an officer or a nurse, delivering the news that a husband, father, or son would not return home from the South.

A Soldier's Life

Before knowing the hardship of battle, a soldier of the 7th Wisconsin complained bitterly of the difficulty of marching while overloaded with equipment.

Camp Opposite Fredericksburg, Va.,
June 20, '62.

Messrs. Editors:— . . . [O]n our way here, we done some very severe marching, and since, in marching from here to Haymarket, Warrenton, Cutlets and back, still harder work has been done, because of the bad roads and hot weather, and the enormous loads the men have been compelled to carry—being in many instances and most of the time—a weight of at least sixty pounds, in order that they may march with everything on or about their persons, that the regulations require in addition to three day's rations in their haversack's, as follows:

One lined blouse; one blue cloth dress coat; two wool shirts; two wool pants; two wool socks; one wool blanket; one rubber blanket; half shutter tent; one pair leggings; one extra pair shoes. Add to this haversacks, with three days rations, canteens, cartridge box and forty rounds of cartridges—Gun, together with two from each company, as pioneer's, who carry in addition to all of the above, one a pick and the other a shovel, and to every ten men in the company one with an ax, and you can form some idea of what a soldier of the army of the Rappahannock carries through the broiling sun or over roads shoe deep in mud, and as greasy and slippery as soap.

Whilst they are robbed of the usual and necessary transportation for even the sick when on a march. Whilst the officers have no other shelter in camp than these same shelter tents, a greater nuisance than which was never imposed upon any human being, and leaves them to huddle up in the wet and mud concentrated on them by these same shelter tents, which goes to prove that the government or the commanding Generals are more saving of horse flesh than they are of human life or suffering, the result of all of which is, that notwithstanding the cry for more men nearly every man here would hail with joy the day of his deliverance from what has become almost an unbearable bondage, and if long continued, a *certain death*—not on the battlefield—but by exposure, disease, and over exertion. . . .

But enough of this, the only question with us now is can nothing be done, if not, for God's sake kill us off in battle and don't "do us to death as jack mules."   Vol. 4, p. 2

Prison

Charles Whittier of Janesville, while serving with the 22nd Wisconsin, endured hunger and exposure during a brief captivity among the Confederates.

Annapolis, April 11 [1863].
Dear Wife:—After a silence of two weeks or over, I am seated to write to you again. I feel that it is through the providence of God that I am spared. I do not know as I can give you a description of what I have passed through since I was taken prisoner, but I have seen the hardest time that I ever did, and am thankful that I am out of the rebels' clutches so soon. We were in their hands 16 days, and the first three days we did not get as much to eat as we ought to have had for one day, and they marched us day and night; but it is past now, and I am alive and well, with the exception of a bad cold. I had everything taken from me but my dress coat, pants, shirt and boots. The rebels took everything we had, even to our overcoats and blankets, and some of the boys lost their boots. The rebels cocked their guns and told the boys to take their boots off.

One man belonging to the 19th Michigan regiment was unable to keep up with the rest, and the devils shot him. We were hurried through to Richmond, and kept in prison one day and night. We were then paroled and started for our lines, and a happier set of men you never saw. It is reported that paroled prisoners are sent to their respective states until they are exchanged, and not knowing how long we shall stay here you had better not write until you hear from me again. The weather here is about like April weather in Wisconsin, pretty cold to sleep on the ground without overcoats and blankets, after marching through rivers and creeks. As I am writing under great disadvantages I will leave the rest to tell you when I get home. I will write as soon as I find out where we are going.
Yours forever,
CHARLES W. WHITTIER.   Vol. 10, p. 176

Lieutenant William Booth of the 2nd Wisconsin, wounded and taken prisoner at Bull Run, wrote from a prison in Richmond, Virginia, to protest that those who did not run from the battle were taken prisoner and treated poorly, while those who fled the battle were "promoted for their fleetness."

Richmond, Va., Dec. 4th, 1861.

DEAR FRIEND:—

My health, is very good, although the time passes slowly. It almost seems that Uncle Abe, had forgotten us; or did not care much for us anyhow. It is now more than four months since we have endured this galling captivity, and we see not, that anything is being done to alleviate it. And to us it begins to look as though nothing could be done. Some of the men are nearly bare, and a great many have died, and more will die, if they are not soon released. Every day is witness of some one being borne to the grave.—The sight of [a] hearse [is] becoming quite familiar to us. Nearly all the wounded have recovered, or are dead. That is, those taken at Bull Run. Some of our Wisconsin men are disabled for life, and are still held as prisoners. A large number of men have been sent South, as the prisons here are full. We think something should be done for us *immediately.* There are some three thousand of us, including more than one hundred commissioned officers, who are looking to their government for succor. They are not the men who ran from Bull Run. But they are those who *did not* run. Thus it is—while we are left here to endure the privations and miseries of prison life, the fast runners are promoted for their fleetness.

This looks to us, rather like a bribe upon cowardice. I don't want you to understand me that *all* were cowards who ran. After the command was given, 'twas *duty,* before that 'twas *cowardice.* Understand me—I claim no merit for not running. The bullet in my leg, put a stop to that; but there are many here, who could have escaped if they had run when the rest did. We understand the reason why we are not exchanged is it cannot be done without recognizing the *rebels as belligerents;* but they have already exchanged five officers, and in this, they have obeyed the scripture which says, "The last shall be first and the first shall be last," for included in the number was one Hale who represented himself as being a Lieut. in the Navy, and a nephew of Secretary Welles, perhaps that accounts for his exchange—while Lieutenants who were wounded, and have been here four times as long as he, are still left. It may be all right but it is hard for us to see the reasoning. However we are not expected to be astute politicians, nor to understand the different approximations towards recognition, exhibited in the exchange of *five or five hundred* prisoners. But it may possibly be explained to our satisfaction, and we, in time, taken to Abraham's bosom.

My wound is entirely healed, though it is affected somewhat by cold yet not enough to prevent, though it may slightly impair, my locomotion. I think I may be able to *run* the next time I fight. That is if they don't shoot in the legs.

I should like to visit you very much, but my friends here cannot spare me just now. I suppose you, all of you, take a hunt once in a while; so do we here, but our game is small, and we don't have to go out of doors to hunt it. You may guess its kind.

Give my love to all my friends, and accept the same yourself, from your friend,

WILLIAM BOOTH. Vol. 1, p. 161

The notorious Libby Prison in Richmond, Virginia   WHi Image ID 70726

Theodore J. Widvey of the 3rd Wisconsin was able to get a letter smuggled out of prison in which he related the conditions under which the Union soldiers had to live.

                                                    Richmond, Va., Aug. 16, '62.

Dear Friend:—I am where least of any place on earth I would be, in a Southern prison. The place is a most horrible one—the room wherein we are is 35x50 feet, and contains 146 prisoners, 36 of whom are officers, including Gen. Prince. It is dark and filthy beyond description. We sleep on the damp, dirty floor, without blankets or bedding of any kind. Our food is bread and fresh beef, *without salt.* We get only half rations, and are excluded from buying anything outside. We are deprived of water, except what is drawn from the filthy James River, which is as warm as if heated over a fire. You have no idea how shamefully we are treated.—The balance of the 146 are men of all classes—generally of the very lowest, being teamsters and camp followers. In the room is the privy, which stinks awfully, as do the men from sweat and filth. We are allowed no liberties, not even looking outside the window. . . . I must close. Farewell.

Your,

T. J. WIDVEY.   Vol. 3, p. 56

Some prisoners were luckier than others. While held in Richmond's Libby Prison, a former tobacco warehouse, members of the 2nd Wisconsin helped themselves to the stock of tobacco and whiskey.

                                                     Arlington, Jan. 13, '62.

Dear Sentinel:— . . . While the Second prisoners were confined in the tobacco factory at Richmond, all the stock [of tobacco], consisting of about four thousand dollars' worth, was carried up into the fifth story or cock loft, and the trap door of this department was nailed down securely.

     More than this, the boys were warned if they troubled it they would be shot. For about two weeks the boys got along very well, but at the end of that time, there came a hankering for the weed, and as they had no funds in bank, they must draw on the Southern stock. By some means a board was lifted up in the floor, then the trap door was forced open, and the way tobacco was distributed around was a caution. Each man laid in a good supply, and hid it securely. The tobacco question was now settled for a time at least. Some time after the owner of the factory came in, and a discovery was made. That he was exceedingly wroth there can be no doubt. He raved, stormed, and even threatened to shoot, etc. Then, more sensibly, went to work and removed all the pressed tobacco from the building, and removing the fine cut to an apartment, nailed it up. When the boys run short again, they sharpened some bits of iron and bored through the floor and from this hole dug out all they wanted. It was a god-send.

Shortly after being confined, two barrels of whisky were found in the building. No sooner was the discovery made than a number got exceedingly intoxicated, making much noise, and fighting. To prevent a repetition of the scene, the more sensible emptied their slop buckets into the barrels, thus destroying the liquor. The drunken ones were placed in irons and kept for a week, but Yankee ingenuity invented a machine which unlocked the irons, and when the officers were absent they were taken off, to be put on again when the officers came. . . .

C.   Vol. 2, pp. 214–15

Arlington, Jan. 17, '62.

. . . From the specimens brought home, the boys must have spent a large portion of their time in making pipes and rings, the former from wood, and the latter from beef bones. Some of these specimens are very ingeniously constructed, and are much sought after by all, as relics. . . .

C.   Vol. 2, p. 221

Escape

Henry Beardsley of Company B, 2nd Wisconsin Infantry, wrote home to relate the adventure of his comrade, George F. Marshall, who escaped from a Richmond prison and made his way to Union lines in western Virginia.

Camp Tillinghast, Va.,
Feb. 3, 1862.

DEAR MOTHER AND SISTER: I should have written this letter last night, but I waited to hear the story of Mr. Marshall, of our company, who has just returned from Richmond. He was taken prisoner at the battle of Bull Run. He escaped from the prison the 25th of December—three days before Bob Burns and his companions were released. He had heard so much about being released that he thought of it as an idle dream, and seized upon the first opportunity to escape. He managed to gain the confidence of the sentinel, whom he had been to work at some time. The sentinel had such confidence in Marshall that he would let him out occasionally, and finally would let him go across the street to a saloon and get liquor. He finally succeeded in getting the sentinel drunk and made good his escape. He stopped in Richmond three weeks, managed to get citizen's clothes, and went around the city as he pleased; saw everything that was worth seeing, and studied the military advantages of the place, which he says amount to nothing, for it would take too much of their forces to protect it, situated as it is—a part of the city in the valley by the James river and a part on the hill, and so chopped up by ravines back that it would take a thousand guns to protect it against any considerable force. They only have two parks of artillery mounted and only four or five hundred well soldiers—just enough to guard the prisoners, &c.

Marshall left Richmond the 14th of January. By the way, I will tell how he fared while there. He stopped at a Union house—he told me the name of the man, but did not wish me to write it (one of the first families of the city)—and fared sumptuously every day. He says there are many Union people in the city who are yet cautious about saying much, but not so much so as they were in the summer.

When Marshall left, a passport was given him by a trader, who advised him to strike for Western Virginia. He took the Virginia Central Railroad and came to Jackson river, the terminus of the road, and took the stage to White Sulphur Springs, forty-five miles, and then came the tug of war—he had to foot it one hundred and twenty miles. It rained and snowed all the time till he got through to our lines. He had to wade creeks and swim the larger streams, traveling nights and sleeping days. He had to come some fine dodges, and was shot at three times by pickets, but fortunately escaped all harm except that he came near dying from fatigue. I should like to give you his story verbatim, but it is too long; so you must be content with what I write.

Andersonville Prison in Georgia, where 12,913 Union soldiers died of starvation and disease WHi Image ID 75547

The country through which Marshall passed after leaving the railroad was desolate, the whirlwind of war had passed over and spread desolation all around. He reached our lines the 21st ult., and was received into the bosom of those braves who have fought the battles of Western Virginia. Rosencranz took him under his care for four days at Charleston, on the Kanawha river, ninety miles from its junction with the Ohio. He took the boat then and arrived in Wheeling on the 28th, stopped over night, and came to Pittsburg, and by rail to Washington. He brought dispatches from Rosencranz to McClellan, with whom he stopped two days and related his story, which was of no small importance to the General.

Mr. Marshall arrived in camp on Sunday, at noon, and was greeted with cheers such as the Light Guard know how to give. He is truly the hero of the company. The narrow escapes, privations and fatigues he has endured, with the important information he brings, place him high on the roll of fame gained in this war.

I will state here that Mr. Marshall was among the first settlers of La Crosse, was clerk in the New England House one year, and then went up

Black river as a lumber clerk, where he has been most of the time since. He is about five feet six inches tall, well built, hair a shade or two darker than mine, and black whiskers, gray eyes; broad, high forehead; sharp nose, and smart enough to get away from almost any *secesh*—a first rate judge of human nature. . . .

HENRY B. BEARDSLEY   Vol. 2, p. 229

Lieutenant A. T. Lamson of Madison and Lieutenant E. E. Sill after escaping from a Confederate prison in Columbia, South Carolina, and making their way back to the Union lines in 1864 or 1865   WHi Image ID 3506

Late in the war, soldiers in the 3rd Wisconsin Artillery were horrified to learn of the suffering endured by Union prisoners held at Andersonville, the notorious prison camp near Americus, Georgia.

Chattanooga, Tenn. July, 1864.

MESSRS. EDITORS: Yesterday P. M. our camp was thrown into commotion by the sudden appearance of our comrade, Thomas Boy[d], who was taken prisoner at the battle of Chickamauga, and who made his escape from the rebel prison at Americus, Georgia, 170 miles south of Atlanta by railroad, on the 14th day of June, and after being captured three times—once by *blood hounds*—and many hair-breadth escapes and thrilling adventures, came into our lines on the Chattahoochee river on the 5th of July.

The tale of horror he tells of the suffering and treatment of our prisoners is almost beyond belief. The barbarous ages give no parallel to it. The sufferings undergone by our men at Belle Isle and Libby Prison were comforts compared to this. . . .

At the time he made his escape, there were confined NINETEEN THOUSAND Federal prisoners in a stockade inclosing TWELVE ACRES of ground, through the center of which runs a *swamp,* that covers about three acres of said twelve. The men are without blankets and many of them almost nude, and all ragged, dirty, and lousy. No soap is allowed them. They have no tents or shelter except *holes in the ground* which they have dug with their hands and sticks for shovels, making roofs (if such they may be called) over them by using sticks for rafters which are covered with dirt. The water they have to use is obtained by digging holes on the edge of the aforementioned swamp. Their rations consist of about three ounces of meat and a piece of corn bread four inches square each day. In lieu of this bread they *very often* get a pint and one-half of corn meal which they have to bake, *without* salt, on a board before a camp fire. Sometimes their bread and meal *fails* and then they get a pint of rice. They very often have to go without their meat ration.

Such treatment seems almost too horrible for well, able-bodied men to undergo; but they are not well, on the contrary, they are suffering the most horrible diseases. Nearly all of the Gettysburg and Chickamauga prisoners, that are yet alive, have the scurvy in its worst form. Two-thirds of the whole number are suffering from the same dread disease. Their limbs are stiff and swollen, teeth dropping out and gums loose and flabby. The soul turns sick from the awful picture. The hospital differs from the stockade or prison only in that there the men have tents, but they are compelled to *lie on the ground without blankets*. The average number of deaths is fifty per day. The rebel surgeons have *no medicine to give the sick*.

At the stockade they have an imaginary line which if our men cross they are shot dead by the rebel guards, and hence it is there called the "dead line." Many of the men's sufferings are so great that they VOLUNTARILY CROSS THE DEAD LINE AND ARE SHOT. Mr. Boyd says he has witnessed many such scenes.

There are very many crazy ones, made so by their intolerable sufferings and loss of all hope of being exchanged.

The dead are stripped of their clothing, if there be any that is at all good on them, and then *piled up* in a cart and drawn off to the burial ground and thrown in trenches about six feet wide and the usual depth that graves are dug and then covered with earth.   Vol. 10, p. 63

Among Secesh

Hiram Calkins of Wausau related the adventure of a sergeant from Company B of the 1st Wisconsin Cavalry who infiltrated a band of rebel marauders to gain intelligence on the band's movements, narrowly avoiding capture in the process.

Bloomfield, Mo., June 19, 1862.
DEAR RECORD:— . . . [I]t was deemed advisable by the commandants, to break up a band of about four hundred rebels, who were encamped about sixty miles in Arkansas, under command of a notorious out-law named Jeffries. . . . The expedition against Jeffries consists of about five hundred men, under command of Majors LaGrange and Torrey. . . .

Before starting, several persons were entrusted with the fearful responsibility of ascertaining the locality of the enemy, their strength, &c. Among these, was one, Sergeant Wase of Company "B," whose appearance, when done in "butternut," would be sufficient to pass him in any rebel camp. He, with others, entered the rebel camp and having learned the rebel vocabulary of phrases, were enabled to curse the Yankees and Black Republicans, in a style apparently original, and satisfactory to genuine traitors, but in one thing only did the Sergeant, lack. He had not learned to drink whiskey and carouse—a necessary qualification for "butternuts"—and for this reason was suspected, and finally arrested as a spy. A guard of four men were placed around him, two of whom were armed with Sharp's rifles. Apparently unconscious of his situation, the Sergeant had doffed his nether garments prepatory to retiring for the night's repose, when observing the guards unmindful of his intentions, he seized the two rifles, and ere they had time to collect their bewildered thoughts, the Sergeant had leveled one of the "six shooters" at their breasts, and without stopping to parley, they "skedaddled" for a hiding place, and when sufficiently remote, the Sergeant made a requisition upon the agility of his feet, which was responded too, in "double quick," leaving nothing visible in the darkness of the night, but the tail of his *unmentionable*. The first house he came to, contributed to his necessity for a horse, and the next supplied a portion of the "butternut," and so on until, when morning came, our notable "secesh" was hasting his way through the country, "in pursuit of the d—d black republicans," prepared, single handed to send into their *cowardly* hosts, twelve ["]leaden messengers of death." Such the people took to be his mission, until he had been able to exchange horses twice on his noble errand of vengeance. Arriving about noon on Monday, at Major LaGrange's camp, he learned that the expedition had already started in pursuit of the rebels, and without waiting to rest his almost exhausted nature, he simply left his trophies, (the rifles and horse) took a fresh "contraband" and started, in pursuit, to join the expedition. From him and the expedition we have not heard, but knowing the men, we have no fears of the result. . . .

Yours &c.,

HIRAM CALKINS   Vol. 7, pp. 135–37

A soldier writing under the name "MACK" thought it easier to travel alone through hostile territory than to endure picket duty.

Bloomfield, Mo. June 3, 1862.

Very soon after I wrote my last letter, our company together with the most of the regiment, left Cape Girardeau for this place, in order to break up some rebel bands that were said to be encamped in this vicinity. The officers thought I was not able to stand the journey, and accordingly I was ordered to stay in camp. After the troops were gone, I was immediately detailed as one of the picket guards, and was kept on duty day and night, rain or shine, most of the time for nearly two weeks, and having become sick of staying in camp, I determined to join my company and see some active service if possible; accordingly, without permission, with neither pass or countersign, I left, rode through six sets of pickets, and arrived safely where our company were encamped at a little village called Hornersville, in the south-east part of the state, and a distant one hundred and thirty miles from Cape Girardeau. There was just enough of danger in the trip to make it interesting, and I enjoyed it very much. When I wanted any thing to eat, I called at some house and demanded food in the name of the Constitution of the United States and generally got the best people had. I fed my horse from the granaries on the route, and camped wherever night overtook me, taking good care that my revolver and musket were where I could grasp them in a moment, and always sleeping within a few feet of my horse. . . .

MACK.   Vol. 7, p. 127

When Lieutenant Albert H. Blake from Sparta was wounded, his brother undertook a harrowing journey to bring him home to convalesce. Along the way, the lieutenant's brother found the country infested with perils, including jayhawkers—marauders ostensibly against slavery—and bushwhackers—irregular Southern militants prone to ambush and robbery.

Upon hearing of the battle at Prairie Grove, Ark., and that my brother, Lieut. A. H. BLAKE, of the 20th Wis., was among the wounded, I determined to go and bring him home if possible. I left home at 3 o'clock, P. M., the 22d of Dec. *en route* for that place. I reached St. Louis at 11 A. M., Tuesday, the 23d. I stopped over here and got the necessary papers for the next day, as passes are to be procured only from one point to another. I took cars for Rolla at 8 A. M., the 24th, and reached that place at dark, 125 miles S. W. of St. Louis. At this place I fell in with Mr. Crane, Sutler of the 20th Iowa Regt., and was happy to learn that he was going through to the battle ground at Prairie Grove. We took the stage next morning for Springfield; this stage was a lumber wagon without seats, and with high side-boards serving us as breast-works as we were traveling through the country infested by bushwhackers and jayhawkers. . . .

We travelled through the day and brought up about 10 P. M. at Gasconade to stop for the night. We were called up in the morning, had breakfast, and started on our way. Nothing remarkable happened through the day. We stopped at a stage house at night, but could get no supper or lodging, so we took our blankets and lay down before the fire. We had a good night's rest although it was rather hard. We left in the morning for Springfield, 13 miles. . . . We stopped at this place over night, and as there was no stage running South from this place we got a carriage and paid $65 to carry us through to the battle-field, 125 miles; the first day's drive was about 65 miles. We stopped at a farm house belonging to one of the "Union" men of those parts. He would not let us have any supper, and said we should have no breakfast, and that our horses might be missing in the morning, and we were of the same opinion, as a member of his family was seen climbing the hills by moonlight, we supposed, to notify the neighbors of the chance of jayhawking our horses; we concluded it was not the place for us, so we hitched up our team and drove about two miles through the woods and camped with a train. We sat in our carriage till morning, when we drove to the battle ground of Pea Ridge. . . . We took breakfast at Elkhorn Tavern, the headquarters of Gen. Sigel at the time of the battle of Pea Ridge. After breakfast we started on our way for Fayettville, Ark., 33 miles. After we had driven a few miles we come up with a company of men, 13 in all; two of this number had been shot a short time before, one was dead and the other was dying.— The bushwhackers had done their work; the circumstances were these: The guerillas came up to an old house where these men were stopping for the night and called for them to come out, and as one came to the door one of the guerrillas said to him: "It is hard, but I am going to shoot you." The man replied, "I guess not." But he shot, and the man fell dead. They then called out another and shot him. Then those that were in the house shut the door and refused to come out. They were told that if they did not they (the bushwhackers) would burn the house down and kill every one of them. They finally yielded and gave themselves up. The guerrillas took their overcoats, pistols and five horses, and left for the mountains. It looked rather hard to see those men standing around their wagon looking upon their dead companions, with their horses gone, and they in an enemy's country. We drove on as fast as possible reaching Fayettesville at 8 P. M. I immediately went to head-quarters and reported what had happened, and the wants of the living men. An escort with an ambulance was sent out in a short time, and they were brought in; but the two men shot were dead and were buried the next day. That is the way things go down in Dixie.

I immediately went to the different hospitals to find my brother. I found him without much difficulty, and much better than I expected. The Surgeon had been successful in stopping the flow of blood, and it was thought that he would be able to be moved in 16 or 18 days. I found him occupying a very good house in company with Major Thompson and Lieut. Stork of the 20th Iowa. . . . I stayed at this place (Fayetteville) 16 days. I employed myself in visiting the different hospitals and calling on what Wisconsin boys I could find. . . . On Sunday, the 11th, there was a rumor going the rounds that the rebel Gen. Hindman was preparing to take Fayetteville, and I heard the landlady remark that the rebel pickets were within 5 miles of the place, and advised her boarders to draw their rations for it was not certain who would run the town within 24 hours, and I having a great deal of caution I thought best to draw *my* rations and start, and being a little *lame* I started early. I got a horse and buggy, got my brother in, drove 33 miles, and put up at Elkhorn Tavern, at which place we overtook Col. Barstow, his son, and Adjutant, on their way to St. Louis, and it being rainy the Col. asked my brother to have a seat with him in his carriage, which was a great favor to him as he was not able to travel in the rain. Nothing occurred on the road to Springfield except that my horse gave out and I was obliged to foot it and push the buggy up hill. We reached Springfield on the fourth day, and stopped over one day to get passes and transfers to St. Louis. . . .

I made up my mind that country did not suit me; so I left Springfield on the 17th of January in stage for Rolla; the weather was pleasant but cool; after we had driven about 25 miles, all at once, and without notice, we were commanded to halt. A man made his appearance at the door of the stage and asked the names of all in the stage, and then rode off; he was well armed; this was about 2 P. M. We had not driven more than two miles further when another called out for us to halt, and the same ceremony was performed, or nearly so. We were stopped eight times that afternoon, I suppose for the purpose of ascertaining how many there were aboard the stage, and what the prospect of a prize was in case they should take us at night, as we drove until late. But they did not make their appearance at night. They were bushwhackers and jayhawkers, and I suppose they thought it would not pay to spend their time on us.—We had no other difficulty in getting thro' to Rolla, and if the sound of the whistle of a locomotive ever suited my ears, it was then. I felt like getting home once more with my wounded brother. We took the cars for St. Louis and arrived there at 6 P. M. At this place I had to go through all the different departments to get a 20 days furlough for a soldier who had been in the service for 18 months without one day's rest or furlough, with a minnie ball through his breast, and a broken foot broken by a gun carriage in taking a battery at Prairie Grove. . . . We left St. Louis at 3 P. M., 20th January, and reached home at 2 P. M., 21st.   Vol. 6, pp. 131–32

Orrin Sanborn of Quincy, Wisconsin, who served in the 10th Wisconsin, learned it was not safe to travel in the South, even in Union-occupied territory.

June 7, 1862.

Dear Father:—I am thankful I am alive yet, and can write you a few lines. Since I wrote you I had a very narrow escape from being shot by rebels. I had been quite unwell for a few days, and some of the other boys were complaining, so when the train came along we got aboard and thought we would go up to where the regiment was staying and see the doctor and get some medicine. Took our guns and cartridge boxes and took seats in the passenger car. I bought a paper and commenced reading, and when we had got about a mile from the bridge and were going through a deep cut, there was a whole volley fired into the passenger car. The Colonel of our regiment, the Major of the cavalry and a Lieutenant were in the car. The rebels were at each end of the cut and on top, so they could fire down on the train. When they fired I turned my head to look out of the window and a ball went through the brim of my hat. There was five boys wounded right around me; one in our company was shot right under the temple; buckshot went nearly through his head and put both his eyes out. He has his senses yet and the surgeon thinks there is some hope of recovery; and another was shot through the leg, one had his arm broke, and another through both arms. The Lieut. was shot through the bowels; all of them were close about me. Three spent balls hit the colonel. Every seat in the car was filled with cavalry, so they couldn't help hitting some of us; two cavalrymen on top of the cars were killed; there was twelve wounded. The engineer didn't know anything about it until we got to the depot which was about 100 rods from the cut. Just as soon as they stopped firing, our colonel jumped up, grasped his revolver and rushed for the door, shouting "stop the train, stop the train, why in —— don't they stop the train!" and then as soon as the train stopped so he could jump off he jumped and ran back, and the cavalry after him; but when they got back to the cut, they could find "nary reb."

When I looked out of the car window I saw one man that I knew we had taken a couple of shot guns from, and I had eaten at his house. After it was all over, I told the Colonel what I knew and he told me, with a wicked wink, to watch for Mr. Cuss, and if we caught him he might suffer; and I'm of the opinion he will suffer, for he lives only two miles from the bridge and I will shoot him if it costs me my life! D— a man that will be "old pie" to my face and shoot me when my back is turned! When we were at his house and after we had searched it all over, he invited us to eat dinner with him. It may be that I am lucky, for I have been right among the bullets as much as any could well be and escape getting a hole in his jacket.

We heard the good news that Corinth was taken and 20,000 rebels captured, and that the Tennessee and Kentucky troops had all deserted Beauregard's army and gone home, also that the Governor of North Carolina had ordered all his troops home, and that the south can't have any more help from him.

I can't believe the war will last much longer, and I shouldn't wonder if before I write again that peace will be declared and published in the papers, and I hope it will for I have not got but one more postage stamp.

As ever your son,

ORRIN C. SANBORN   Vol. 4, pp. 208–9

A woman who accompanied her husband to the war related to a friend the experience of trying to find her husband after he sustained wounds at a battle in Mississippi.

Oh, my friend! how can I tell you of the tortures that have nearly crazed me for the last three days! Pen is powerless to trace, words weak to convey one tittle of the misery I have endured. I thought myself strong before. I have seen so much of suffering that I thought my nerves had grown steady, and I could bear anything; but to-day I am weak and trembling like a frightened child.

But do not wonder at it. My dear husband lies beside me, wounded unto death perhaps. I have lost all hope of him, tho' I thank God for the privilege of being this moment beside him. And being in agony. There has been little time to tend them, poor fellows. True, the surgeons are busy all the time, but all the wounded have not yet been brought in, and it seems as if the time will never come when our brave men shall have been made comfortable as circumstances may permit. It is awful to look around me. I can see every imaginable form of suffering, and yet am helpless to aid them of any consequence.

Since night before last I have not left my husband's side for a moment, except to get such things as I required, or to hand some poor fellow a cup of water. Even as I write my heart throbs achingly to hear the deep groans and sharp cries about me. He is sleeping, but I dare not close my eyes, lest he should die while I sleep. And it is to keep awake, and in a manner to relieve my over-burdened heart, [that] I am writing to you now under such sad auspices.

On the morning of the 3d instant the fight began. The attack was made on Gen. MacArthur's division, and we could plainly hear the roll of artillery here, as it is only about two miles and a half from this place. Oh! the fearful agony of that awful day! I had seen F. a moment early in the morning, but it was only for a moment when he bade me good bye, saying hurriedly, as he tore himself away: "Pray for me, my wife; and, if I fall, God protect you!" There was something in his look and tone that struck a chill to my heart, and every moment after I knew the fight had begun I felt as if he had indeed fallen. I cannot tell how long it was before I heard that Ogelsby's Brigade was engaged, but it seems an age to me. After that my agony was nearly intolerable. I never had a thought of fear for myself, I was thinking only of F. Then I got the word that he had been hotly pursued by the rebels and had fallen back.

Late in the afternoon I succeeded in gaining a little intelligible information.

Poor General Hackelman was shot thro' the neck while giving command, and fell mortally wounded. He died between ten and eleven o'clock the same night, I have since learned. Up to this time of receiving the wound he had acted with the greatest bravery and enthusiasm, tempered with a coolness that made every action effective. When dusk at last put an end to the first day's conflict, I learned that General Ogelsby had been dangerously wounded, but could gain no intelligence from my husband. I could not bear the suspense. Dark as it was and hopeless as it seemed to search for him then, I started out for the battle field.

Oh, how shall I describe the search of that night? It looked like madness. It was madness. But all night long I straggled amongst bleeding corpses, over dead horses, trampled limbs, shattered artillery—everything that goes to make up the horror of a battle-field when the conflict was over. They were removing the wounded all night. Oh, think how awful to stumble over the dead and hear the cries of the wounded and dying, alone, in the night time. I had to start off alone, else they would not have let me go.

As you may suppose, I could not find him, either among the living or the dead. But the next morning, just after sunrise, I came to a little clump of timbers where a horse had fallen—his head shot off and his body half covering a man whom I supposed dead. His face was to the ground, but as I stopped to look closer, I perceived a faint movement of the body; then heard a faint moan. I stopped and turned the face upward. The head and face were both covered with blood, but when I turned it to the light I knew it in spite of its disfiguration. Oh God, the agony of that moment sickened me almost to suffocation. With strength I thought impossible in me, I drew him crushed and bleeding, from beneath the carcass of our poor old horse, whom we had both so loved and petted, and dipping my handkerchief in a little pool of water amongst the bushes, bathed his face and pressed some moisture between his parched, swollen lips. He was utterly insensible, and there was a dreadful wound in his head. Both limbs were crushed hopelessly beneath the horse. He was utterly beyond the reach of human skill to save, but as soon as possible I had him conveyed to the hospital. I have nursed him ever since, hopelessly and with a heart breaking with grief. Oh! how many wives, how many mothers, are to-day mourning the dead and dying, even as I mourn my dying! He has not opened his eyes to look at or speak to me since he fell. Oh! could he but speak to me once before he dies, I should give him up with more resignation. But to die thus—without a look or word! Oh, my heart is breaking!   Vol. 5, p. 163

The Dangers of Medicine

Surgeon General William Hammond famously noted that the Civil War occurred near "the end of the medical Middle Ages." Soldiers often gave readers a feel for the medical treatment provided by incompetent doctors.

Baton Rouge, La.

June 13, 1862.

FRIEND MILLS:— . . . I am unable to state as to other regiments from our State, but truth and duty to the friends of volunteers at home, compels me to state that our Surgeons and assistant Surgeons are totally incompetent, and I may say, inhuman. I will illustrate a scene at Surgeon's call—an every day occurrence. At 5 P. M. the Surgeon's call is sounded. The 1st Sergeants of companies take the "Sick Book" and those desiring to attend, the names of which are placed on the book, and proceeds to the Surgeon's quarters. Then something like the following ensues:

DOCTOR—"What book comes first?"

SERGEANT—"Co. A."

DOCT.—"Co. A. What's first name?"

SERGT.—"Smith."

DOCT.—"Well Smith, what's the matter with you?"

SMITH.—"Bad darrhoea—bones ache—sick in stomach."

DOCT.—"Here, (taking two papers of powders from a pile), take one of those now, and if you don't feel better, take the other, sometime during the day. Who comes next?"

SERGT.—"Brown."

DOCT.—"Well, Brown, what's the trouble?"

BROWN—"Have a severe headache—and billious—feel very sick."

DOCT.—"Here, (takes two papers out of the same pile that he gave Smith), take one of them now, and if you don't feel better, take another.— Who comes next?"

SERGT.—"Jones."

DOCT.—"(Well, Jones, what's the matter with you?")

JONES—"Sprained my ankle while on picket yesterday—it is very pain-ful—I am unable to duty."

Doct.—"Here, (takes from same powders that he gave Smith and Brown) take one of them now, and in two hours take another. Who comes next?"

And so the miserable farce goes on until all have been *attended* to. The same remedy is given for sore throat as for a sprained ankle. A volunteer in the U. S. army considers himself as a doomed man when he is once in the clutches of the Hospital. . . .

Yours &c.,

High Private.   Vol. 3, pp. 115–16

A Union surgeon examining patients in Tennessee   WHi Image ID 33583

I lived—or rather existed—in a hospital something over two months, during which time I saw considerable that was interesting and instructive, and occasionally a little that was very amusing. I was moved twice, and both removals had nearly proved fatal; but I sometimes think a man will endure what would kill anything else. For instance: When I was taken ill I was conveyed to the hospital tent which belonged to the command. This was an ordinary bell tent, containing some ten or twelve men, all lying on the ground. It was very disagreeable for a well man, for the frequent rains had filled the low, swampy soil with water till it was as soft as a well saturated sponge; but, according to the Surgeon in command, it was good enough for soldiers. The way this *worthy* treated those who were unable to do duty, and yet able to crawl to his quarters, was, to say the least, *amusing*. At eight in the morning he would have them brought to his tent by the Orderly Sergeant, there to await the coming of His Highness, sometimes half, sometimes a whole hour. Arrived at last, he would enter, light his meerschaum, elevate his feet something higher than his head, when the performance would commence. The Assistant would call the first name on the list. The man would enter, and as we hardly ever take off our caps in camp, perhaps he would forget it now. Immediately the clerk would be ordered to "knock that man's hat off." The hat off, the next thing is, "Well, sir, what's the matter with *you?*" The man would commence to tell, perhaps, get half a dozen words said, when, "That's all, sir; call the next man," would ring in his ears, and after waiting nearly an hour, he would get his regular dose of "Quinine." But I have spent far more times with this brute than I intended. Were I to wish him ill, it would be that he might fall sick and receive the same treatment he bestowed on others.

As the command was ordered to move, those who could not travel were sent to a hospital about one mile distant; and as I was of this number, I had the satisfaction of knowing that I was to take no more quinine. Yet my strength was nearly gone, and the kind old doctor who came and *felt my pulse,* spoke encouraging words, and gave me medicine suited to my wants, told the attendant, as I was afterward informed, that I could hardly live four hours. But his kind care soon told on me, and I was better, and enabled to look around. The room where I was confined was, as near as I can remember, about 12 by 14. There were seven of us to occupy it, no two with the same disease. The beds were built up against the sides of the room, the same as berths in a steamboat, and so near together that between my face and the boards above there was a space of three of four inches. There was no window to the *house,* and the door was a hole in the wall with a blanket hung up before it. I lay here some two weeks. One day a chap was brought in with a wound in the head. The Surgeon found the ball resting on the skull, considerably flattened; but his thick head had saved his life. After remaining for a few days he returned to camp, giving as a reason that he wanted fresh air—in which he showed his good sense. Had the old physician whom I found at this hospital remained, matters would have been different. But he staid only two or three days, his time being up. He was succeeded by a little chap, who was entirely incapable of tending the number of men who were here, and it was hard work for a fellow who couldn't go to the cook room, to get anything to eat. For two weeks all I got to eat I bought, the burnt, half-cooked rice, sloppy coffee, and crackers, being unpalatable. It was a happy day to me when I left the swamps of Virginia. I was conveyed in a steamer to Annapolis, Md. On the way I saw another physician who did not consider a sold[i]er good enough to speak to him. So for two long weary days I received no medicine, or anything that I could eat. There were no ladies aboard the boat. But I was destined to see a better day. The boat was hardly tied when I was taken to a very pleasant room, where everything was clean and neat, the air pure and fragrant with the perfume of a number of large boquets of flowers placed there by the fair hands of ladies. Oh, there is a dearth of WOMAN's care in the army, and I had felt it sadly! But now everything was changed; all that could be done to hold together the brittle thread of life was immediately attended to, and I soon began to mend. Thanks to a kind physician and the ladies!

This is said to be the best conducted hospital in the country, and the average of deaths is much less than at other places, from which we may learn, that as we value the lives of those we love—those who are freely enduring danger, sickness and privation of every kind, all for the good of the country—as we value these, so should our efforts be to secure for them suitable places in which they may recover, when by the bullet or disease, they are for the time being disabled.

There is much more that might be said on this subject: but if the reader's curiosity is awakened, let him "Go and see;"—but not unless he wishes to help.   Vol. 3, pp. 149–50

Camp Whittier, Jefferson Co., Mo.,
Feb. 18, 1862.
. . . Oh! it must be a hundred times sweeter to die for one's country, on the field of battle, than to linger for days at the point of death in a cold, dreary hospital.   Vol. 4, p. 268

Hospital No. 4, Newport News, Va.,
April 15, 1862.
EDITOR TIMES:— . . . The diseases here are of different kinds, such as mud

fever, typhoid and remittant fevers, consumption, diphtheria, &c.—But the most fatal, the most uncalled for and deplorable complaint known here, is *positive starvation!* The majority of invalids who come here, are those who are reduced by constant exposure and low diet, (crackers and coffee,) and need a little stimulus and nutritious food, good nursing, bathing, &c. But, on the contrary, what do they get? They are literally crammed with drugs—morphine, quinine, pills and powders of different kinds; and all are fed on the same rations, viz: dry bread, with untrimmed coffee, 98 per cent. water, the balance *ex't of peas.* At noon, all are allowed a small plate of beef stew and dry bread; or beef tea, 99 per cent. water, and same. No matter how low and feeble, how inflamed the stomach and bowels of the person, he must eat this or go without. . . .

Most respectfully yours,

S. R. KNOWLES
Vol. 3, pp. 177–78

Being wounded was only the beginning of an excruciating and months-long odyssey to find the right treatment for a broken thigh suffered by William Bugh.

27, South Howard Street,

Baltimore, Md., June 17th, 1862.

U. Carruth, Esq.

MY FRIEND: . . . I was wounded on the 5th of May. The 10th of May I was carried to the hospital in this city. On the 13th of May the Physician in charge, after a very superficial examination, pronounced the bone in my hip or thigh fractured, put a splint on my leg, and suspended it in a swing. I remained in this position three weeks, when the Physicians in the hospital changed, and the new Physician, after making some considerable examination of my leg, decided that there was no fracture of the bone. He removed the splint from my leg, and took it out of the swing in which it was suspended, and told me I would be able to be up in a few days. I was very much encouraged, and under these circumstances wrote the letter of the 27th ult. I remained in the hospital until Saturday the 7th inst. and was then removed to my boarding house. I discovered no improvement. My removal was effected by placing me, bed and all, on a stretcher, and being carried by four men. I had been directed by my physician to exercise my leg as much as possible, so as to recover its use and vitality. I followed his advice. I suffered intense pain both day and night, and could find repose only through the influence of morphine. And although my wound was healing kindly, my leg was not improving any. I was yet unable to move it myself, and suffered much pain to have any one move it for me. Finally on Thursday last (the 15th inst.) a friend of mine suggested to me that he would have his family Physician, Dr. Reiley, a very eminent Doctor in the city, call and see me. The Doctor accordingly called Sunday evening. He examined my hip and thigh, and immediately pronounced the thigh bone fractured. He then demonstrated the fact in two or three different ways. The fracture is a little below the hip joint. He informed me that it would be necessary for me to lie flat on my back four or five weeks longer, remaining perfectly quiet, in order to let the bone knit together. I was perfectly overcome with discouragement: and what most overwhelmed me was the unwelcome information that my wounded leg would be an inch or so shorter than the well one.

I had remained there six weeks flat on my back, had suffered the most excruciating pains, and was flattering myself with the hope that I would be up in a few days; and to be thus informed that I was not so nearly well, that I must remain in one position four of five weeks longer, was almost too much for me to bear. I slept none until two o'clock the next morning, and then through the influence of morphine. But I made up my mind that it was God's will that I should suffer longer, and trust that I have gathered fortitude enough to bear it all. Under these circumstances, when I shall be able to visit Wisconsin or join my company I am unable to judge. If I am so crippled as to be unable to do military duty, I suppose I shall have to resign, and forego the ambition of winning, as you say, "more glory in the army."

I shall be exceedingly happy to hear from you or any of my friends. My address now is, 27 South Howard Street, Baltimore, Md.
Yours, Respectfully,
WM. A. BUGH.   *Vol. 3, p. 220*

When mislabeled bottles led to an overdose, the aggressive action of a Milwaukee soldier helped save a life.

Camp No. 2, in the Field, Near Alexandria, Va.,
March 18th, 1862.
ED. TIMES:— . . . I must not close without giving you an account of the sad

incident which befel four of our men at Flint Hill. On Wednesday morning last, when the sick were marched up to the Surgeon's quarters to get their medicine, Dr. Crane administered to four of them what he supposed to be, and what was labeled—Quinine, but which was in reality morphine. He gave them large doses, as they were threatened with some bilious disease, and in a few moments the men fell into a stupor, and the doctors were called to administer to them. The symptoms being so unusual, and all of them alike, the vial was examined, and the mistake was discovered; but not in time to save all of them. They were all in a dying condition. Sergeant Cutts, of Co. E, (and a finer fellow never lived,) survived only three hours. A little brandy was given, followed by a little strong coffee, and directions to keep them awake were given, as the only remedies. One of Co. F's men were said to be dying and I called in to see him. The boys were trying various methods to keep him awake, but no use; he was dead to all appearances save his breathing. He was black in face, his eyes turned up so to show their white. Something must be done at once and your humble correspondent has the consolation of having saved the life of a fellow soldier. I mentioned to a stalwart fellow that stood near me, to take hold of the dying man by one arm, while I took him by the other. The boys wanted to know what we intended to do with him. "Why not let him die in peace?" But I just told them if they would stand back and let us alone, the fellow shouldn't die. They stared at us some, at first, and the more, as we began jerking him around first one way and then the other, tripping him up, cuffing him, pinching him, &c., &c. In short, if he had been a well man it would have been a severe case of assault and battery. Well, we persevered with him for two hours, with no effect only to get him to open his eyes, and immediately close them again. Finally, we made another vigorous effort to arouse him by the same rough treatment, and the young man began to cry! this was a good sign. Vomiting soon followed, also a passage of wind; a little brandy was then administered, and he went to sleep quietly, and in the morning was all right. I went in to the tent about sunrise to see how he got along. I inquired how my patient was. Said he, "He is well. You saved my life last night!" I must confess that my feelings were a little touched, although I have seen something of suffering and blood; and you must not think of me as a faint-hearted soldier, if I tell you that the tears came into my eyes as he stretched out his hand to shake hands with me. You may deem me a little egotistic in giving you these details, but

I thought they might interest your readers. . . .
My love and respects to all.
Yours Truly,
S. R. KNOWLES,
Of Mil. Zouaves.   Vol. 3, pp. 165–66

Death

Oh, war is a great thing, fine victories, and grand battles are glorious to read of, provided that when carefully examining the list of killed and wounded, no loved name appears to start up the spectral form to whom it belongs. . . .
John W. Barlow   Vol. 3, p. 219

Arlington, Va., Jan. 14th, '62.
EDITORS SENTINEL:— . . . Have you ever attended a funeral in camp? Of all the solemn ceremonies ever witnessed, the burial of a brother soldier is the most solemn. As we gaze upon the cold face of the departed hero, and think of the dear friends he has left to serve his country, of the loving wife, perhaps the darling little children, who so willingly gave up their dear friend but a short time since, the tears cannot be hid, and low weeping is heard in the mournful gathering. Poor fellows, they die in a noble cause, but the loss is none the less great. May a just God have mercy on the widows and orphans of our departed braves, and speedily terminate this wicked rebellion. . . .
W. J. A.   Vol. 2, pp. 216–17

Although soldiers witnessed a great deal of sickness and death, the death of a close friend could still be difficult to bear.

Baton Rouge, La.,
May 20, 1862.
FRIEND O. D.:—I now take the earliest opportunity of writing a few lines to you with a heart full of sorrow. I have sad news to tell you. Orrin is no more in this world. He was taken sick at Ship Island with typhoid fever, and

when our regiment was ordered to march we had to leave all our sick on the Island.—He died on the 13th of May. The news came to us last night and I assure you we were almost struck dumb. Orrin and myself have slept and messed together ever since we have been soldiers, and I cannot become reconciled to his death. A few days before he was taken sick we were walking on the beach together picking up shells. He was talking about his children and said he would carry home the shells to them. I will bring them if I live. . . .

Respectfully Yours
N. F. BREED.[1]   Vol. 3, pp. 108–9

                                                        June 10th, 1862.
Dear ———:
    I am melancholy to-day and have been so for several days—ever since Charley died I have felt as though I had not a friend left. Charley was my friend, and a braver or better boy never shouldered a gun or slung a knapsack; always ready to do his duty, kind, and pleasant to all—ever ready for fun when fun was the order of the hour; he had won the respect of his officers and the love of his comrades; As our chaplain said at his grave: "It does seem as though our truest and best boys were taken from us first." Charley's parents, God help them in the hour of their sorest trial! tears come unbidden to my eyes while thinking of the sorrow his death will cause in the far off home of their's. They cannot help but think that this calamity might have been averted if they had only listened to the dictates of their own hearts and kept their darling boy at home. Vain regrets! Charley has gone we trust to a fairer and better land where sickness and sorrow are unknown. . . .
    I sometimes wish that a few thousand of our northern and southern demagogues were obliged to decide this war at the swords point and to the death of every one of them.
E.   Vol. 5, p. 155

One of the more unpleasant duties an officer had to undertake was writing to the families of soldiers who had died.

---

1 Norman F. Breed of Chilton served in Company K, 4th Wisconsin Cavalry, and died of disease August 13, 1862, in New Orleans.

Colonel Halbert E. Paine, who wrote to the wife of a deceased soldier, started practicing law in Milwaukee in 1857. He rose to the rank of major general and lost a leg after being wounded at the Battle of Port Hudson in 1863. He returned to Wisconsin, where he served three terms as a US congressman.   WHi Image ID 43556

Colonel H. E. PAINE, of the Fourth Wisconsin Regiment, writes the following letter to Mrs. LYNN of this village:

NEAR VICKSBURG, JULY 21 [1862].—*Madam*—It becomes my painful duty to inform you that your husband was killed, yesterday, in a contest between the gunboat Arkansas and the Federal gunboats. On the 14th inst., twenty men were sent as sharp-shooters, under his command, up the Yazoo River, on the gunboat Tyler. Early in the morning our boats met the Arkansas, and the fight commenced. At the second fire from the ram, Captain Lynn was instantly killed by a shell which exploded on the Tyler, killing five and wounding six of his men.

I am informed that his conduct in the engagement was marked by the utmost coolness of judgment, combined with daring gallantry. This report did not surprise me, for he had already shown himself second to none in the regiment, in all the qualities which constitute the true soldier. I was so impressed with his worth, that on the day before his death I had written to the Governor of our State, recommending his promotion.

The portraits of his family were found upon his person—a touching proof of the magnitude of their loss. I tender them my heart-felt sympathy in this calamity, which has made their home desolate. The intelligence of his death did not reach me till in the afternoon. We were then under arms, awaiting an apprehended attack, and I could not leave my post, but I immediately sent orders to preserve his body for burial in Wisconsin. This, however, I found to be impossible, and he now sleeps by the side of the brave young men who fell with him, on the bank of the Mississippi, nearly opposite Vicksburg. As soon as the exigencies of the war will permit, his remains will be forwarded to Wisconsin.

Your sincere friend,

HALBERT E. PAINE,

Col. Fourth Wis. Reg.   Vol. 3, pp. 131–32

Fewer than four months after he enlisted in the 21st Wisconsin, William Hume took his own life in Kentucky.

In Camp near Mitchellville, Tenn.

Nov. 12th, 1862.

MRS. HUME.—I cannot express to you how painful it is to communicate to you the intelligence of the death of your husband. He died at Lebanon, Ky., on Sunday evening the 9th inst., under painful circumstances. He had been unwell and in the hospital for nearly a month. While we did not consider him at all dangerous, I discovered that he was very much depressed in mind the last time I saw him, which was on the 28th day of October, the day before we left camp at Lebanon. He was then, and until his death, very comfortably cared for at the principal hotel in Lebanon. I received a letter from him about a week ago, at Bowling Green asking me to assist him in getting a furlough to go home. Col. Hobart and myself made such inquiries as enabled me to give him directions about obtaining the necessary certificates to get the furlough. I expected to hear that he was on his way home to recruit his health, and was very much shocked to learn instead, that he had gone to that home from which there can be no return to the duties, dangers, and hardships of the soldier's life. His long continued ill health, his necessary absence from the Regiment and associates, and the delay in getting a furlough, had engendered a depression of spirits, which in his weakened condition, caused a temporary insanity, under the influence of which, he either fell or threw himself, from a third story window in the hotel, upon the pavement below. He lived about an hour and a half after he was carried in, but was insensible, and suffered no pain, and of course made no communication before his death.

You know how deeply I sympathize with you in this affliction—more than I can tell you. I have passed through afflictions also, and know what you must suffer. He was, and had been for years, my friend—therefore I have a share—although light compared with yours—still, no small share in this affliction.

What shall I say, what can I say, that will soften or lighten this dispensation?—I know that I can say nothing. You know better than I can [tell] you, better than I know, where to look for consolation, where alone consolation can be found—that He who tempers the wind to the shorn lamb, can alone heal the heart so sorely wounded. Look to Him.

I shall always feel a deep interest in the welfare of yourself and children, and it would give me great pleasure to hear from you, and that you and yours are well, and more than all, that you had learned to see in this dispensation the hand of Him that doeth all things well.

Very Respectfully your Friend and Servant,

CHAS. H. WALKER.   Vol. 6, p. 153

A nurse in a hospital in Evansville, Indiana, took the time to write to the wife of Samuel Fish, who was mortally wounded at the Battle of Shiloh, detailing the last hours of his life.

Evansville, Indiana,
Monday even, April 21, 1862.

MRS. FISH: I am an entire stranger to you, and know you only from the lips of your husband. But I know you have a feminine heart, loving and susceptible of grief, and therefore I can feel for you on the subject on which I write. Your husband, Samuel Fish, was wounded in the late battle at Pittsburg, and arrived in this city Friday evening last. He was carried to Hospital No. 3, where he was very kindly cared for, and rested very well during that night. The next morning he seemed quite smart when the physician came around to dress his wound, though they knew it would be a miracle if he survived. He ate some breakfast, and a little dinner, but grew worse toward evening. About three o'clock in the afternoon I visited said Hospital, and found him very low. I asked him if he wanted anything, or if I could do anything for him. His first reply was that his nurse was very kind to him, and did every-thing he could for him. But upon my insisting upon doing something for him, he told me I might bring him a cup of tea. I went directly to the kitchen and got some for him, and he took it and drank a part of it, and pronounced it good. I then asked him if his family knew of him being wounded, and he thought not. I then asked the privilege of writing for him. He wished me to write to you, his wife—to tell you where he was, and was taken just as good care of as he could have been at home, but would like to see you if you could come immediately, for he knew he could not live many days. He felt he must die, and that very soon, and he knew you could get here in time, if I should have telegraphed to you which I wanted to do. He wanted me to write to you to do the best you could with the family without him, for he was going home. He seemed prepared to die, and willing to go. After telling me this, he became so weak that I was alarmed, and sent for the Dr. to come up. He came immediately, and sent all the visitors away, (for there were several around him,) and then did what he could for him. But he said he could not live through the night, he thought. A nurse sat beside him all the time, bathing him, and giving him stimulants, to keep life in him. I [was] with him till late in the evening, hoping he would revive and say something more about his family. But he seemed to sleep all the time, and I left him in the care of his nurse and two men who were to [sit] up with him, with the intention of going down the next morning to see him. I bade the nurses pay strict attention to him, and see if he said anything about his family. Owing to a heavy shower of rain, and the illness of my mother, I did not go till the afternoon, (and then through drenching rain,) and found him still alive, though past speaking. As I went in I met a physician who said he was just going to send for me, for Mr. Fish way dying, and he wanted me

to hear his last words. I went directly to him, and as the crowd gave way for me he looked up as if he knew me, but he could not speak. I sat by him for hours, trying to get him to speak to me, but he could not. I left him at a late hour, and he was dozing. Just at eleven o'clock last night, (Sunday, April 20th,) his sprit severed its prison walls, and flew to its Saviour. He died very easily—just as if he were sleeping—without a mutter, groan or struggle. He is out of this world [of] affliction and sorrow, and now rests in that quiet home, to which we shall all go by-and-by, where all is peace and quiet. No wars there, nor suffering. He is free, but he died nobly in a glorious cause. And though you were not by his bedside to soothe his dying hours, yet kind and loving hearts stood round his sinking form and tears fell thick and fast from the eyes of all who looked upon him. Though he was far from home, there were those who stood round his dying couch, who felt that for them, as well as others, he fought and fell—that felt that for us, our homes and firesides, he left his home and all that was near and dear to him, to defend his country against an internal foe, and to meet them in battle array. I feel that he fought, bled and died for my interest as well as his own: therefore I felt as if he were my own father. He received the very best of attention that could be given to any one, and he seemed very thankful for it. His remains will be interred in Oak Hill Cemetery, to-morrow. His wound, which was received on Sunday, (the first day of the battle,) was a very severe wound by a ball, through the right leg, just above the knee. If you would like to make any more enquiries about him, I shall take pleasure in assisting you all that I possibly can, for I heartily sympathize with you in your affliction.
Miss SUSIE JONES,
Evansville. Ind.   Vol. 5, p. 252

CHAPTER 6

Reflections

WISCONSIN'S SOLDIERS shared freely their thoughts on a variety of topics, from the Southern countryside through which they passed to the people they were trying to subdue. Correspondents often felt compelled to share their observations of the Southern landscape, both physical and intellectual, as if documenting a Gulliverian expedition. The South was often viewed as a foreign country whose inhabitants seemed to speak another language and whose way of life was foreign at best, but probably backward. Devastation and destruction were noted with a mix of remorse and Schadenfreude.

Wisconsin's soldiers often found time to ruminate on the causes behind the hardships they suffered. Although soldiers disagreed about why they fought—most fought to restore the Union, many fought to end slavery—the reasoning behind the fight was necessary to make it through hard times, as difficult conditions, sickness, and even death seemed to be ameliorated by knowing why they fought and affirming the rightness of their cause. However, invective was often aimed at those held responsible for the war, be it the leaders of the rebellion or politicians from the North and the South.

Serving in an army far away from friends and loved ones inevitably carried the soldiers' thoughts toward home, family, and the joys and comforts of life that were given up in order to fight. Days spent at home before the war took on an almost mythical status to the soldier serving on picket duty or enjoying a few minutes of rest between marches. The soldiers knew that war causes changes in the men who fight it, and upon their return to Wisconsin it was clear that a terrible price had been paid by the survivors lucky enough to be mustered out.

On the South

Being in the South was something like being in a foreign country for Ed Living-
ston, who made a study of the Virginia countryside, which he appreciated, and the
people, which he didn't.

On Picket, near Harrisonburg, Va.,
May 6th 1862

MR. EDITOR:—Seated beneath an ancient chestnut which adorns the bank
of the Shenandoah, my musket within reaching distance ready to respond to
the call of my companions, using my haversack for a desk, I will use the four
hours allotted me off duty, in giving you a short narration of our sojourn in
the Old Dominion. I have no scenes of carnage to depict, or conduct of some
favorite officer to eulogize, for we have as yet been in no general engagement
with the enemy, though we have for the greater part of the time since the
battle of Winchester, formed the advance of Bank's Division. But for long
marches through mud and rain, climbing steep mountains, fording deep
streams, and doing arduous and dangerous picket duty, we have proven the
3rd Wisconsin not inferior to any regiment in Bank's Division. After Jackson's defeat at Winchester, he retreated up the Shenandoah river, following
the Winchester and Staunton turnpike, closely pressed by the advance of
our infantry and the Vermont 1st Cavalry, between whom and the celebrated
Ashby Cavalry frequent skirmishes took place, convincing the chivalry that
the Green Mountain Boys had not degenerated since the days of Ethan
Allen. We frequently came in sight of their rear guard, the long roll beaten
throughout our lines, the line of battle formed, field pieces hurried to our
front and those of the enemy to their rear, a few shells exchanged and the
rebels were off in double quick; then a smoke ahead, the clattering of horses
feet, rattling of sabres, and the Vermont boys were off to extinguish the
flames of some bridge which the rebels had fired to retard our advance. Thus
we have followed them for 70 miles, until the Shenandoah valley, the gar-
den of Virginia, is once more under the protection of the stars and stripes,
and Jackson's army, disheartened by defeat, and decimated by desertion, is
driven across the Blue Ridge, to seek safety farther down in Dixie; but the
coils of the Boa Constrictor are tightening around him, and fly where he
may he cannot avoid its deadly volume.

THE PEOPLE AND COUNTRY.

The villages through which we have passed are almost entirely deserted by the white male population; the few that remain look careworn and haggard, and if ignorance is bliss, they live in an enviable state of felicity. I went to one house near Newmarket to exchange flour for bread. 'The lord of the manor,' a man of forty-five or fifty years of age, who owned 400 acres of cultivated land and 84 slaves, asked me what regiment I belonged to. I told him the 3rd Wisconsin. "Wisconsin," echoed he, "*Is that in Massachusetts?*" A six foot Vermonter who was with me told him that it was, that it was only another name for Bunker's Hill, but that he was from Kentucky. So secesh sold him the bread, but would have nothing to do with me. They are very poorly posted in war matters, and differ materially as to its origin, one lady declaring "that Breckenridge received the most votes for President, but the Yankees got Lincoln to Washington first and made him President, and the South wouldn't stand it!"

I did not expect to see such ignorance in Virginia, the birth-place of so many Presidents and statesmen; but I have seen but *one* schoolhouse since leaving Harper's Ferry! The slaves are as well posted in political and war matters as their masters, the only information in vogue being tradition or hearsay, which is alike acceptable to white and black. And these are the people that call us 'mudsills!' They may have had intelligent people here, but if so they have certainly gone to the war.

The Shenandoah or valley of Virginia is productive and well cultivated, most of the farms or plantations are sown in wheat, which is now about knee high, and looks well. This valley extends from Harper's Ferry to Staunton, a distance of 106 miles. It is bounded north by the Shenandoah, and south by the Mapanutten mountains, which run parallel to the Blue Ridge. We are camped at Harrisonburg, 26 miles east from Staunton.

That it is healthy here, it is sufficient to say that we have but eight sick in the hospital.

CURRENCY.

The only money or representation of money (as they have no money,) in circulation is Jeff's promise to pay, or shinplasters. I send you two specimens of the latter, which if you refused to take at par here, your loyalty to the Southern Confederacy would be at once questioned, and, before our advent, summarily dealt with. My four hours have nearly expired, and I must take my post. All from Richland Co. are well.

Yours, &c.,

ED. LIVINGSTON.   Vol. 3, p. 22

A Civil War–era envelope illustration depicting Northern views of the Southern nobility   WHi Image ID 76242

Already in the fall of 1861 Virginia was adversely affected by the presence of armies.

Fort Corcoran, August 19, 1861.

I have been over some portion of Virginia since we crossed the Potomac, and I find it in a deplorable condition. Surely the chariot wheels of war have already made deep marks on the "Old Dominion,"—marks that will require the rain and sunshine of many years to wear away. Our tents are pitched in what has been a beautiful peach orchard—the orchard still remains, but the beauty has long since fled; and the house of the owner, surrounded by ornamental shrubbery of the most beautiful species, is now occupied by the sutler of our regiment. And wherever I have been I have found the country in the same ruined and desolate condition—houses are converted into shops and barracks, and plantations into commons; fences are torn down and crops are going to waste for the want of care—the Unionists have fled to Washington, and the Secessionists to Manassas, leaving a wide extent of country almost depopulated. We passed, on our march to Centreville, many houses, and even villages, entirely deserted, or occupied only by a few of the sable sons and daughters of Africa, which the South generally, and Virginia particularly, delights to see upon her soil so thick, that wooley heads and coal black faces darken all the land. The nearer we approached the rebel lines, the more desolate the country became, having been scoured in every direction by their foraging parties. To the honor of our officers, let me say that all foraging, taking by stealth or by force, was strictly prohibited by our army, but it is impossible for 20,000 or 25,000 men to pass through a country without leaving their footprints, and to a great extent, destroying its beauty. One can have no idea of the appearance of a country in time of war, unless he has been there, and with his own eyes seen the utter desolation that reigns, like the "King of Terrors" over a silent grave yard, wherever a great army has passed! I now, perhaps, have some feint conception of the appearance of the Old World when scourged by the devastating armies of the middle ages.— When reading of the crusades; of the overrunning of Europe by the followers of Mahomet; of the fearful and horrible devastations of the armies of Alaric and Attila; or the brilliant and triumphant, though destructive, successes of the first Napoleon. I never could realize that they were one-tenth part true, but looked upon them as exaggerated war stories. But here I see, in Virginia, the birth place of the "Great Father of his Country," our revered Washington, the same scenes reacted, though on a smaller scale, and I have a foundation upon which imagination can build a superstructure that may, perhaps, equal, but never exceed, the awful reality of those Eastern wars.

In all probability there is not another State in America that will suffer during this contest, as Virginia must and has suffered. I have seen but a small portion of that part where the hand of war has destroyed every green thing, but I have seen more real desolation than in all my life besides, and I have seen much of the world. Virginia must hereafter be styled the Battle Ground of America, as Belgium is of Europe, for here the forces of the

North and South have met, and must meet again and again in battle, until her thousand hills shall run red with human gore. . . .

R. K. BECHEM.   Vol. 1, pp. 134–35

DEAR TRIBUNE:— . . . The Sunny south begins to be with us a term of no idle meaning. It is as warm as June. The days are perfectly lovely; with our tents wide open, pleasant sunshine, chirping of Robins, budding of trees, the green grass peeping from the earth, the whole county in bloom, the whole air vocal with the songs of birds; it needs no consultation of the map or geographical knowledge to divulge the fact that we are gradually penetrating to the warm latitudes. But nevertheless war has devastated this once beautiful prosperous and happy country. But a year, and what scenes have intervened, three different armies, two rebel and one Union, have been encamped here; numerous skirmishes and battles have been fought in the neighborhood; and innumerable skirmishes between pickets and guerilla bands in every direction, and for a great distance around. My heart sickens over the dreary scenes and prospects which meet my view on every side. May God staunch the bleeding wounds of this unhappy country.

Yours Fraternally.

AOTA.   Vol. 4, pp. 276–77

*Movements through the countryside ending up at Falmouth, Virginia, led "C."
to wonder how it was that former countrymen were inflicting such harm on one
another.*

Camp Opposite Fredericksburg, Va.,
May 18th, 1862,

DEAR SIR:—As to-day is the Sabbath, and as beautiful a one, too, as man ever enjoyed, I thought I would, again, employ a few moments in speaking of things in this branch of the army of Uncle Samuel.

Well, we have been marched, since I last wrote you, some thirty miles, to the banks of the Rappahannock, striking it at a small village called Falmouth—a dirty dilapidated, antidiluvian-looking apology of a place for either a nigger or a white man to live in; yet it contains quite a respectable Cotton Factory, and possesses natural advantages, which, if they were possessed by any one of the villages of Marquette, would have made it a city of thousands of inhabitants in one tenth of the time that Falmouth has been struggling to die; as judging from the tombstones in its grave yard, it must have been settled one hundred years ago—some of them bearing date, A. D. 1758. . . .

It is strange what different feelings and promptings govern us in our desires, to shed the blood of our fellow man, and that man our brother. I fully believe that nine out of ten of us would rather run the risk of death on the battle-field than to return without a fight.

I see that Gov. Harvey's body has been recovered, of which we were glad to hear. Our flag, and our officers' arms are draped in mourning for his loss—not as a hollow or empty show, but as a genuine evidence of our grief at his loss, not only to his family and State, but more particularly to us and all of the soldiers from our State. But he is only one of the many good men that have and are yet to die for the good of their country. His loss is but a tithe of that which has been suffered to save our land. Oh, when the history of this war, in all of its consequences, its horrors, its sufferings, and its ago-nies shall have been written, it will leave a record for the future, such as the past, in its bloodiest horrors, has failed to have furnished. . . .

C. Vol. 3, pp. 297–98

The ruins of a house near Chattanooga, Tennessee, damaged during the Chatta-nooga Campaign of October and November 1863, also known as the Battle Above the Clouds WHi Image ID 74487

Harsh Words for Missouri

Several Wisconsin regiments spent time in Missouri during the course of the war, and few had any good things to say about the state.

Camp Burnside, Iron Co., Mo.
November 15th, 1861.

. . . Civilization—if it can be called civilization—exists in this country in its lowest forms. The houses are nearly all built of logs, with shake roofs and puncheon floors. Farming is carried on in the most primitive style. Such things as threshing machines, reapers and fanning mills are unknown. The houses are without stoves, and the women are without crinoline.—Books and newspapers are very rare, and schools and churches are like angels' visits—few and far between. The ignorance of many of the people is equalled only by their credulity. Their leaders have made them believe the most absurd and atrocious falsehood with regard to the Administration, and the people of the North. On the second day we were out, I stopped at a house, to get a drink of milk. The proprietor appeared more respectable and intelligent than the average of the people we had seen. We entered into conversation. He admitted that he sympathised with the South, but had never taken up arms against the Government. He said that until within a short time, he had such an idea of our troops, that had we come along two weeks before, we should have found his house deserted, and himself hiding in the woods. He evidently regarded the war as one of the North against the South; not as one of ambitious rebels against a just and free government. Finally, after talking with him some time, he told us that he could not read, and that all he knew of national affairs he had to learn from others.—Many—probably the majority—are in his condition.

At Greenville they had a story in circulation that Washington had been taken, and that Lincoln and his Cabinet were prisoners. Further on they had another story that Lincoln was down in Arkansas freeing the negroes, and that Gen. Scott was after him with an army to drive him out. In conversation with a prisoner, who has been a Captain in Thompson's army and who is evidently a man of great intelligence, for this country, he told me that he had taken up arms under the belief that the Administration intended forcibly to emancipate all their slaves, and introduce negro equality among them. He said that some time before the late battle at Fredericktown he became convinced that he had been deceived, and that he applied for a discharge and had returned to his home, where he was found when arrested. The ignorance of the masses in the South is one great cause of this rebellion. Slavery has entailed upon them ignorance and poverty—social, intellectual and moral degradation—yet they seem unconscious of the fact. "A fire is kindled around them, yet they know it not; and it burns them, yet they lay it not to heart." It may be this war will open their eyes.

M. Vol. 2, pp. 21–22

Cape Girardeau, Mo. Dec. 1st., 1862.
Friend Ballou.—About two weeks since, all of the 1st Wis. Cavalry remaining here, except a few who were left at the hospital or had been detailed on extra duty, started for the little town of Patterson, where Gen. Davidson has his head quarters. On their arrival there the Regiment was joined to a Brigade, and placed under the command of Col. Heartman, of the 13th Ill. Cavalry. Whether they will go directly south into Arkansas, or first come to this place and proceed down the river, is uncertain, but it is considered certain that they will participate in the grand movement southward which is to be made by the whole western army.

The boys felt no little regret at leaving this city, for in all their military experience in this State, they had fared better here and felt more at home, than in any other place, and the prospect of going back into the "country" again, and repeating their former hardships and trials, was rather unpleasant. There is scarcely any thing agreeable, or even tolerable, to a Northern man, in the region which lies to the west and south west of this city. More than half of it is irreclaimable swamp, and the rest is generally barren and rocky. And what is worse, the inhabitants are no honor or ornament to the country. We came here with high notions respecting Southern refinement, elegance and "chivalry;" but eight months' experience has revealed the sad truth, that nine-tenths of the people are an ignorant, indolent, drunken and cowardly set, whose redeeming qualities are yet to be discovered. The settlers of this section came from all the Southern States, but principally from Kentucky, and Tennessee; they consider a log house a palace, wear "butternut" homespun, and raise for food, corn and a breed of animals, thin, lean and agile as a deer, called by way of courtesy, "hogs." They spend three fourths of their time in sleep or hunting, and own more rifles than Bibles, build more distilleries than mills, have a hundred doggeries to one church or school house, raise more tobacco than wheat, and one and all enjoy a dog fight better than a newspaper or a good speech. Nearly all women and children, as well as men, are greatly addicted to whiskey, tobacco and profanity; my good opinion of southern gentility was greatly dashed when I first heard more oaths rolled from the glib tongue of a woman in five minutes, than I had ever heard before in twice the time, and it entirely vanished when I saw a "right smart" young lady coolly bite a cud from a plug of tobacco, and in a short time begin to "expectorate" as genuine tobacco juice, and as much of it, as any old veteran in the service could produce. It may be a great privilege to enjoy the society of the "high bred, genteel southerners," but I am too obtuse to see it, and shall be content when the war closes to spend my life among the "mud-sills" of the north.

The way in which the Missourians murder the "Kings's English," is enough to condemn them. I might give examples of their peculiar idioms by the page, but will spare the infliction. They also make it a point never to give a direct, positive answer to any question, even respecting things they understand perfectly, but always so qualify, modify or reduce it by "may bes," "perhapses," and "I reckons," that you are but little wiser for asking. For instance, ask how far it is to the next town, and the questioned person will probably tell you he "Should call it a right smart way." "But how far," you repeat; and you get, "Wal, I reckon it mought be two looks and a half, or three looks perhaps." Should you question him half an hour, with all skill and ingenuity of a lawyer, it is doubtful if you could wring from him a reply much more direct or unequivocal. Their whole character partakes of the suspicion and distrust which their conversation indicates. They are sly and treacherous as Indians, and this State has "patronized" the latter so far as to adopt their code of tactics in war. They delight in shooting at Federal soldiers from secure hiding places, and if caught are ready at once to swear by all the oaths the Bible forbids, that they are good Union men and were "pressed into the service." I have not seen a dozen who would own they were "Secesh," but I have seen hundreds of "good loyalists," who would shoot a Federal soldier if his back was turned, and they could escape unhurt. The fact is, there is no chance for any love or admiration for them, and were they not such near neighbors, I consider that any union or connection with them whatever, would be far from an advantage. . . .

EQUES.   Vol. 7, p. 170

Old Abe, the Wisconsin War Eagle, in 1861   WHi Image ID 78929

Southerners

A Southern lady commented on Old Abe, the eagle carried throughout the war by the 8th Wisconsin.

OXFORD, Miss., Dec. 12, 1862.
Editors Gazette: . . . As we marched through the streets of Oxford, yesterday, a young lady, who was standing on the sidewalk, asked us what kind of bird that was we carried. We told her an eagle. She replied, "You can't fool me; that's a Yankee buzzard you carry." . . .
W. B. BRITTON,
Eight Wisconsin Volunteers.   Vol. 4, p. 139

An errand of mercy grew complicated for a soldier attempting to deliver a mes-sage from a dying Confederate officer to the officer's brother in Mississippi. Several days' captivity, however, allowed him to gauge the thoughts of his adversaries on a variety of topics.

Corinth, Miss., Oct. 25.
Wednesday, Oct. 8th, four days after the battle of Corinth, and while our army was yet in pursuit of Price, found me, a "solitary horseman," on my way to armed rebeldom. I left Corinth for the purposes of conveying a message to the confederate outposts, from a dying confederate colonel to his brother, a surgeon, residing about one hundred miles south. I reached Rienzi, a dis-tance of fifteen miles, after dark, and was escorted to headquarters by a Union guard, who had picked me up two miles out of town as a "suspicious individual." The colonel commanding being satisfied with my "credentials," directed me to report to Gen. ——, then in town, and dismissed me. Gen. —— received me kindly, flattered my vanity by saying "but few men could be found bold enough to attempt the journey under existing circumstances," and suggested a postponement until our army returned and the country was more quiet. I demurred, and was ordered to report myself to him next morning.

In searching for lodgings I was again arrested by a Union soldier, marched a distance of two miles, reporting to different officers, and finally brought before Col. R——, who had previously, first disposed of me. He kindly sent an aid with me to a planter's in the neighborhood, where myself and tired horse found food and rest.

Morning found me at Gen. ——'s, who informed me "that for a humane object, I would be allowed to pass his lines, but I must leave all military papers behind, except the telegraph message, and depend upon my personal address for my safety." Judging from my experience the night before with the Union pickets, the prospect was not flattering.

I was passed out of the lines by an aid, about 9 o'clock A. M. I found but few improvements on the road to Boonville, and fewer inhabitants. Boonville was deserted; every store and public building was vacant, and only two families remaining. Seven miles south of this place I found the confederate outpost—cavalry pickets—to whom I made known my errand, at the same time presenting the telegram and asking to be allowed the privilege of returning to Corinth. My honest face, personal address, and persuasive eloquence was of no avail. A "live Yankee" was caught, and he might prove one of Lincoln's emissaries or a scout of Rosencrans. The lieutenant commanding forwarded the dispatch, with a note, to the Colonel, and I was informed that it would be necessary for me to remain with him until the Colonel's pleasure concerning me was known. While waiting, I had my horse fed, and listened to the remarks and conversation of my captors. Their ideas of the war, its present and future, the compromise and final end of the difficulties, were both amusing and instructive; but of this anon.

At sundown a courier came with orders to fall back, and soon we were all in saddle, "skedaddling" through highways and byways, through swamps and fields, wading streams and climbing hills, until we reached another deserted village, Baldwin, where I was placed under a new guard, assigned a "bed" in the church, (made by placing two high-backed benches together and my blanket for a covering) given a dry biscuit for my supper, and soon after was asleep, with an armed guard around me.

The next morning, after a repast of dry biscuit and pork, broiled on a stick, we were in our saddles and again moving southwardly. About four miles traveling brought us to a plantation, where feed for the horses was obtained for the whole command, a halt was ordered and the corn appreciated.

From here we passed through Guntown, another nearly deserted village, and near night reached a plantation between Guntown and Saltillo, where I was presented to the Colonel commanding, my guards dismissed, and permission given me to occupy his room until further orders. Up to this time I had been surrounded with cavalry privates, a class supposed to be as reckless and daring as any in the Southern army. For the next three days I associated with the Colonel, his Adjutant, Captains, and Surgeons—men well educated, and who ought to understand the true issues of the war. The men echo the baser expressions of the officers, without qualification, or attempted reasonings, having all the prejudices against the north that editors and officers have sought to inculcate, and never questioning the truth of the reports they are told against the Yankees, and very stubborn to believe any good of them. The officers charge the abolitionists of New England with the war, (a la *"Times, News & Co.,* state that if Lincoln had not called upon the States for men, the south would have whipped South Carolina back into the Union &c., &c.;) that every man of the south will die before they submit to any compromise that will bring them back into the Union as *it was.* They freely admit that the North is too strong for them, and that in the end they must be defeated unless the *Democracy* of the north can succeed in controlling civil affairs, thereby stopping supplies of men and means to carry on the war, obtain an armistice, and eventually a favorable compromise—and that compromise a dissolution of the Union—or a reconstruction favorable to their peculiar institutions. They insist, and endeavored to make me acknowledge as a fact, that "the policy of Lincoln's Administration is to subjugate and then confiscate their property, to pay the expense of the war, personal first, and then real estate, the latter to be held as government property, not to be sold, but to be *leased out* to the present occupants, if they desire it; if not, then to any who will pay the annuity. Tax gathers will be placed in every township and collections forced at the point of the bayonet." These and other similar statements were made as to Lincoln's policy, and then the question was asked whether I thought the chivalrous sons of the south would submit, short of extermination. Other statements were to the effect that "the northern army *desired,* and if they could, would *enslave* every white male inhabitant [of the] south, prostitute their females and lay their country waste." They charge upon the army the violation of women, and mention numerous cases which *they have heard from reliable* sources, but have not witnessed. Also the forcing of slaves to leave their masters, and as an evidence of this, state that our army under Gen. Ord, near Iuka last month, hung three slave men, and whipped a slave woman upon the naked back until she fainted, for refusing to accompany our troops back to Corinth. They also charge us of bayoneting their wounded and shamefully abusing our prisoners.

Their admiration of Gen. Buell was unbounded, and he received more praise from them than any General in their own army. I supposed the rumors in the Northern papers to the same effect were the offspring of the

Tribune's imagination, but it is true "*Buell is their ideal of what a Northern commander ought to be.*" Their hatred of Butler and Mitchell is as intense as human passion can make it. They laugh at McClellan and Halleck, but are afraid of Rosencrans. The North-West, under Grant, have whipped them into a respect for our Western army, and the *surgeon* went so far as to say that "the Southern army would be willing to, at once, throw down their arms and leave their future interest to the magnanimity of the people of the North-West, provided: First, that New England should not be allowed to join in the *new* union of States.["] A majority of this regiment were very anxious to have the war close, and both officers and men, in private conversation, admitted themselves deceived as to the real feeling of the North towards the South, and charged our troubles equally to the political Southern "fire-eaters" and Northern "Abolitionists." I had expected, after getting south of where our army had yet marched, to find some evidences of a prosperous farming community, protected by their armies. In the whole distance traveled by me (fifty miles) and for twenty five miles farther south, as I learned from them, their own army has stripped the fields of their crops, have appropriated the cattle and hogs for subsistence, and the mules and horses for their cavalry. The few inhabitants remaining are almost destitute of the commonest necessaries of life. Many who have never known want are anxiously devising plans to protect themselves and families from starvation. The women of the South are worthy of praise for their sacrifices and devotion—not to their unholy cause—but to their fathers, husbands and brothers. Delicate and unused to labor, they work as best they can in the field and on the home loom. Among the many mothers, wives and sisters of the confederate soldiers I met (with but one exception) there was a sincere, agonizing prayer for an end to this unholy war. It must be near the truth to say that not a Southern home remains but what has lost its inmate. In the South-West there is a universal feeling of unsafety. Disheartened and with gloomy forebodings they are deserting home, property—all, and seeking a place of refuge with little hope of finding it. The people of the North may think these hard times, but their trials can give them no conception of the misery experienced at the South. It is like one man *lashing* another, it is hard work to give the blows, but harder to *receive* them. The blockade is severely felt by them. The scarcity of many articles has caused them to reach almost fabulous prices. A planter told me he had offered one hundred dollars for a barrel of salt, but was refused. Boots are worth from twenty to thirty dollars. Brogan shoes ten dollars. Common "Kossuth" hats five to twelve dollars. Overcoats and blankets, none to be had, and the dread of winter, without them, is great.

After four days' detention, I was allowed to return to Corinth with, I must acknowledge, some change in my opinion of the Southern view of the war.

Lincoln's emancipation proclamation is made an instrument to obtain recruits from the border States, and I think it has and is giving them many; but it has also, with the recent vigor of the Western army in Mississippi and Kentucky, convinced them that they are to expect earnest work, and that every available means will be used to bring the war to a successful termination. They are waiting anxiously to hear from the Northern elections [if] the *peace democracy* can show any substantial gain in Congress, it will help them more than the winning of "many battles," for then there is encouragement for them to hold out a little longer. If the result is otherwise, they *have no hope but in a reconciliation.* They have not the means to carry on the war many months longer.

Every vote cast for a *peace* candidate is worth more to them than two armed recruits. The man who now will, for political advancement, cast his vote for men or measures advocating anything less than the most stringent support of the administration in crushing the rebellion, is in my opinion, a *traitor* to his country, doing more to encourage the enemy and whiten Southern battle fields with the bones of Union soldiers, than an armed rebel.
W. G. M.   Vol. 4, pp. 129–30

Experience rooting out poorly equipped Southern marauders led "Private" to question the fitness of Southern soldiers, while giving credit to Southern women for their courage.

Camp Murphy, Victoria, Mo.,
January, 1862.

Editors Journal:—

. . . A few days since seven deserters from Jeff. Thompson's army, whose families live near here, came home. As soon as their return was made known, a scouting party was sent out, and they were arrested and brought into camp.—After detaining them two days they were released, in accordance with orders, and the usual mode of treating such persons. . . .

The farther South I go, the more I see of what I only heard before—the stronger is my conviction that events will soon transpire that will require a more rigorous policy on the part of our government. The men that were released were poorly equipped with old rifles and shot guns, and horses, poor, jaded and worthless.—They were a pitiful sight. They returned poor and ragged, having received no pay, and wore back the clothes, or rather rags, they wore away. With a reckless indifference, and with the stain of treason upon them, these ignorant men came forward and renewed their allegiance, or took the oath—to the government they had betrayed, and that too without knowing any good and valid reason for so doing. When called upon to sign their names, but three of the seven could write down their names.

Is this a fair specimen of a large portion of the men that compose the Southern army! If so, how unenviable will be the task of the future historian, who shall write the sad commentary on this rebellion, which is seeking to destroy "the edifice of constitutional American liberty." We have a good deal of guard duty, as from twenty to thirty men are on guard every day. The pickets at the bridge are occasionally fired upon, but none as yet have been shot. Scouting parties are sent out every few days to look after noted secessionists, who are returning home from Jeff. Thompson's army.

That there is danger leaving camp to go any great distance, is true. One Union man near here, says he has not left his home for three months, for fear of being assaulted by the Secesh. Still there is something so exciting and interesting about such expeditions, that one leaves all thoughts of fear and danger behind. Ten picked men, which is the usual number that compose our scouting parties, feel equal to any 100 apologies for men the enemy can muster, and if some of our Wisconsin friends were with us to see the *effect* they would have the same feeling of confidence, for it is contagious. I have been twenty-five or thirty miles from camp with such an expedition. When we surround and search 'secesh' houses the men cower, grow pale, and accede with alacrity to every demand. It is *real sport* to see them move at the beck of our bayonets glittering in the candle light, for you must know that these are nightly visits, as we prefer darkness rather than light for such work.

To some of the *women* I will give more credit. I have seen them sitting in bed (our duty compels us sometimes to disregard ceremony in searching the different apartments of a house) with perfect nonchalance, bid defiance to all intruders—but they soon follow the example of their husbands and the rest of the "men folks." . . .

Yours very truly,

PRIVATE.   Vol. 4, p. 37

Recruits wanted for the Brave Southern Army—Good pay, (in Confederate Bonds) and good quarters, (in a horn.)

An envelope illustration of the quality of Southern recruits   WHi Image ID 75990

On the War

After fighting difficult battles in the fall of 1862 at Second Bull Run, South Mountain, and Antietam, "Lance" reflected on changes to the men and their reputation.

Head Quarters 6th Wis. Vols.
Gibbon's Brigade, near Sharpsburgh,
October 14, 1862.

Editor Courier:— . . . We that are left of company C, Prairie du Chien Volunteers, have yet a lively remembrance of our good friends at the Prairie and Crawford county; and at times when seated around the camp fire, the conversation will turn to the earlier days of the company, when we used to assemble at the old Fort, raw recruits, to learn our first lesson in that which now cannot be equaled by the regulars.—Then the bible presentation. The American flag and its maker, and the fair young lady who presented it—all these are mentioned, and all seem to wish to do honor to our oft remembered friends. . . .

You have probably seen, before this, the complimentary notice given us by "Little Mac," I will give it though. In a letter to the Governor, he wrote:

"I beg to add to this endorsement the expression of my great admiration of the conduct of three Wisconsin regiments in Gen. Gibbon's Brigade. I have seen them under fire acting in a manner that reflects the greatest possible credit upon themselves and their State. They are equal to the best troops in any army of the world."

The above, coming from one whom we all esteem and admire, made us feel proud, and it let us know we had done our duty to his satisfaction.
LANCE.   Vol. 3, pp. 266–67

Seeing the destruction in Arkansas elicited no mercy from "L. K. H."

Pine Bluff, Arkansas,
June 21, 1864.

Editors Sentinel:— . . . This country is fast becoming depopulated from various causes, all growing out of the war. All who are at all fit for service, from 15 to 50 and 55, are forced into the rebel army, being hunted from their homes and hiding places in the woods by a swarm of rebel conscriptionists with horses, guns and bloodhounds, or are compelled to leave the country, and their property taken and their farms laid waste; while those who are not able to serve are made to pay a fearful tribute in stock provisions, &c. Those who escape either turn to bushwhacking and robbing indiscriminately friend and foe, or are themselves plundered of everything, and finally escape to our lines with little else than their worthless lives remaining.

Little or no crops are being raised in the country, and the balance of last year's crop is fast disappearing. Every boat leaving for the north is literally crowded with men escaping the coming desolation, carrying with them their families, hoping to find shelter and protection from the very people they have lately taken great delight in literally hating.

Truly have they learned that the way of the transgressor is hard—but there are thousands yet in arms in whom the rebellious spirit can be cured only by death and on whom all proclamations and amnesty oaths are only wasted, and may God, or Grant, hasten the day when we shall be so reinforced as to move forward to their utter destruction. . . .

L. K. H.   Vol. 10, pp. 340–41

A new year and new additions to the list of men who had died led a soldier serving in Missouri to reflect on the loss of men to sickness and the meaning behind the sacrifice.

                                    Camp Curtis, Sulphur Springs, Mo., Jan. 6th.
Messrs. Editors:— . . . During the year that is gone, all over our land, thousands of graves have been opened and closed over the remains of those who a few short months ago left their homes amid the tears and benedictions of parents and wives, brothers and sisters, upon whose faces they shall look no more. It was not their privilege to fall upon the field of glory, and early they have gone down to unknown graves. No historian will record their names and no marble monuments will preserve their memories. Others perhaps, who have suffered and sacrificed far less for their country will reap the renown and share the rewards of success. Tears will be shed in distant places and hearts will be sad that are far away; but the great tragedy of life will go on and they will be forgotten. However it may be with others, I can hardly avoid a feeling of veneration for the memory of the private soldiers who are daily dying in our military hospitals. Many of them were moved to enlist by as pure motives as ever led men to take up arms in any cause; and as I stand by their graves while their comrades pay them the last honors of war I am often reminded of Grays familiar lines—

"Full many a gem of purest ray serene
The dark, unfathomed caves of ocean bear,
Full many a flower is born to blush unseen,
And waste its sweetness on the desert air."

Eighteen hundred and sixty-one has closed upon a drama enacting on this continent unparalleled in human history, and which in its results must effect the destiny of the race for all time to come.—One year ago, the clouds of civil war began to loom up above Charleston harbor and it has continued to spread until it darkens the land. Under its baleful shadow, a million men have rushed to arms, on the one side to overthrow and on the other, to defend a Government, which notwithstanding all the defects that have been visible in its administration—has conferred more benefits and inflicted fewer injuries than any other the world has yet known. To support this government in this its hour of peril, six hundred thousand men have left the peaceful pursuits of civil life—the comforts and endearments of home—for the perils and privations of the camp and the battle field—for wearisome marches, midnight watchings, hunger and cold, disease and wounds, and death. None of these are the unwilling conscripts of a hated despotism—but of their own accord they have come to "do or die" in defence of the government founded by Washington, and sanctified by the sufferings which won Freedom in "the times that tried men's souls." Dark as are the days, and evil as the times upon which we have fallen, there is something in this great fact which must be cheering to every patriotic spirit. Ten righteous men, could they have been found, would have saved Sodom in the days of its greatest guilt—surely amid all this mighty host of patriotic soldiers there are enough to save our country from the ruin threatened by perjured demagogues and their phrensied followers.

M.   Vol. 4, pp. 35–36

> Head Quarters First Division, Army
> of the Mississippi. Camp "Big Springs,"
> July 14th 1862.

FRIEND MILLS:— . . . Still scarce a day passes in which we do not hear the solemn strains of the "death march" telling us that another has been added to the many thousands who have already fallen martyrs to the sacred cause of constitutional liberty; then soon we hear the boom of musketry of some distant company or squad firing over the grave of a loved and departed comrade.—Alas! how many hearts have been made desolate in consequence of this wicked rebellion. How many are to-day mourning the loss of sons and brothers slain in defence of their country's honor, and whose bones lie buried unmarked, in the forests and on the battlefield of a distant land. It may appear hard to some to die thus away from home, in a strange country, with no kindred hand to alleviate his dying agonies; no kind and familiar voice to whisper sweet words of comfort and consolation during the last moments of his existence. But O! none can imagine the inexpressible pleasure experienced in the dying hour of those who yield up their lives for their country's good. I have witnessed several instances of this kind since I have been connected with the army. While visiting the general hospital the day following the battle at Farmington, I saw a young man a sergeant, apparently about 21 years of age who was mortally wounded by a piece of shell which had cut away his right hip. He was in most awful agony, yet he bore it all without a murmur. As I seated myself at his bed-side, he grasped my hand, and turning his mild blue eyes upon me with an expression I never shall forget, asked me to "grant a favor to a dying soldier." He handed me a pencil and a piece of paper, and gave me the address of his father, and some directions respecting the disposition of his money and little effects, and told me to tell his father that he *died at his post*. When I assured him that his request should be granted, he smiled and said, "O how sweet to die for one's country, protect it from traitors in arms, and treason at home." The effect seemed to exhaust him, and he fell back on his pillow and died, poor fellow!

What a fearful responsibility rests upon the leaders of this rebellion. The blood of the brave and noble, which flowed so freely at Donelson, on the field at Shiloah and on the contested ground before Richmond, cries aloud for *vengence*. Let it be meted out to traitors at home and abroad.

Vol. 4, pp. 103–4

Longing for Peace

Enthusiasm for the war had faded markedly by the fall of 1862 as casualties mounted and military gains evaporated.

Gallipolis Ohio, Oct. 28, 1862.

. . . The people are becoming sick of this long and tedious strife. Too many homes are already made desolate; too many hearts are now writhing in

Sergeant Jefferson Coates of Company H, 7th Wisconsin Infantry. Coates was a native of Boscobel, Wisconsin. He was wounded at the Battle of South Mountain and later lost both eyes at Gettysburg, after which he was awarded the Medal of Honor for his bravery.   WHi Image ID 3898

anguish[;] too many widows and orphans are found in our land; there are too many childless mothers and too much suffering to be tolerated much longer by our people, unless something more is accomplished by our armies. The soldier too is becoming discouraged. He is obliged to abandon grounds gained by hard marches, and in many instances by bloody and sharply contested battles, obliged to destroy large quantities of Government stores and ordinance, which cost him many hours labor to transport, and obliged to march for miles without tents, blankets, and upon short rations, with poor and scanty clothing and less pay. Is it then to be wondered at that he should wish for the day to arrive when he can once more say "I am a free man and my country is at peace with all the world!" ...

D. W.   Vol. 7, p. 250

PITTSBURGH LANDING, May 11, 1862.— ... In strolling over the battle fields of the 6th and 7th of April, yesterday, I came upon the camping ground of the Wisconsin 16th. at the time of the attack. Near by are the two graves of Capt. E. Saxe, Co. A, 16th Regt., and J. H. Williams, 2nd Serg't of same company. Williams, I believe, was formerly editor of the Green Lake Spectator. I travelled at least sixteen miles upon the battle field in different directions, and at every step the forest trees and the earth bore evidence of the terrible nature of the conflict. In some places, the dense under-brush was swept off clean, about three feet from the ground, for half an acre, by the grape and canister.

Large trees were cut down by cannon balls, limbs chopped off, which in falling, proved fatal in many instances. The different positions of the different batteries are indicated by the dead horses lying around, only partially covered or burned up. The graves of the dead lie every where. Here a single one without the frailest indication of name or mark; there a long row, with board records in ink or paint, or rudely carved thereon with friendly jack knife. In wandering through the bushes we now and then stumble upon large portions of the human body unburied, and now and then upon a grave from which the feet of the dead protruded.

War is really not a pleasant occupation, however agreeable and attractive soldiering may be. Did the instigators of wars have to bear its actual pains and penalties, there would be an universal peace. Could the two armies now in the field—Confederate and Union—have the settlement of the pending difficulties, we should have peace in ten days. . . .

H.   Vol. 5, pp. 261–62

On the Battle-field
Prairie Grove, Ark. Dec. 10th 1862.

DEAR PARENTS:— . . . What a terrible thing is war. When I look over this fine country, once the abode of peace, and see the havoc made by the armies—fences and buildings burned, every corn crib emptied, families in need of bread, and more especially when I looked over to yonder trenches

The discharge papers of Sergeant George W. Noble of the 3rd Wisconsin Cavalry WHi Image ID 71573

and think of the fathers, husbands and brothers lying there, and of the many, many bleeding hearts broken by their fall, I cry out—"How long, O Lord, how long." When will peace, a peace satisfactory to us, overshadow our country. . . .

SIDNEY H. NICHOLS.

Vol. 6, pp. 127–28

On the Weather

Soldiers often found misery or solace in the changing state of the weather. A pleasant spring morning in Missouri led "Crackers" to utter lofty thoughts and poetry.

Point Pleasant, Mo.,
March 19th 1862.

DEAR PRESS:—

Imagine yourself seated at the foot of some noble oak, that has withstood the storms of years; that while others have fallen it still stands, a monument of strength, and like some lordly knight towering above its more diminutive companions. The distant booming of cannon "sounding from afar"—the twitter of merry forest songsters, which the return of spring has brought to us, once more,—while everything seems to put forth renewed energy—and with this, picture to yourself the scene of a thousand men—some lounging on the ground, basking in the warm southern sun, dreaming of friends and times "that were." Some singing snatches of old familiar songs as they bake their corn-dodgers; while a few, who, as they partake of the good things of this world, are spending their leisure time in obtaining that knowledge, from the volume of inspiration which will enable them to make their calling and elevation sure,—and you will have a very good idea of my position and circumstances while I write. While sitting here this pleasant morning is it strange that our thoughts should go back and rehearse the many scenes that have been enacted in the drama of our short lives.

"Our busy thoughts—can they be chained,
What bars or bands can hold them fast?
They are ever passing—nor restrained;
Reach to the future, scan the past,
Swifter than the rays of morning light
Are flitting through earth'[s] climes afar,
Or rise to friends in realms so bright,
So far above the distant star,
Or dart through space on rapid wing
To soar among their twinkling orbs,
That shine in glory to their king
Who ever all is Lord of Lords."

We ask is it strange that we could wish to exchange the bustle and tur-moil of camp for the quiet life at home? Exchange these "days of strife and nights of working" for those days when we could go forth in the morn-ing and preform the days labor in peace and safety—and their nights for improvement and quietude? Now, don't think we are suffering under any Hypochondriacism, or that our patriotism is on the wane—No indeed we would rather spend a lifetime here lending our strength to crush rebellion, than to see it triumph. . . .

This morning the word is ["]Onward to Memphis."

Will write when I get there.

Receive this while I remain yours &c,

CRACKERS.

Vol. 4, pp. 58-59

Fine weather in Kentucky inspired a soldier to appreciate the natural beauty of the South and then pontificate at length on the Southern mind and the cause of the rebellion.

Camp Wood, at Munfordville, Ky.,
Thursday, Dec. 12.

Our advance is now encamped on the Green River hills looking over into Dixie. . . .

Nothing could be more inspiring than the sight I was looking upon. Nature never gave birth to a more beautiful scene than this. We have escaped from the swamps and dark, overshadowing forests of Nolin Creek to these beautiful and romantic hills, and a general joy pervades the army. The men look brighter and step brisker; the officers salute each other in gay humor; the drill, which day before yesterday was a laborious drag, is executed with new-born alacrity this morning; patients whom the murderous delay among the miasmas of Nolin had sent to the hospital, and almost to the grave, are out this morning standing on the knolls, looking at the canvas cities which crown the swelling fields and deck their sloping sides, drinking in fresh life from the bright unclouded sun and pleasant breeze.

September has returned upon us, or rather, in a march of twenty miles, we seem to have transported ourselves from the pole to the tropics. A few days ago we were wallowing in snow and mud—we waded through fog by day and slept in the mire at night—the hospitals were crowded with sick, and every day's clouded and uncertain close beheld a fearful addition to the new-made heaps, beneath which many a victim of mismanagement lies dead; our horses, chilled by December rains, and pelted by sleet and snow, were almost unfit for service, and more than one regiment, wasted by disease, and demoralized by unavoidable relaxation of discipline, was in a ruinous condition. But this morning we are new beings, in a new world. This advance, simply in its effect upon the army, is a most wholesome measure. It was a great mistake that we were not allowed to come here a month ago. . . .

Kentucky is in a perfect ferment over the President's message and CAMERON's report. Let the work go on; good will come of it. The public intellect of Kentucky is just beginning timidly to ask itself what is the cause of the rebellion. This is a most decided advance from the status of last Summer and Fall. Then our Unionists utterly blinked the Slavery question by making the extraordinary assertion that there was no manner or description of cause whatever for the rebellion. So completely did this extraordinary idea possess them, that it would be impossible to instance an article or a speech of that period of which it did [not] form the substratum. Absurd as the position may appear, it was nevertheless perfectly logical; for the narrow premises within which the moral and political condition of Kentucky compelled her to compress the crisis would permit her to draw no other conclusion. And as the rebellion was supposed to spring from no far-reaching, wide-sweeping and all-powerful cause, it was very naturally set down as a bubble which would soon burst as spontaneously as it was generated; a delusion, which, like all the creations of enchantment, would vanish at a touch. But honest, brave Kentucky, has now sufficiently progressed towards that full consciousness of the condition of our age and nation, which we shall all reach by and by—to begin to inquire earnestly for the cause of this swelling tide of woes. The Northern mind has already undergone a similar process, and asked the same question. That all reflecting minds in the North and in the loyal Border should reach the same conclusion on this momentous inquiry—the most momentous that has engaged man's attention from creation's dawn till now—is not to be expected. In fact they have reached the most opposite conclusions, and both conclusions contain much truth and much error. The ages are measurably self-conscious, yet they possess no oneness of self-consciousness. In no one opinion or set of opinions is there embodied a perfect knowledge of the age; but when school is compared with school, and creed with creed, it is discovered that the ages are not without a knowledge of themselves. Not from one speculum, but from a thousand reflecting surfaces and in fragments, are the giant images projected on the curtain of all time. To one who comprehends somewhat of the sublime, far-reaching laws which govern the rise and fall of empires and civilizations, the present hour and this divergence of opinion which is now revealed between Kentucky and Northern thought, possess a deep and melancholy interest. The North believe that Slavery is the cause of the war, and they are about to act on that truthful, yet not all-truthful, opinion. If Slavery is not the cause of the war, there remains apparently but one other opinion—that man is incapable of self-government, and that republics are necessarily destroyed by the degree of freedom they accord their citizens. This opinion, I am sad to say, the public mind of Kentucky, under the stimulus of the late news from Washington, seems about to adopt. The leading intellects of the State assert that if Congress attempts to free the slaves, the Union is forever lost; and I believe they are right. Yet I know that if Slavery were removed, the Union would to-morrow coalesce into a grander and more glorious nation than ever before, and that while Slavery lasts the Union can never be restored. I have longed for emancipation, but it is emancipation by the States themselves. If Congress attempts the task, not only will the Union never be reconstructed, but necessities will have been inaugurated which will at length destroy both our liberties and our civilization. Our only hope—at least, my only hope—was that an enlightened spirit would display itself in the loyal border, and that they would prove themselves equal to the great mission which they may now accomplish. Perhaps this may yet be, and under the spur of the necessity which the hour presents, great minds and hearts along the border may rush rapidly to the work. Unless this shall be, I repeat that our civilization will perish beneath despotism, civil strife and freed barbarians, as the civilization of the ancients did. I will not enter into the subject; for this generation is not yet ready to hear the truth. But let any man consider the ancient civilization and the parallel course of the modern; let him trace the history of literature, philosophy, religion and government in the two great developments; let him contrast the universal republic in which the ancient civilization culminated, with the universal republic which civil strife is now rending asunder, and he will have food for melancholy reflection. The opinion into which Kentucky seems drifting, an opinion which her leading journals and statesmen have already openly proclaimed, possesses a deep and fearful significance; yet that opinion is not only false, but a crime against mankind. It may be that in every civilization, man after having emancipated himself from superstition and tyranny, and thus produced the era of freedom, proceeds in the same course till he has destroyed every conservative force, and thus rendered a dissolution of society sooner or later inevitable. It was this spirit of license, this wanton, reckless ambition, that destroyed the Roman Republic, and even the age of MARIUS and SYLLA, of CÆSAR and POMPEY, of OCTAVIUS and MARC ANTONY, never witnessed an act of more wanton wickedness than the present rebellion. Only we have more room for hope than CATO or BRUTUS had; for while no question of sublime morality relieved the darkness of Rome's hour of death, our higher civilization produces such a one. And if we are to sink beneath exhaustion and military despotism, our fall will not prove man incapable of self-government more than did Rome's. It will only prove that in our civilization, he had not yet become wise and pure enough for continued and undying self-government. There has been more freedom, a higher, purer and better freedom, in our civilization than in the ancient, and hereafter there will be yet more and better freedom. Then, why should we repine? All things are in the hands of that All-disposing Power who has marked out for our age and nation, and for all ages and nations of men, their destiny.   Vol. 4, p. 167

Snowfall in Tennessee reminded "Grape" of home in Wisconsin. Yet the war needed to be won, and Grape believed the Emancipation Proclamation was a necessary weapon in that war.

Humboldt, Tenn., Dec. 9, 1862.

DEAR SENTINEL:—The "glorious summer," which has so long smiled upon us, and which our Generals (except in the Western Department) have improved by also "*smiling*" occasionally, if not oftener, ("only this, and nothing more,") has closed his benignant reign, and "the winter of our discontent" has commenced its "rain" in earnest. On the 5th inst. we had a fall of snow which would be called *respectable* in Wisconsin, and which beat the memory of the "oldest inhabitant" here. It fell to the depth of *five inches*, and the earth is still mantled in its glistening robe of white. The trees, which, a few days since, bloomed in summer verdure, to-day present a spectral and dreary appearance—their naked arms and each tiny finger gleaming in a chrystal coating like so many weird spirits of the Northland, transplanted by a supernatural hand to "the region of vine and of song,"—the "Sunny South,"—to mind us Northmen of our own ice-bound home, throned in chrystaline beauty and magnificence, by the "great water." One's thoughts instinctively wing themselves to the scenes of home, and nestle with the "loved ones," wearily "watching and waiting" there. Reminiscences of the "gay and festive" occasions of hilarity and pleasure enjoyed with them in "by-gone houre," during the merry season of the "Ice-King's" reign, throng one's brain; visions of parties, where "youth and pleasure met;" merry sleigh rides, and the "tintinabulations of the bells;" "raids" on Wauwatosa; "fair women and brave men" gliding in sylphid beauty and graceful evolution over "the pond's" mirrored surface, and the many bright scenes painted on the memory's canvas rise before the soldier in his lonely tent, "way down in Tennessee." He involuntarily sighs for a return of the halcyon days of peace, and to be wafted to the sounds and scenes of "home, sweet home." But war's stern and bloody path is before him. He knows not what hardships, dangers and carnage lie before him. His life is in the hands of the "God of Battles," and he can only *hope* that he may be spared for a happy re-union, to resume his seat by the sacred hearthstone.

Winter, here, is very properly termed the "rainy season." In a few days it will be dreary and desolate enough with us. We shall have incessant rains, cold, damp nights, very disagreeable for camping, and impassable roads. Just as we are entering upon this season our army is ready to "do something." There is no fault to be found, however, with the army of the West, for Gen. Grant's force was so decimated by the campaign and the battles through which it had passed, and reduced by the numbers drawn from it to reinforce Buell and guard the hen-roosts and potatoe patches in his department, that he *could not with safety* make any aggressive movements, until strengthened by the new levy of troops assigned to him. . . .

The President's message is *well received* in the army. Soldiers are universally pleased to see that the President has not been swerved from the course he had previously marked out, by the pressure brought to bear upon him, by tender conscienced politicians and rebel sympathizers. The army stand by the Proclamation. No one can be in active service six months, no matter what his political predelictions were when he entered the army, without having the conclusion forced upon him that that very blow struck at slavery is a blow to crush the rebellion and restore the Union. Observation soon teaches him that African slavery is the foundation, the moving spirit of this unholy war against the best and noblest government upon God's footstool; that it is in itself an aggressive anti-republican institution, totally antagonistic in its nature to our form of government, and that until that cursed system is crushed out, there can be no permanent or honorable peace established in this country.

Such is the universal sentiment of those who have fought the battles of the Union, and borne the starry emblem of our National Sovereignty upon many a sanguinary field. . . .

We were favored with a "right smart" shock of an earthquake here last week. It lasted several seconds.

Yours, &c.,

GRAPE.   Vol. 5, pp. 70–71

Reflections on a New Year

With a new year approaching, a soldier reminisced on his year spent in the army in a letter to his father.

Abbeville, Miss. Dec. 16th, 1862.

DEAR FATHER:—Again I find myself pen in hand, trying to scratch off something on this little sheet, for it is the only way in which we can have a little chat together; and as it is raining to-day we have nothing to do but to talk over our adventures for the past year. It is now nearly 1863. One year ago I left home, shortly after returning from a hard summer's work, and had my wishes been gratified, would have passed the winter at home with a kind father and mother who have always been so good to their son, at times too when that son did not appreciate the kindness and love he always received at home.

I had a brother who, although younger in years, was older in Patriotism and love of Country. He had already left the comforts of home; had taken the hands of dear ones, had spoken the last good-bye, and gone, as all true

American born citizens should go, to punish those who dare to trample upon our Flag which has so long floated in triumph over our heads, and which our father and mother taught us to love, the noble old Flag the Green mountain boys fought so well under; yes that dear brother was gone, and should his brother stand and look on when his country was in danger? Should he stand with folded arms and see a part of those bright stars plucked from that dear old Flag without lending a helping hand? No! No, but go and with that dear brother help replace those stars, and if it is so to be, give our lives up before we will see the old Flag without them.

One year ago I asked my dear Mother one Sunday afternoon if she was willing that I should enlist. Like the mothers in the days of the Revolution, she told her son if he thought his country was in need of him to go, and with that younger son, stand by the Union to the last. And if there were more such mothers in the Northern states there would be an army in the field to-day large enough to drive every rebel both North and South into the sea. And I have not forgotten, when I first enlisted my Father in neither word or action, tried to discourage me. No but had he been in circumstances so that he could, would also be engaged in this noble cause.

But my dear Father you have done more good by being at home with your pen, than you could have done with the old "Belgian;" you must not think that your sons have the idea that their Father would not stand fire, or that we think he would not make good use of the old "Belgian" if he had the chance, far from it; but I believe those kind, long letters we have received every week, have done more towards keeping us in good health than all the surgeons in the army could have done. Not only have they done your sons good, but there is not a soldier in the whole company who does not like to hear from you. And when the mail comes in they all want to hear what you have to say, and then you will hear them say "I wish I could get such good and cheerful letters as your father writes."

A *soldier* far away from home, does not care to hear of all the little troubles his friends are undergoing, for he cannot help him, as he has enough on his mind without having his letters filled with gloom, but if his friends would only show the bright side of the picture it would encourage them and make them altogether different from what some of them are.

The boys are all well and anxious to be on the move again, but how long we are going to stay in this place is more than any of us can tell. The boys send their respects to you. As dinner is ready I shall have to bid you all good-bye for this time.

From your Son,

W. J. E. R.   Vol. 5, pp. 169–70

What a Private Thinks of Copperheads

I have an Enfield rifle that I took form a rebel, and have turned it against them to pretty good advantage. I mean to shoot as many rebs. as I can while I am here, and would shoot a COPPERHEAD *just as quick!* If the editor of the Markeson *Journal* knew with what *contempt* his paper is received in Co. I of the 11th, I think he would keep them at home. Such men would not be safe down here. It is considered to be a Copperhead sheet, and it is men of just such principles, that give the rebels courage and prolong the War. They are the ones THAT ARE RESPONSIBLE *for the widows and orphans and homes that are made desolate,* and are despised down here by even the rebels themselves.

*   *   *   *   *

Now is the time for these northern sympathisers—Copperheads, traitors, or whatever else you may please to call them, to show their hand. Why don't they come down here and help their southern friends out of this "bad scrape" they have got themselves into? I think I can tell you the reason. It is this: They are too "big cowards" to fight for their friends or the Government under which they have lived so long in peace and prosperity.—This is not only my opinion, but the opinion of three-fourths of the Army.

Vol. 9, pp. 94–95

An Execution

Witnessing an execution in Maryland gave "E. E. B." of the 3rd Wisconsin the opportunity to wonder which was worse, a soldier who murdered someone in a moment of rage or the executioners who put him on the gallows.

Head-quarter's 3d reg't Wis. vol.
Camp Brownlow, Frederick City, Md.,
Jan. 27, 1862.

Since my last writing, nothing has occurred aside from our regular routine of duty, except the execution of John Lanahan, a private of the 46th Pennsylvania Regiment.

It will be remembered that, while maddened with liquor, this man shot the Major of that Regiment, last September, near Darnestown, killing him instantly, because the Major had ordered him punished for drunken and disorderly conduct. Lanahan was tried by a court martial, and sentenced to be hung. The sentence of the court was confirmed by Gen. McClellan and ordered to be carried into execution. Gen. Banks, as Division commander, fixed the time of the execution on the 23d of December.

Col. Ruger, as Provost Marshal, was required to execute the sentence. Our Regiment, as Provost Guard, was required to guard the prisoner, [until] he expiated his crime.

At 12 o'clock of the fatal day we marched to the guard post, where he was confined and escorted the prisoner to the gallows, erected some four miles out of the city. His arms were pinioned to his side, he was drawn in a covered carriage, surrounded by a heavy guard, the Regiment marching behind. Arrived at the place of execution, the regiment formed square around the gallows, the prisoner mounted the steps first, and alone, and with a light step, mounted upon the platform, from which he was to be launched into eternity. A thrill of mournful admiration went through the assembled soldiery, to see him step with so bold a stride, so erect, so manlike. He seemed perfectly prepared to die, and to hail with gladness, the hour of his release. In answer to the inquiry "Have you anything to say?" he shook his head and told them he was ready. A white cap was drawn over his eyes, Capt. Bertram, Assistant Provost Marshal, slipped the fatal noose over his head, adjusted it, bound his limbs, and left the scaffold. All being ready, Col. Ruger dropped his handkerchief as a signal, and the hangman, who was disguised, and his face and head shrouded with black, struck the spring, the drop fell, a shudder ran along the lines, as the rope straightened with a twang. A few contortions and writhings of the body for perhaps a half-minute, and it hung lifeless, swayed to and fro by the fierce northwester then blowing. As the men looked on with blanched faces, whispered exclamations of horror could be heard in the ranks. I am proud to be able to say that most of the members of our Regiment were unwilling spectators of the horrid scene. Such is the improved sentiment of our time, that the gallows is looked upon with disgust, and regarded by men prepared for the bloody vicissitudes of war, as a relic of a barbarous age. The scene was well calculated to banish any lingering doubt, we might have, of the propriety of abolishing the death penalty. The startling question was suggested to me,— was not his execution a more *cold blooded* murder than the one for which his life was taken? Instinctively we looked upon him, blood-stained as he was, as a martyr, meeting death with a fortitude that enlists those sympathies the deepest, because they spring alike, form pity and admiration. . . .

E. E. B.   Vol. 3, pp. 3–4

Return of the Second Wisconsin

The return to Madison of the 2nd Wisconsin, part of the famed Iron Brigade, in July 1864 was an occasion for celebration, mourning, and reflection. Having left Wisconsin "eleven hundred strong," the remnant numbered less than one hundred. During its three years' service, the 2nd Wisconsin proved to be one of the finest combat outfits in the Union army, and it suffered the greatest percentage of losses of any Union regiment. Although there was joy at the return of the 2nd, the correspondent also reflected on the scene of the regiment's parting and the "horrid consequences of war."

The return of this gallant regiment brings to our mind most vividly the scene of their departure. We remember it as if it were but yesterday. It was a bright June day, in 1861. Camp Randall was alive with the bustle of preparation— soldiers marching and countermarching, while the air was made vocal with martial music, and the ground shook under the tread of stalwart men. None connected with that scene probably dreamed of the return which took place on Saturday last. Few of those who had been mustered into that regiment imagined that full three years would elapse before the war closed. Many of them doubtless indulged in the prevailing error that the South was not in real, solid earnest, and that the overthrow of the rebel power was going to be a holiday task. But it was not our design to indulge in these speculations. It was an error in which a great many people participated, and let it pass. We have taken the pen for the purpose of paying a tribute of praise to the noble Second, so justly its due. It left us amid a shower of encomiums. They were a splendid body of men—strong, brave, and full of ambition. The people were justly proud of them, and on many a hard-fought field have they gratified the pride and fulfilled the predictions so freely expressed at their departure. They left Madison amidst the shouts of the people, and the small remnant of them, after three years of hard service, have returned to be greeted with shouts of welcome from the same people. Would that all who went might have been here, to have heard those shouts, and to have been gladdened by the sound of those ringing bells, and that roaring cannon, which welcomed home their living companions. Hundreds of those absent ones are gone where "no sound can awake them to glory again." They have passed beyond the reach of praise They have gone to that "bourne from whence no traveler returns."[1]

At the time this regiment left Camp Randall, nearly eleven hundred strong, we remember of wondering to ourself how many of those strong, healthy, able-bodied men would return; and when we beheld their shattered, decimated ranks marching around the public square of our city, memory brought back the mental question of three years ago, and the scene before us presented the sad answer, and we turned gloomily away, to meditate upon the horrid consequences of war.

The reception which greeted this regiment on its return was well deserved. The boys of the 2d have earned it right nobly. They enlisted in an early stage of the war, stimulated by no promise of large bounties, and they have served faithfully and fully redeemed the pledge they made. Their valor has been well tried and well proven on many a sanguinary field through all the campaigns of the gallant army of the Potomac. They richly merit all the honors of veteran soldiers, and while we mourn over the gallant dead, we congratulate

---

1 From Hamlet's famous "To be, or not to be" soliloquy: ". . . who would fardels bear,\To grunt and sweat under a weary life,\But that the dread of something after death,\The undiscovered country from whose bourn\No traveller returns, puzzles the will,\And makes us rather bear those ills we have\Than fly to others that we know not of?" (Act 3, scene 1).

the equally gallant living upon their safe return to their homes and their friends, and hope they may long live to enjoy the honors they have won.

We understand that they are to be mustered out of the service to-day. When that event takes place, the 2d Regiment of Wisconsin volunteers will cease to exist as an organization, but its history will still survive. It will share in the glory which has shed so pure a lustre upon the fame of the long abused but now vindicated McClellan. It has stood the brunt of the fierce onset of battle under Meade, Hooker, Burnside and Grant. History has already erected imperishable monuments to its renown. They are scattered along the blood-soaked fields of Virginia, almost as thick as mile stones, pointing the way to Richmond. The 2d Regiment is mustered out of the army, but its fame cannot be mustered out of the memory of men.

God speed the day when peace shall muster out all of our gallant soldiers. May that day bring with it a restored Union, a vindicated constitution, and a government of laws under which civil liberty and the rights of the people will find a secure shelter from the encroachments of power. God speed the day!   Vol. 10, p. 115

Veterans and family members at a September 1887 reunion of the Iron Brigade in Milwaukee WHi Image ID 10695

Index